Creativity, Heritage and the City

Volume 3

Cities are faced with various problems, including terrorism, energy challenges, and environmental issues, as well as inter-urban competition brought about by expanding globalization forces. What is required is to gather theoretical insights from various scientific areas, not only social science– humanities but also natural science, and connect them to the practical insights already gained through numerous efforts to deal with these issues on the ground. In this way, paradigms for urban creativity can be developed and we can start to accrue dependable practice and theoretically based intelligence that can be used for improved policymaking. The keywords for this book series are "urban creativity", "(cultural) heritage", and "social development". Developing cultural and natural resources, including heritage, so as to take the lead in evaluating, implementing, and suggesting urban or regional designs that harmonize ecology, society, and people, and to further develop urban and regional culture is essential. There is a particular focus in this book series on fostering individuals who can design, manage, and direct models, technologies, and tools for promoting interfaces between such actors as policymakers, urban planners, engineers, and residents. The above-stated goals can be implemented through cooperation with international research communities and networks, international organizations, and natural history institutions, academies of science, and research institutes.

More information about this series at https://link.springer.com/bookseries/13785

Jihon Kim

Non-State Actors in the Protection of Cultural Heritage

An Analysis on Their Rights, Obligations, and Roles

Springer

Jihon Kim
Korean National Commission for UNESCO
Seoul, Republic of Korea

ISSN 2366-4584 ISSN 2366-4592 (electronic)
Creativity, Heritage and the City
ISBN 978-981-16-6658-2 ISBN 978-981-16-6659-9 (eBook)
https://doi.org/10.1007/978-981-16-6659-9

This Springer imprint is published by the registered company Springer Nature Singapore Pte Ltd.
The registered company address is: 152 Beach Road, #21-01/04 Gateway East, Singapore 189721, Singapore

Foreword

International treaties for the protection of cultural heritage have become, in the past half a century, an important component of multilateral policymaking. The field gradually expanded from an initial intent to protect heritage in case of conflict (1954) to include the fight against illicit traffic of cultural objects (1970), the protection and listing of world heritage sites (1972), the conservation of underwater archaeology (2001), and the safeguarding of intangible heritage (2003).

To these five conventions, all administered by UNESCO, a sixth was added by UNIDROIT in 1995, aimed to strengthen the fight against illicit traffic of cultural objects. Other international cultural conventions exist, but are either focused on cultural policies (such as the 2005 UNESCO Convention for the Protection and Promotion of the Diversity of Cultural Expressions) or have a regional scope (such as the European Landscape Convention or the Faro Convention, among those administered by the Council of Europe).

Parallel to these developments, the role of civil society organizations in the field of cultural heritage has greatly expanded, engaging not only management of heritage sites but also protection and conservation of cultural objects, cultural heritage advocacy, studies and research, advisory services, and direct involvement in emergency actions for the conservation of monuments and sites in case of conflicts and natural disasters, often in partnership with official bodies.

Civil society is certainly a general term—with meanings varying according to the different social and political contexts—that needs to be articulated and detailed. This book's choice of the term non-State actors (hereinafter, 'NSA(s)') intends to emphasize the difference of legal status between the governmental systems that are the legitimate owners of the conventions and the great variety of social actors that are directly or indirectly involved in the implementation of international cultural policies. It is a term that encompasses a variety of entities, ranging from international and national NGOs to representatives of communities or special interest groups, specialized institutions, public and private training and research centers, experts, and concerned individual.

In the past decades, a great number of international organizations have become important stakeholders in the implementation of the international cultural heritage conventions, due to the emergence of new policies on common heritage and cultural rights. As a result, international cultural heritage law has become gradually inconsistent with States' claim of the sole authority over the protection of cultural heritage.

How is the role of NSAs recognized, promoted, and valued within the international treaties aimed to protect cultural heritage? While researchers have often discussed the role of NSAs within individual conventions, a comprehensive analysis on their role in international cultural heritage treaties had not yet been done.

With this book, Jihon Kim aims to fill the gap, by presenting a thorough analysis of the international cultural heritage conventions and of their operational texts, to map the changes in the rights, obligations, and roles of NSAs since the mid-twentieth Century. A series of case studies illustrates this evolution.

The analysis of the rights and duties of NSAs to participate in the implementation of cultural heritage conventions clearly indicates that along the years their roles have significantly expanded. The relationship between State and NSAs actors has indeed evolved from an initial approach, that saw civil society organizations essentially as 'beneficiaries' of the governmental action or at most as 'service providers' for the functioning of the treaties, to a greater recognition of the relevance of communities and local, national, and international organizations to ensure accountable and transparent policy implementation processes, and to contribute to achieve the goals of the conventions.

However, the analysis also reveals great discrepancies between the different conventions and divergent approaches from one to another. Some of these divergencies are explained by the different time of adoption of the treaties. The 2003 Intangible Heritage Convention, for instance, provides a greater role to communities in the identification, promotion, and management of intangible heritage elements than the 1972 World Heritage Convention, which foresees a very limited role for NSAs.

But a better explanation points to the increasing politicization of the management of the treaties. The current political polarization of the global context inevitably finds a reflection in international cultural heritage policies. Heritage, as a repository of collective identity, can easily trigger cultural conflicts, as several incidents concerning world heritage or intangible heritage have shown in recent years.

At the same time, the States are increasingly privileging the 'labelling' value provided by some of the conventions, especially those managing a list, over their primary heritage conservation and safeguarding goal, and have found sophisticated ways to collude in overcoming the technical and scientific recommendations of the advisory bodies whenever they do not go in the desired direction. This process has shown a dangerous progression during the past decade, and has now reached a critical point.

Recognition of civil society's role has also lagged for purely political reasons. For example, it took no less that 16 years for the World Heritage Committee to adopt a policy for the indigenous people after the 2001 rejection of the proposal to create of a specialized council of experts, due to the resistance of many government to recognize the very existence of indigenous people. And it should be noticed that this policy was adopted 10 years after the adoption of the United Nations Declaration on the Rights of Indigenous Peoples (UNDRIP) by the UN General Assembly in 2007.

In the past half a century, civil society has been able to expand its participation to the global effort to protect heritage for the present and future generations. These advancements are not reversible and they require operational frameworks that are different from the one established in the post-war period, when States exercised a de facto monopoly in all operations related to heritage, from its identification to its conservation and safeguarding, to its economic use.

Today NSAs are playing a major role in supporting the governmental tasks. They also play an irreplaceable role as watchdogs to anticipate and prevent possible threats to heritage and mobilize the public interest in support of preservation.

Following a complete analysis of the legal, procedural, and operational frameworks of the different treaties, the book emphasizes the need to explore innovative and practical mechanisms to enable NSAs to assume a proper status and take on practical roles within international cultural heritage laws.

This is a pre-condition to ensure sustainable protection of cultural heritage, respect of human rights, promotion of cultural diversity, and, ultimately, foster peace and dialogue in our changing societies.

Paris, France Francesco Bandarin

Francesco Bandarin has been Director of the UNESCO World Heritage Centre (2000–2010) and UNESCO Assistant Director-General for Culture (2010–2018). He is currently Advisor to ICCROM, the Aga Khan Trust for Culture, and the Smithsonian Institution. He is a founder, and member of the Advisory Committee, of OURWORLDHERITAGE, a global initiative aimed to promote the role of civil society in the implementation of the World Heritage Convention.

Preface

The international community has witnessed significant developments concerning the status and roles of non-State actors (hereinafter, 'NSA(s)') in international law during the last century. Apart from the traditional State-centric international legal system, particularly in consideration of the fact that States hold the sole authority to conclude and enforce international treaties, NSAs have become important participants of international law, with procedural and substantive rights and responsibilities, and with specific roles in the implementation of international law.

In this context, this book reviews the status and roles of NSAs in international cultural heritage law, and aims to contribute to the understanding of NSAs in international law in general, while providing a different angle from which to understand the current implementations of international cultural heritage conventions. Indeed, due to the emergence of new ideas on common heritage and cultural rights in the twentieth century, international cultural heritage law has become inconsistent with States' claim of the sole authority over the protection of cultural heritage. However, the rights, obligations, and roles of NSAs have not yet been clarified; some NSAs are still exposed to the danger of abuse by state power as well as the pressure of globalization, and hence, more attention to ensuring their participation in heritage protection is required. At the same time, it is noteworthy that as the international impact of NSAs' behavior has increased, more duties to protect cultural heritage have been sought for and by them.

This book analyzes the texts of international cultural heritage conventions as well as their operational texts to track the changes in the rights, obligations, and roles of NSAs since the mid-twentieth century. As the operational guidelines for the conventions are regularly updated to reflect the changing environment of the conventions, they become an important source for analysis. Practical cases on the status and roles of NSAs are introduced in order to glean empirical ideas concerning the operation of the relevant provisions of the conventions and guidelines, as well as to facilitate in-depth understanding of their effectiveness in reality. In this analysis, diverse forms of cultural heritage such as tangible, intangible, movable, and immovable heritage, all covered by different international conventions, are taken into consideration. The different categories of NSA, including the secretariats of international organizations, experts, NGOs, local communities, and the general public, are also duly accounted for in analyzing their status and roles in each different convention.

This book reveals that the NSAs in international cultural heritage law have substantive rights, obligations and roles, as prescribed in the legal and operational texts, as well as in practice. At the same time, the operational guidelines of the conventions have imparted more concreteness to the status and roles of NSAs. In the course of those changes, some NSAs have become more vocal than others. At the same time, discrepancies between text and practice, as concerns the status and roles of NSAs, are observed as well, which have occurred for various reasons, one of which is the politicization of conventions' governance.

In general, NSAs do have rights and duties to participate in the implementation of cultural heritage conventions, and their roles have been further recognized. This phenomenon is most prominent in the field of intangible cultural heritage, in that individuals and communities bearing heritage play a pivotal role in safeguarding non-material cultural values of society and transmitting them to future generations. A similar situation can be found with regard to the status and roles of NGOs and local communities in the protection of World Heritage. Pari passu, the international obligation of NSAs to protect cultural heritage, has increased as well, with the increasing dissemination of ideas on common heritage. Destruction of the common cultural heritage of humankind by individuals has become subject to the jurisdiction of international courts, and so too, higher moral and legal standards have been required of NSAs involved in the movement of cultural property.

However, the value of cultural heritage is easily ignored in the process of globalization and development. In addition, the top-down approach of the States in the management of their cultural heritage often is applied in the implementation processes of cultural heritage conventions. In the process, NSAs and, in particular, local communities, are easily left out. At the same time, technological advancement has enabled freer and less restricted flow of assets and properties, which phenomenon accelerates illicit trafficking and destruction of cultural property. These challenges to the protection of cultural heritage cannot be tackled only by the actions of the States; rather, they require the consolidated efforts of various groups of society. Doubtless, to the extent that protection of cultural heritage has become a common concern of the international community, Westphalian-inspired notions of state-centricity are no longer valid in the field of international cultural heritage law. It is time to explore innovative and practical mechanisms to enable NSAs to assume a proper status and take on practical roles to achieve the ultimate goal of international cultural heritage law: sustainable protection of cultural heritage.

Seoul, Republic of Korea Jihon Kim

Acknowledgements

The kernel of this book grew out of my experiences in the field of cultural heritage, where I could witness the interesting phenomena of co-existence and confrontation as well as cooperation between States and non-State actors (hereinafter, 'NSA(s)'). The roles of various NSAs including local communities, NGOs, experts, and the secretariats of international organizations seem to have increased with further recognition of their rights and obligations in the texts of various international conventions for the protection of cultural heritage. This notwithstanding, there has been a degree of discrepancy between text and practice. In an effort to bring clarity to the question of the rights, obligations, and roles of NSAs, this book explores the textual changes made to various international cultural heritage conventions and analyzes relevant cases.

This book is based on my doctoral thesis completed at Seoul National University, under the supervision of Prof. Jin-Hyun Paik, for whom I would like to express my deepest appreciation. For more than 10 years, since the entrance to my master's course, he has patiently encouraged me to grow academically enough to be a doctor. I am deeply indebted to his generosity in sparing his valuable time during the cases at the ITLOS and his term as president, and I could move forward only with his kind support.

I also would like to extend my sincere thanks to the professors who have made this research possible: my thesis examiners, Dong-Joon Jo who has carefully reviewed the thesis and led entire processes for the screen, Taekyoon Kim who has provided warm support and encouragement, Keen-Gwan Lee who has long been my role model both at work and study, and Sangmin Shim who has spared no effort for my improved work. All of them have permitted me to indulge my experience in bringing the practice of an international organization into the light of the academic world. I would not have been able to complete the thesis without all of their kind commitments.

My research benefitted from the valuable contributions of many eminent experts in the field of cultural heritage, who have supported both work and study of mine continuously. In particular, Francesco Bandarin, Marina Schneider, Lyndel V. Prott, and Ahmed Skounti have provided helpful assistance to my research by sitting for interviews with me. In addition to an interview, Kishore Rao added his valuable comments that guided the entire research.

There are numerous professors and experts to whom I feel grateful for giving me the motivation and inspiration in the journey of mine to finish this research: Hyo-Jai Im, Dawnhee Yim, Kidong Bae, Kyung Rip Park, Hae Un Rii, Kyung Koo Han, Utak Chung, Inho Song, Chul-In You, So Hyun Park, Jae Heon Choi, Sangmee Park, Ho-Young Song, Dong Ju Choi, and In Uk Kang. In addition, I am also grateful to many colleagues at the Korean National Commission for UNESCO, Permeant Delegations to UNESCO, UNESCO Secretariat, and Ministry of Foreign Affairs and Cultural Heritage Administration of the Republic of Korea.

I dedicate any good parts in this work to my parents whom I love and respect the most. My father, Taesoo Kim, and my mother, Malbong Kim, instilled in me the value of study and that of hard work and I would like to follow their life paths. I am blessed with a wonderful companion for my life, LJ, who have been the source of my courage, hope, and trust. I am indebted to my mother-in-law, Ae-Sun Kim, who has always cared for me with generosity, my beloved late father-in-law, Yong Chul Lee, and my sisters and brother, Minjeung, Hyejung, and Daekyu. The friendship of my old friends as well as many colleagues at Kooksa Kendo dojo has been indispensable to the completion of my research.

This book could not have been finished without the support, consideration, and care of many people at Springer, such as editorial board of the Creativity, Heritage and the City series led by Prof. Hiroshi Okano and the coordinators of my book, Kowsalya Raghunathan and Gowtham Chakravarthy V. There remains much room for improvement in this research, and I will further commit myself to research with a beginner's humble attitude. And I hope that this commitment will eventually lead to another chance for me to convey my sincere thanks to all, but with better work.

Seoul, Republic of Korea Jihon Kim
September 2021

Contents

About the Author

Dr. Jihon Kim is a senior program specialist at the Korean National Commission for UNESCO. Since 2006, she has coordinated external relations between UNESCO and the Republic of Korea, particularly in the field of cultural heritage, and organized various projects, such as research projects, international conferences, and fundraising campaigns with government and private sectors. She has participated in many intergovernmental meetings of UNESCO including World Heritage Committee and Intangible Cultural Heritage Committee as an advisory member of the delegation of the Republic of Korea and served her diplomatic mission at the Permanent Delegation to UNESCO from 2019 to 2020.

As an adjunct professor, she has lectured on international cultural heritage law and policy at Sungkyunkwan University and Konkuk University since 2016. She was a research fellow at the International Institute for the Unification of Private Law (UNIDROIT) and an editorial member of the Korea Institute of Traditional Landscape Architecture. Since 2018, she has been serving as a public legislative officer at the Ministry of Government Legislation in the areas of culture, sports, and tourism. She is currently a member of the International Council on Monuments and Sites (ICOMOS), and the Advisory Committee of OUR WORLD HERITAGE, an international NGO to promote the role of civil society in the implementation of the World Heritage Convention.

She received her B.A. in Art History (*summa cumme laude*), and M.A. and Ph.D. in International Studies at Seoul National University. She also studied at John F. Kennedy School of Government at Harvard University, University of British Columbia, and University of International Business and Economics in China through various programs. She has written numerous articles on the cultural heritage law and policy, such as "1970 UNESCO Convention and its Legal Implementations in the Republic of Korea" and "National Response to International Conventions: The Case of the 2003 UNESCO Convention and the New Korean Legislation." She is a co-author of several books on cultural heritage and UNESCO, including *The Role of UNESCO in the Search for Peace*, *Our Sustainable City* and *Associative Values of Tangible and Intangible Heritage under the World Heritage Convention*, and edited Korean version of UNESCO publications on heritage such as *World Heritage: Benefits beyond Borders* and *World Heritage: Challenges for the Millennium.*

Abbreviations

AIMA	Australasian Institute for Maritime Archaeology
CCAAA	Co-ordinating Council of Audiovisual Archives Association
DOALOS	UN Division of Ocean Affairs and the Law of the Sea
ECHR	European Convention on Human Rights
EEZ	Exclusive Economic Zone
ICA	International Council on Archives
ICBS	International Committee of the Blue Shield
ICC	International Criminal Court
ICCROM	International Centre for the Study of the Preservation and Restoration of Cultural Property
ICJ	International Court of Justice
ICOM	International Council of Museums
ICOMOS	International Council on Monuments and Sites
ICOMOS-ICUCH	ICOMOS International Committee on Underwater Cultural Heritage
ICRC	International Committee of the Red Cross
ICTR	International Criminal Tribunal for Rwanda
ICTY	International Criminal Tribunal for the Former Yugoslavia
IFLA	International Federation of Library Associations and Institutions
ILA	International Law Association
INTERPOL	International Criminal Police Organization
IOS	UNESCO Internal Oversight Service
IUCN	International Union for Conservation of Nature
NAS	Nautical Archaeology Society
NGO	Non-Governmental Organization
NSA	Non-State Actors
STAB	Scientific and Technical Advisory Body
UN	United Nations
UNCLOS	United Nations Convention on the Law of the Sea

UNESCO	United Nations Educational, Scientific, and Cultural Organization
UNIDROIT	International Institute for the Unification of Private Law
UNODC	United Nations Office on Drugs and Crime
UNTOC	UN Convention against Transnational Organized Crime
WCO	World Customs Organization
WIPO	World Intellectual Property Organization
WTO	World Trade Organization

List of Tables

List of Cases

Ancient Coin Collectors Guild v. US Customs and Border Protection, Department of Homeland Security, et al., 801 F. Supp. 2d 383 (D. Maryland 2011).

Ancient Coin Collectors Guild v. US Customs and Border Protection, 698 F.3d 171 (4th Cir. 2012).

Autocephalous Greek Orthodox Church in Cyprus v. William O.A. Lans, District Court of Rotterdam, Case n. 44053, 4 February 1999; confirmed in Appeal, Hof Den Haag, 99/693, 7 March 2002.

Autocephalous Greek-Orthodox Church of Cyprus v. Goldberg and Feldman Fine Arts, Inc., 717 F.Supp. 1374 (S.D. Ind. 1989).

Autocephalous Greek-Orthodox Church of Cyprus v. Goldberg and Feldman Fine Arts, Inc., 917 F.2d 278 (7th Cir. 1990).

Beyeler v. Italy, Application No. 33202/96, European Court of Human Rights, Judgement of 5 January 2000.

Bulankulama and Others v. Secretary, Ministry of Industrial Development and Others (2000), LKSC 18.

Coal Contractors Limited v. Secretary of State for the Environment and Northumberland County Council [1993] EGCS 218.

Commonwealth v. Tasmania [1983] HCA 21; (1983) 158 CLR 1 (1 July 1983).

Dispute regarding Navigational and Related Rights (Costa Rica v. Nicaragua), Judgment, I.C.J. Reports 2009.

Glamis Gold Ltd. v. United States, Award (NAFTA Arb. Trib. 2009).

In re An Application by the Tasmanian Aboriginal Centre Inc [2007] TASSC 5.

Jurisdiction of the Courts of Danzig, Advisory Opinion, 1928 P.C.I.J. (ser. B) No. 15 (Mar. 3).

Parkerings-Compagniet AS v. Republic of Lithuania, ICSID Case No. ARB/05/08, Award of 11 September 2007.

Prosecutor v. Ahmad Al Faqi Al Mahdi, ICC-01/12-01/15, Judgement and Sentence, 27 September 2016.

Prosecutor v. Al Hassan Ag Abdoul Aziz Ag Mohamed Ag Mahmoud, ICC-01/12-01/18.

Prosecutor v. Biljana Plavšić, IT-00-39&40/1-S, Sentencing Judgement, 27 February 2003.

Prosecutor v. Duško Tadić, IT-94-1-AR72, Appeals Chamber, Decision, 2 October 1995.

Prosecutor v. Jadranko Prlić et al., IT-04-74, Judgement, 29 May 2013.

Prosecutor v. Miodrag Jokić, IT-01-42/1-S, Sentencing Judgment, 18 March 2004.

Prosecutor v. Mladen Naletilic & Vinko Martinovic, IT-98-34-T, Judgement, 31 March 2003.

Prosecutor v. Pavle Strugar, IT-01-42-T, Judgement, 31 January 2005.

Prosecutor v. Radoslav Brdanin, IT-99-36-T, Judgement, 1 December 2004.

Prosecutor v. Tihomir Blaškić, IT-95-14-T, Trial Judgement, 3 March 2000.

Reparations for Injuries Suffered in the Services of the United Nations, Advisory Opinion [1949] ICJ Rep. 175.

R.M.S. Titanic, Inc. v. The Wrecked and Abandoned Vessel, 924 F.Supp. 714 (E.D. Va. 1996).

R.M.S. Titanic, Inc. v. The Wrecked and Abandoned Vessel, Civ. No. 2:93cv902 (July 28, 2000 E.D. Va.).

R.M.S. Titanic, Inc. v. Wrecked and Abandoned Vessel, 742 F. Supp. 2d 784, 790 n.6 (E.D. Va. 2010).

Salvors, Inc. v. Unidentified Wrecked & Abandoned Vessel, 861 F.3d 1278 (11th Cir. 2017).

United States v. Frederick Schultz, 333 F.3d 393 (2nd Cir. 2003).

List of Legal Instruments

African Charter on Human and Peoples' Rights (1981)

Agreement Concerning the Shipwrecked Vessel RMS Titanic (Titanic Agreement) (2000)

American Convention on Human Rights (1969)

Arab Charter on Human Rights (2004)

Convention against Torture and Other Cruel, Inhuman or Degrading Treatment or Punishment (1984)

Convention concerning the Protection of the World Cultural and Natural Heritage (1972)

Convention for the Protection of Cultural Property in the Event of Armed Conflict (1954)

Convention on Stolen or Illegally Exported Cultural Objects (1995)

Convention on the Elimination of All Forms of Discrimination against Women (1979)

Convention on the Means of Prohibiting and Preventing the Illicit Import, Export and Transfer of Ownership of Cultural Property (1970)

Convention on the Protection and Promotion of the Diversity of Cultural Expressions (2005)

Convention on the Protection of the Underwater Cultural Heritage (2001)

Convention on the Rights of the Child (1989)

Convention on the Rights of Persons with Disabilities (2006)

Convention for the Safeguarding of the Intangible Cultural Heritage (2003)

European Convention for the Protection of Human Rights and Fundamental Freedoms (1950)

Hague Convention (II) with respect to the Laws and Customs of War on Land and its annex (1899)

Hague Convention (IV) respecting the Laws and Customs of War on Land and its annex (1907)

ICOMOS Charter for the Management and Protection of the Underwater Cultural Heritage (1996)

Instructions for the Government of Armies of the United States in the Field (Lieber Code) (1863)

International Charter for the Conservation and Restoration of Monuments and Sites (Venice Charter) (1964)

International Covenant on Civil and Political Rights (1966)

International Covenant on Economic, Social and Cultural Rights (1966)

International Convention on Salvage (1989)

International Convention on the Protection of the Rights of All Migrant Workers and Members of Their Families (1990)

Geneva Convention (IV) relative to the Protection of Civilian Persons in Time of War (1949)

Guidelines for the Implementation of the 1999 Second Protocol to the Hague Convention of 1954 for the Protection of Cultural Property in the Event of Armed Conflict (2019)

Operational Directives for Convention for the Safeguarding of the Intangible Cultural Heritage (2018)

Operational Guidelines for the Convention concerning the Protection of the World Cultural and Natural Heritage (2019)

Operational Guidelines for the Convention on the Means of Prohibiting and Preventing the Illicit Import, Export and Transfer of Ownership of Cultural Property (2015)

Operational Guidelines for the Convention on the Protection of the Underwater Cultural Heritage (2015)

Proclamation of Masterpieces of Oral and Intangible Heritage of Humanity (1998)

Protocol Additional to the Geneva Conventions of 12 August 1949, and relating to the Protection of Victims of International Armed Conflicts (Protocol I) (1977)

Protocol Additional to the Geneva Conventions of 12 August 1949, and relating to the Protection of Victims of Non-International Armed Conflicts (Protocol II) (1977)

Protocol to the Convention for the Protection of Cultural Property in the Event of Armed Conflict (1954)

Recommendation on the Means of Prohibiting and Preventing the Illicit Export, Import and Transfer of Ownership of Cultural Property (1964)

Recommendation on the Protection of Traditional Cultural and Folklore (1989)

Rome Statute of the International Criminal Court (ICC) (1998)

Second Protocol to the Hague Convention of 1954 for the Protection of Cultural Property in the Event of Armed Conflict (1999)

Statute of the International Tribunal for the Prosecution of Persons Responsible for Serious Violations of International Humanitarian Law Committed in the Territory of Former Yugoslavia since 1991 (ICTY) (1993)

Treaty on the Protection of Artistic and Scientific Institutions and Historic Monuments (Roerich Pact) (1935)

United Nations Convention on the Law of the Sea (1982)

Chapter 1
Introduction

1.1 Background

The question of the legal status of non-State actors (hereinafter, 'NSA(s)') has been discussed actively since the 17th century, when Gottfried Wilhelm Leibniz used the term 'international legal person' for the first time (Nijman 2004, p. 29). The concept of legal personality intended to address those entities that 'the legal system has cast to appear on the stage of the law' (Cheng 1991, p. 24). In the system, 'only those *personae* that played a direct role could appear on the stage, in spite of the other entities that might participate in the production of the play' (Bianchi 2009, p. xiv). The former has been actively discussed among legal scholars, while the latter caught the interest of political scientists, particularly the New Haven School, which introduced the process-based approach to international law, as well as constructivists, who showed that the interaction among different actors constitutes the structure of the system (Arend 1998, p. 129).

The rise of international organizations from the end of the 19th Century (Bederman 1995), the development of international humanitarian law and human rights law, and appearance of new actors such as non-governmental organizations (NGOs) and multinational corporations (MNCs), have further stimulated research on NSAs (Aldrich 1996; Randelzhofer 1999; Stephens 2002; Hodgson 2003; Tomuschat 2003; Thürer 2005; Damgaard 2008; Bonafè 2009). The participation of various NSAs in international law-making, law-adjudication and law-enforcement has been evident in different specific settings, and scholars have come to pay more attention to international law's various domains, among which are the environment, labor, and investment (Peters 2016; d'Aspremont 2011). Study of the status and roles of NSAs is relevant also to another specific domain of international law: international cultural heritage law.

International cultural heritage law is one of the subject areas wherein the evolution of NSAs can be observed. Traditionally, the protection of cultural heritage, in particular immovable heritage, has been under the strict jurisdiction of States. However,

J. Kim, *Non-State Actors in the Protection of Cultural Heritage*, Creativity, Heritage and the City 3, https://doi.org/10.1007/978-981-16-6659-9_1

with globalization in the 20th Century, the development of two important ideas—common heritage and cultural rights—has challenged the sole authority of States over the protection of cultural heritage. The former can be found as early as in 1954 in the preamble of the Hague Convention for the Protection of Cultural Property in the Event of Armed Conflict,[1] but it was reflected further in other conventions adopted later, as well as in the increased general concern of the international community over common heritage (Cançado Trindade 2010, pp. 327–352). In addition, pertinent to the development of the concept of international criminal responsibility of individuals, international courts started to exert their jurisdiction over crimes involving the destruction of instances of cultural heritage important to humankind.[2] Higher legal standards for private art trade have been formulated as well.[3]

Cultural rights, being the rights of individuals concerning their own heritage, were recognized for the first time in Article 27 of the Universal Declaration of Human Rights (1948).[4] It was proposed by the United Nations Educational, Scientific, and Cultural Organization (UNESCO), the only specialized agency of the United Nations dealing with culture. Cultural rights were reaffirmed in Article 15 of the International Covenant on Economic, Social and Cultural Rights (1966).[5] International efforts to strengthen protection of the cultural rights of NSAs (Stamatopoulou 2007), in particular those of local communities and indigenous peoples, are closely connected to the protection of cultural heritage. Most of all, cultural rights related to heritage are vulnerable to the spread of globalization and arbitrary State-led development and protection policies. In this vein, recently adopted international conventions not only require States to protect the rights of local communities concerning their heritage,

[1] Para. 2 reads: "Being convinced that damage to cultural property belonging to any people whatsoever means damage to the cultural heritage of all mankind, since each people makes its contribution to the culture of the world."

[2] For example, *Prosecutor v. Miodrag Jokić*, IT-01-42/1-S, Judgment, 18 March 2004; *Prosecutor v. Pavle Strugar*, IT-01-42-T, Judgement, 31 January 2005; *Prosecutor v. Jadranko Prlić et al.*, IT-04-74, Judgement, 29 May 2013; and *Prosecutor v. Ahmad Al Faqi Al Mahdi*, ICC-01/12-01/15, Judgement and Sentence, 27 September 2016.

[3] For example, the 1995 UNIDROIT Convention on Stolen or Illegally Exported Cultural Objects requires "due diligence" on the part of a bona fide acquirer of cultural property based on the Article 4(4). See Chap. 3 of this book for further details.

[4] Article 27 reads: "(1) Everyone has the right freely to participate in the cultural life of the community, to enjoy the arts and to share in scientific advancement and its benefits; (2) Everyone has the right to the protection of the moral and material interests resulting from any scientific, literary or artistic production of which he is the author."

[5] Article 15 reads: "(1) The States Parties to the present Covenant recognize the right of everyone: (a) To take part in cultural life; (b) To enjoy the benefits of scientific progress and its applications; (c) To benefit from the protection of the moral and material interests resulting from any scientific, literary or artistic production of which he is the author; (2) The steps to be taken by the States Parties to the present Covenant to achieve the full realization of this right shall include those necessary for the conservation, the development and the diffusion of science and culture; (3) The States Parties to the present Covenant undertake to respect the freedom indispensable for scientific research and creative activity; (4) The States Parties to the present Covenant recognize the benefits to be derived from the encouragement and development of international contacts and co-operation in the scientific and cultural fields."

but also guarantee their ownership rights as related to the safeguarding and transmission of heritage.[6]

This tendency is in line with the democratization of the legal order or enforcement process, with its increased accountability of States and the incursion of international law into domestic policies (Hafner 2009, p. 33). NSAs became empowered to pursue their rights against States in domestic and international courts, and 'double protection for rights of NSAs' were conferred by both domestic and international law (Gaja 2010, p. 14). However, as Cassese (2005, p. 145) pointed out concerning individuals' 'corresponding rights' with respect to their obligations regarding the important values of the international community, NSAs still lack remedies under international law in general (Clapham 2010, p. 27). Except for the European Court of Human Rights, where individual applications can be accepted,[7] NSAs do not enjoy the full enforcement of their rights. In the domain of international economic law, investors can submit claims directly to international arbitration without exhausting local remedies; but these are considered to be cases of *lex specialis* having no impact on the traditional doctrine of diplomatic protection by States (Parlett 2011 p. 122).

With substantive obligations imposed by international law, but with partial procedural standing requiring consent of States and limited enforcement of their rights, it can be generally asserted that NSAs have an imbalanced international status concerning their rights and duties. Their roles in the process of law application are limited as well. However, along with the recognition of the dominant status of States in international law, a balance between the status and roles of States and those of NSAs is required. In particular, the international community needs to pay more attention to the areas wherein individuals are most vulnerable to the abuse of State power (Orrego Vicuña 2003, p. 196). Meanwhile, globalization has strengthened connectedness among people, and as such, has increased the impact of the behavior of each NSA on the entire international community. Although it may yet be premature to ascribe Cassese (2008, pp. lxxviii–lxxxi)'s dreamed-of 'community sentiment' to the international community, shared goals of international law need to be pursued by not only States but also NSAs as members of the global community.

Increased involvement of NSAs is necessary also in international cultural heritage law. Indeed, many attempts have been made to create more room in which NSAs can participate, together with States, in the protection of cultural heritage. Some conventions on cultural heritage have reflected this idea by including NSAs in legal texts, and other conventions have accommodated such changes of ideas by revising their operational guidelines. And in the process of international cultural heritage law implementation, there have been numerous cases of changes to NSA status and role; sometimes, however, such changes as stipulated in the texts of conventions or the relevant operational guidelines have not been fully implemented in practice.

---

[6] For example, the 2003 UNESCO Convention for the Safeguarding of the Intangible Cultural Heritage.

[7] Article 35(3)(b) of the European Convention for the Protection of Human Rights and Fundamental Freedoms.

Notwithstanding the development and expansion of NSAs' legal status and roles in international cultural heritage law, academic attention has been rather fragmented thus far. Many scholars have paid attention to the issues of cultural rights and human rights, in particular those of indigenous peoples (Blake 2014; Langfield et al. 2009; Ashworth et al. 2007; Anaya 1996; Brown 2003; Daes 2007). Legal analyses concerning individuals' ownership of tangible and intangible cultural heritage have been conducted (Correa 2001; Posey and Dutfield 1997; Greenfield 1989; Brodie et al. 2000; Kowalski 1998), and studies on individual criminal responsibility for destruction of cultural heritage during armed conflict have increased in number as well (Ehlert 2013; Lenzerini 2013; Nowlan 1993; Chapman 1994; O'Keefe 2010; Frulli 2011; Lostal 2015). And whereas in-depth analysis of the development and implementation of multiple conventions on cultural heritage exists (Blake 2015; Forrest 2010), there has been little research focused on the status and roles of NSAs considered as active participants in the implementation of international cultural heritage law. Therefore, this book aims to provide a different, hitherto neglected angle from which current implementation of international cultural heritage conventions, specifically from the NSA perspective, can be understood. Analysis of the provisions of the international cultural heritage conventions and their operational regulations as well as cases related to those texts will enable determinations of where the legal system for the protection of cultural heritage stands at present concerning the status and roles of NSAs. Comparative studies on different NSAs respecting different conventions on cultural heritage will provide additional insight into their participation in heritage protection. Ultimately, these attempts will suggest a way forward concerning the promotion of the status and roles of NSAs for better protection of cultural heritage.

1.2 Research Framework

1.2.1 Research Questions

This book aims to provide insight into changes in the international legal system as they relate or pertain to the status and roles of NSAs in international cultural heritage law. What is the status of NSAs in international cultural heritage law, and what are their roles in its implementation? Do the provisions of international cultural heritage conventions and their operational guidelines stipulate rights, obligations and roles of NSAs? How have those texts on the status and roles of NSAs been implemented in practice? Have there been any changes in those texts, or in practice, concerning the status and roles of NSAs over time? What are the reasons for any discrepancies that exist between text and practice?

While surveying the status and roles of NSAs in cultural heritage law, the considerable divergences among different international conventions in terms of the main contents, governance, as well as the actors involved and their rights, duties and roles will be duly accounted for. It is anticipated that these factors will be found to influence the status and roles of NSAs according to the relevant categories and conventions. This analysis will enable a closer look at the status and roles of each kind of NSA in different contexts of cultural heritage law.

Finally, in the process of examining the current status and roles of NSAs in international cultural heritage law, this book also intends to identify existing obstacles to the promotion of their status and roles, and will suggest some future directions to pursue for better protection of cultural heritage.

1.2.2 Research Scope and Methodology

Currently, six international conventions and two protocols in terms of cultural heritage protection are in effect: the Convention for the Protection of Cultural Property in the Event of Armed Conflict (1954; hereinafter, '1954 Convention') and its Two Protocols; Convention on the Means of Prohibiting and Preventing the Illicit Import, Export and Transfer of Ownership of Cultural Property (1970; hereinafter, '1970 Convention'); Convention concerning the Protection of the World Cultural and Natural Heritage (1972; hereinafter, '1972 Convention'); Convention on Stolen or Illegally Exported Cultural Objects (1995; hereinafter, '1995 Convention'); Convention on the Protection of the Underwater Cultural Heritage (2001; hereinafter, '2001 Convention'), and the Convention for the Safeguarding of the Intangible Cultural Heritage (2003; hereinafter, '2003 Convention').[8] The Convention on the Protection and Promotion of the Diversity of Cultural Expressions (2005; hereinafter, '2005 Convention') also can be considered to be related to several issues of heritage protection, but will not be dealt with in this book, as its main focus is the promotion of cultural expressions, not the protection of cultural heritage.

Many of these conventions have their own intergovernmental committees that decide key issues concerning their implementation, including management of the relevant international lists under them. Those intergovernmental committees are positioned at the intersection of States and NSAs, and therefore are included within the research scope of this book, which is summarized in Table 1.1.

Legal texts of each convention and its operational directives or guidelines are the main material objects of this book for analysis. The operational directives or guidelines of conventions, unlike conventions themselves, which are difficult to amend,[9] can be revised regularly to reflect the changing environment of conventions' implementation. The analysis of these texts is important, in that they are flexible enough to accommodate international discussion on the changing status and roles of NSAs

[8] All of the conventions are deposited with the Director-General of UNESCO, except for the 1995 Convention, the depository of which is the Government of the Italian Republic, where UNIDROIT (the International Institute for the Unification of Private Law) is located.

[9] For example, for the amendments of the 2003 Convention, a two-thirds majority of States Parties present and voting at the General Assembly of the Convention is required (Article 38).

Table 1.1 Overview of international cultural heritage law

Subject/domain	Relevant international cultural heritage conventions	Intergovernmental committee for governance	Relevant international list(s)
Protection of cultural property in armed conflict	1954 convention and its first protocol (1954) and second protocol (1999) Guidelines for the implementation of the second protocol (2009~)	Committee for the protection of cultural property in the event of armed conflict (under 2nd protocol)	International register of special protection (under 1954 convention), and List of cultural property under enhanced protection (under the second protocol)
Restitution of cultural property	1970 and 1995 conventions Operational guidelines for the implementation of the 1970 convention (2015~)	N/A (Intergovernmental committee for promoting the return of cultural property to its countries of origin or its restitution in case of illicit appropriation stands independently from relevant conventions)	N/A
Protection of world heritage	1972 convention Operational guidelines of the 1972 world heritage convention (1978~)	Intergovernmental committee for the protection of the cultural and natural heritage of outstanding universal value ('World Heritage Committee')	World heritage list (including the list of world heritage in danger)
Protection of underwater cultural heritage	2001 convention Operational guidelines for the implementation of the 2001 convention (2013~)	N/A	N/A (Register of the best practices of underwater cultural heritage created by the meeting of states parties)
Protection of intangible cultural heritage	2003 convention Operational directives of the convention (2008~)	Intergovernmental committee for the safeguarding of the intangible cultural heritage ('Intangible Cultural Heritage Committee')	Representative list of the intangible cultural heritage of humanity, list of intangible cultural heritage in need of urgent safeguarding, and register of good safeguarding practices

Source Author

in the course of heritage protection. This will be one of main contributions of this book in terms of scope of analysis.

To comprehend the effectiveness of those legal texts in articulating the rights, duties, and roles of NSAs in practice, cases will be scrutinized. In particular, the cases at statutory meetings will be closely observed together with the legal cases at courts. This extensive review of relevant documents will be another added value of this book in assessing the status and roles of NSAs. In addition, this empirical exercise will facilitate identification of possible disjunctions between the text and practice and provide clues to their origins and rationales.

Last but not least, a comparative analysis of the status and roles of different categories of NSAs in various cultural heritage conventions will be made as well. This approach will allow us to better understand the interactions and communications among multiple actors within diverse international legal systems for the protection of cultural heritage.

1.2.3 Research Structure

This book is structured in three parts: introduction, main body, and conclusion. This chapter is the Introduction, which includes overviews of the general trends of the changing status of NSAs in international law as well as in international cultural heritage law. It also will define several key terms used in the book and will suggest relevant research questions and designs.

From Chaps. 2 to 6, which are the main bodies of this book, specific international cultural heritage conventions will be analyzed one by one. According to the chronological adoption of the convention (from 1954 to 2003) and the domain of the cultural heritage for protection, a total of five chapters will deal with the status and roles of NSAs in six conventions and two protocols. After summarizing relevant conventions including the background of their adoption and key contents at the beginning of each chapter, provisions of the convention as well as those of the operational documents related to the rights, obligations, and roles of different NSAs will be analyzed.

With regard to the analysis of the state of implementation of those provisions related to NSAs in practice, different methodologies will be chosen due to the various governance systems and history of implementation of each convention; accordingly, the specific focus of analyses of each chapter will vary. For example, in some conventions that have a strong intergovernmental committee, such as the World Heritage Committee of the 1972 Convention and the Intangible Cultural Heritage Committee of the 2003 Convention, roles played by each NSA in practice are scrutinized at the meetings of committees rather than in court cases.

Chapter 7 is a conclusion. Based on the findings in previous chapters on the status and roles of NSAs in each cultural heritage convention, this chapter will attempt to draw conclusions on the status and roles of each category of NSA. Based on this, a general synthesis of the status and roles of NSAs in international cultural heritage law will be provided. These analyses will enable identification of obstacles to further promotion of NSA participation in international cultural heritage law, and will also suggest means of involving them for better protection of cultural heritage by international conventions.

1.3 Terminologies

1.3.1 Non-State Actor (NSA)

There is no clear definition of 'NSA' in international law. Indeed, it is a deeply ambiguous term. Defined in the negative sense, it means the whole set of non-State actors, from natural individuals, NGOs, MNCs, to armed opposition groups. They can be broken down by characteristics into smaller categories such as international organizations, civil society organizations, political parties, indigenous peoples, epistemic communities, and others. The tendency to class all NSAs as one legal entity has been criticized as an oversimplification of the different characteristics of each (Alston 2005, pp. 3–36). Indeed, unlike fairly concise and homogeneous groups of some 190 and more States in the world, it is rather difficult to indicate similarity and dissimilarity among NSAs.

Mostly, NSAs have been treated as 'individuals' in international law. First of all, individuals can be defined as a single human being or a natural human person. However, in a broader sense, the term can refer to more than a single human being, including groups, corporations, and NGOs. This definition cannot be synonymous with NSAs, which includes all participants in the international system that are not States or State-like entities (Gorski 2007, para. 6), such as intergovernmental organizations. In fact, groups can refer to more than a single person literally, but in some contexts, they may mean terrorist groups and transnational criminal organizations that are subject to sanctions of the UN Security Council.[10]

Concerning international criminal responsibility, individuals tend to be confined to natural persons, as the Rome Statute of the International Criminal Court (ICC) provides.[11] This is in line with a narrow definition of individuals, and can be referred to as 'private individuals' as well, as stated by the Permanent Court of International Justice (PCIJ) in its advisory opinion of the *Jurisdiction of the Courts of Danzig*.[12] Scholars also use this term to focus on individuals as natural persons (Tomuschat 2010, pp. 317–329).

For the purpose of this book, the definition of NSAs follows that of all non-State actors mentioned in the text of international cultural heritage law and those involved in their implementation. Therefore, according to the specific issue concerned, NSAs

---

[10] For further discussion on non-state actors, see also Peters et al. (2009).

[11] Article 25(1) reads: "The Court shall have jurisdiction over natural persons pursuant to this Statute."

[12] *Jurisdiction of the Courts of Danzig*, Advisory Opinion, 1928 P.C.I.J. (ser. B) No. 15 (Mar. 3), at 37.

Table 1.2 NSAs in international cultural heritage law

Subject/domain	NSAs				
	Int'l Orgs (UNESCO, etc.)	Experts (advisory bodies)	NGOs	Local communities	Individuals (General Public)
Protection of cultural property in armed conflict	v	v	v	–	v
Restitution of cultural property	v	–	–	–	v
Protection of world heritage	v	v	v	v	v
Protection of underwater cultural heritage	v	v	v	–	v
Protection of intangible cultural heritage	v	v	v	v	v

Source Author

can include not only natural human beings in a narrow sense but also groups that share a direct nexus with them.

Various NSAs according to different international cultural heritage law are summarized in Table 1.2. As can be seen, there are several kinds of NSA that are mentioned in international cultural heritage conventions, such as groups of experts,[13] NGOs, and international organizations. As their rights, duties and specific roles are set out in the provisions of the conventions and observed in the course of their implementation in various ways, they will be analyzed as separate categories of NSA in this book. For example, NGOs are mentioned in several international cultural heritage conventions, and some NGOs identify themselves as a spokesperson of the civil society or local people when they take part in the process of rule-making or monitoring. Although there remain problems of accountability, transparency, and governance of NGOs (Lindblom 2005; Dupuy and Vierucci 2008), those are beyond the scope of this book. Other NGOs, those consisting of experts, also play some advisory roles in the enforcement process of international cultural heritage law.

Similarly, individual or groups of experts play substantive roles in the implementation of conventions based on their own expertise, and international organizations,

[13] Among the experts, there exists some differences in terms of the characteristics of their participation in the implementation of conventions. For example, the ICOMOS and IUCN, the two advisory bodies for the nomination of the World Heritage List, stand independently from States based on the provisions of the 1972 Convention. Meanwhile, the evaluation body for the 2003 Convention consists of six representatives of accredited NGOs of the Convention and six individual experts who are selected by the Member States of the Intergovernmental Committee of the Convention. The specific characteristics of experts according to the different conventions will be duly discussed in the relevant chapters.

mostly UNESCO in this book, also have explicit roles as per the provisions of international cultural heritage conventions.[14] Therefore, within the specific legal context of each convention to be addressed in Chaps. 2 to 6, these entities will be dealt with as categories of NSA as well.

The term "local communities" is mentioned in the texts of several conventions, and therefore will be dealt with as a separate category of NSA. For example, in the aforementioned 2003 Convention, the individuals, groups and community that bear and transmit intangible cultural heritage are referenced, and these will all be categorized as a local community for convenience's sake. Local communities can be regarded as individuals as well, but they will be dealt with separately, as some conventions pay special attention to their rights, duties and roles respecting implementation.

1.3.2 Rights, Obligations, and Roles of NSAs

As specific elements indicative of the status of NSAs, 'rights' are defined in terms of both substantive rights and procedural rights. Indeed, the international community has witnessed dramatic progress in international law over the last century as concerns the rights of NSAs. Departing from the traditional view defining international law as a body of rules applicable to States in their relations with each other, a more multifaceted and cosmopolitan view toward international legal relations emerged (Parlett 2011, p. 3). In fact, under the Westphalian system wherein States were the dominant players, non-State actors were considered inferior to States, and were considered to be, rather, simple subjects, beneficiaries, or indirect subjects (Gorski 2007, paras. 11–12).

However, after World War II, scholars started to place more emphasis on the international personality of NSAs. George Scelle's radical idea of considering States as fictions and individual human beings as the only real subjects of international law (Orakhelashvili 2001, p. 244) no longer receives harsh criticism. As the International Court of Justice (ICJ) Stated in its Advisory Opinion in the *Reparations* case in 1949, "the subjects of law in any legal system are not necessarily identical in their nature or in the extent of their rights, and their nature depends upon the needs of the community".[15] Although the capacities of States and NSAs are different in degree and character, it cannot be denied that the latter have acquired international legal personality to some extent (Nijman 2004).

The considerable development of international human rights law as well as humanitarian law has contributed to the upholding of the status of NSAs, particularly natural

---

[14] International organizations are established based on the inter-state consent, but their secretariats will be the object of study in this book. For UNESCO, in addition to its basic role as the secretariat of the conventions, it has contributed to the implementation of international cultural heritage conventions as a specialized agency of the UN in the field of culture. Its concrete roles will be discussed in each of the chapters reviewing the respective conventions.

[15] *Reparations for Injuries Suffered in the Services of the United Nations*, Advisory Opinion [1949] ICJ Rep. 175.

persons, as true subjects of international law (Cançado Trindade 2011, p. 3). Since the Universal Declaration of Human Rights was adopted in 1948, many international and regional treaties have strengthened the protection of individuals.[16] International humanitarian law has been extended to provide for their protection during armed conflict. Under the scope of these legal mechanisms, individuals enjoy their substantive rights internationally.

Procedural rights guarantee the direct access of NSAs to national and international forums (Shelton et al. 2006, p. 250). These include participation in rule-making processes as well as implementation and monitoring mechanisms. Substantive rights are set out in the provisions of conventions and their relevant texts. These rights are enforced by individual claims based on the relevant provisions.

In terms of the obligations of NSAs, international criminal law has shown clearly that individuals are subject to it (Cassese 2008, pp. 403–527). From the Nuremberg Tribunal after World War II to the International Criminal Tribunal for the Former Yugoslavia (ICTY) and the International Criminal Tribunal for Rwanda (ICTR) in the 1990s, individuals have been indicted for war crimes. Currently, as a permanent international forum, ICC is revolutionarily challenging State sovereignty by subjecting individuals to prosecution for four categories of international crime: genocide, crimes against humanity, war crimes, and the crimes of aggression.[17] Other obligations prescribed in international human rights law or civil law can be included, though they are, rather, political messages without enforceability or require broader consensus for more concrete contents.

Concerning the roles of NSAs, this book aspires to offer insight into the consequences of the participation of the multitude of NSAs in the enforcement of international law, and looks at those NSAs both as participants in international cultural heritage conventions as well as objects of regulations. Indeed, the roles of NSAs have not been without influence on international legal rules (d'Aspremont 2011, p. 7). It has been acknowledged that NSAs are subjects or legitimate actors of international law, and their roles in the implementation of the law have been duly recognized in the international legal system (Bianchi 2009, p. xix). Therefore, this book, when addressing questions on the legal status of NSAs, includes cross-referencing inquiries into the roles of NSAs from the political science scholarship. Indeed, a closer look at the specific roles played by different NSAs will provide clues to understanding the

---

[16] Some of the major international treaties are as follows: the International Covenant on Civil and Political Rights (1966), International Covenant on Economic, Social and Cultural Rights (1966), Convention on the Elimination of All Forms of Discrimination against Women (1979), Convention against Torture and Other Cruel, Inhuman or Degrading Treatment or Punishment (1984), Convention on the Rights of the Child (1989), International Convention on the Protection of the Rights of All Migrant Workers and Members of Their Families (1990), and Convention on the Rights of Persons with Disabilities (2006). As for regional legal mechanisms, there are the European Convention for the Protection of Human Rights and Fundamental Freedoms (1950), American Convention on Human Rights (1969), African Charter on Human and Peoples' Rights (1981), and Arab Charter on Human Rights (2004).

[17] Article 5 of the Rome Statute of the International Criminal Court (1998).

complex interaction, amounting sometimes to power struggles, between States and NSAs.

In this work, the roles of NSAs will be analyzed for all of their categories, including international organizations, experts, NGOs, local communities, and individuals; however, the statuses of NSAs will be reviewed only for the categories of local communities and individuals, because rights and obligations under international cultural heritage law in general can be observed from only in those two contexts. Other NSAs, for example UNESCO, expert bodies or NGOs, play certain roles in the implementation of cultural heritage conventions without any explicit rights conferred to, or duties imposed on, them.

1.3.3 Cultural Heritage[18]

There exist some discrepancies in the terms relating to the main subject of the conventions analyzed in this book: cultural heritage. However, there is no single or universally accepted definition of terms such as 'cultural property', 'cultural heritage', and 'cultural object', though scholars have vigorously debated the different legal meanings of the respective terms (Prott and O'Keefe 1992, p. 307; O'Keefe 1999, p. 26; Blake 2000, p. 61; Frigo 2004, p. 367; Francioni 2007, p. 221). The term 'cultural property' was first used in a legal context in the 1954 Convention, which states that cultural property is something 'of great importance to the cultural heritage of every people', whether movable or immovable.[19]

The same term is defined more exhaustively in the 1970 Convention, which provides that 'cultural property' is "property which, on religious or secular grounds, is specifically designated by each State as being of importance for archaeology, prehistory, history, literature, art or science" (Article 1). The 1970 Convention then lists categories of cultural property that may be designated by States. This list has been openly criticized for its vague and broad definitions, but it has nonetheless served an important function by compelling each State to specifically consider which objects should be available for inclusion as cultural property (Forrest 2010, p. 23).

---

[18] Some parts of Sect. 1.3.3 have been borrowed from the earlier publication of the author (Kim 2013, pp. 5–7).

[19] Article 1 of the 1954 Convention reads: "For the purposes of the present Convention, the term 'cultural property' shall cover, irrespective of origin or ownership: (a) movable or immovable property of great importance to the cultural heritage of every people, such as monuments of architecture, art or history, whether religious or secular; archaeological sites; groups of buildings which, as a whole, are of historical or artistic interest; works of art; manuscripts, books and other objects of artistic, historical or archaeological interest; as well as scientific collections and important collections of books or archives or of reproductions of the property defined above; (b) buildings whose main and effective purpose is to preserve or exhibit the movable cultural property defined in sub-paragraph (a) such as museums, large libraries and depositories of archives, and refuges intended to shelter, in the event of armed conflict, the movable cultural property defined in sub-paragraph (a); (c) centers containing a large amount of cultural property as defined in sub-paragraphs (a) and (b), to be known as 'centers containing monuments'."

Compared to 'cultural property', the concept of 'cultural heritage' is evidently broader in scope, expressing a 'form of inheritance to be kept in safekeeping and handed down to future generations' (Blake 2000, p. 83). In the Article 1 of the 1972 Convention, this term encompasses all kinds of immovable cultural heritage, such as monuments, groups of buildings, and sites (Yusuf 2008, pp. 23–50), with clear indications of the duties of State parties in the Article 4 for the protection of said heritage. The 2001 Convention has similar denotations and connotations, but additionally includes movable underwater cultural heritage as well (Article 1).

In the 2003 Convention, 'cultural heritage' becomes associated with non-material cultural items, including "practices, representations, expressions, knowledge, skills—as well as the instruments, objects, artifacts and cultural spaces associated therewith—that communities, groups and, in some cases, individuals recognize as part of their cultural heritage" (Article 2(1)). This intangible notion of heritage is extended further, in the 2005 Convention, to 'cultural expressions,' specifically to "those expressions that result from the creativity of individuals, groups and societies, and that have cultural content," and 'cultural activities, goods and services' such as "those activities, goods and services, which at the time they are considered as a specific attribute, use or purpose, embody or convey cultural expressions, irrespective of the commercial value they may have" (Article 4(3) and (4)).

In the midst of this conceptual shift from property to heritage, the term 'cultural object' appeared in the negotiations leading to the 1995 Convention (Prott 1997, p. 17). Still broader than 'cultural property' or 'cultural goods', 'cultural objects' are defined as objects and works of art, and need to be included in the specific categories. An interesting point with regard to this definition is that it does not require any State action to entrust cultural objects to national inventories for their protection (Article 2).

Depending on the purpose of each legal doctrine, the definition of cultural property, cultural heritage, or cultural object can be more or less selective, as it usually is preceded by the phrase 'for the purpose of this convention', or something similar. Therefore, in this book, one or another of three terms will be used according to the specific provision being discussed. However, in more general contexts, 'cultural heritage,' for convenience, will be used as representative of all three terms.

With respect to the specific categories of cultural heritage, there exists a general division between tangible and intangible forms. Tangible heritage can be further divided into movable and immovable forms. Intangible cultural heritage includes cultural expressions, cultural activities, goods and services. The scope of application for each convention is indicated in Table 1.3. These different types of heritage will be duly considered for analysis in this book, as they are each closely related to the status and roles of NSAs. A detailed explanation of the subject of heritage according to each convention will be provided in the respective introductions of Chaps. 2 to 6.

Table 1.3 Types of cultural heritage subject to different international cultural heritage law

Convention	Type of cultural heritage for protection		
	Tangible		Intangible
	Movable	Immovable	
1954 convention and two protocols	v	v	–
1970 convention	v	–	–
1972 convention	–	v	–
1995 convention	v	–	–
2001 convention	v	v	–
2003 convention	–	–	V

Source Author

References

Aldrich GH (1996) Individuals as subjects of international humanitarian law. In: Makarczyk J (ed) Theory of international law at the threshold of the 21st century. Kluwer, The Hague

Alston P (2005) The "Not-a-Cat" syndrome: can the international human rights regime accommodate non-state actors? In: Alston P (ed) Non-state actors and human rights. Oxford University Press, Oxford

Anaya SJ (1996) Indigenous peoples in international law. Oxford University Press, Oxford

Arend AC (1998) Do legal rules matter? International law and international politics. Virginial J Int Law 38:107–153

Ashworth GJ, Graham B, Tunbridge JE (2007) Pluralising pasts: heritage, identity and place in multicultural societies. Pluto Press, London

Bederman DJ (1995) The souls of international organizations: legal personality and the lighthouse at cape spartel. Virginia J Int Law 36:275–379

Bianchi A (2009) Introduction: relativizing the subjects of subjectivizing the actors: is that the question? In: Bianchi A (ed) Non-state actors and international law. Ashgate, Farnham

Blake J (2000) On defining the cultural heritage. Int Comp Law Quart 49(1):61–85

Blake J (2014) Exploring cultural rights and cultural diversity: an introduction with selected legal materials. Institute of Art and Law, Leicester

Blake J (2015) International cultural heritage law. Oxford University Press, Oxford

Bonafè BI (2009) The relationship between state and individual responsibility for international crimes. Martinus Nijhoff, Leiden

Brodie N, Doole J, Watson P (2000) Stealing history: the illicit trade in cultural material. ICOM and Museums Association, UK

Brown MF (2003) Who owns native culture? Harvard University Press, Cambridge

Cançado Trindade AA (2010) International law for humankind: to-wards a new jus gentium. Martinus Nijhoff, The Hague

Cançado Trindade AA (2011) The access of individuals to international justice. Oxford University Press, Oxford

Cassese A (2005) International law. Oxford University Press, Oxford

Cassese A (ed) (2008) The human dimension of international law. Oxford University Press, Oxford

Chapman J (1994) Notes: destruction of a common heritage: the archaeology of war in Croatia. Bosnia and Hercegovinia. Antiquity 68(1):120–126

Cheng B (1991) Introduction to subjects of international law. In: Bedjaoui M (ed) International law: achievements and prospects. UNESCO and Martinus Nijhoff, Paris and Dordrecht

Clapham A (2010) The role of the individuals in international law. Eur J Int Law 21(1):25–30

Correa CM (2001) Traditional knowledge and intellectual property: issues and options surrounding the protection of traditional knowledge. Quaker United Nations' Office, Geneva

D'Aspremont J (ed) (2011) Participants in the international legal system: multiple perspectives on non-state actors in international law. Routledge, Abingdon

Daes E-I (2007) The protection of the heritage of indigenous people. United Nations, New York

Damgaard C (2008) Individual criminal responsibility for core international crimes: selected pertinent issues. Springer, Berlin

Dupuy P-M, Vierucci L (eds) (2008) NGOs in international law: efficiency in flexibility? Edward Elga, Cheltenham

Ehlert C (2013) Prosecuting the destruction of cultural property in international crimi-nal law: with a case study on the Khmer Rouge's destruction of Cambodia's herit-age. Martinus Nijhoff, Leiden

Forrest C (2010) International law and the protection of cultural heritage. Routledge, London

Francioni F (2007) A dynamic evolution of the concept and scope: from cultural property to cultural heritage. In: Yusuf AA (ed) Standard setting in unesco vol. 1: normative action in education, science and culture. Martinus Nijhoff, Leiden

Frigo M (2004) Cultural property v. cultural heritage: a battle of concepts in international law? Int Rev Red Cross 86(854):367–378

Frulli M (2011) The criminalization of offences against cultural heritage in times of armed conflict: the quest for consistency. Eur J Int Law 22(1):203–217

Gaja G (2010) The position of individuals in international law: an ILC perspective. Eur J Int Law 21(1):25–30

Gorski S (2007) Individuals in international law. In: Wolfrum R (ed) The Max Planck encyclopedia of public international law. Oxford University Press, Oxford. (Online edition, www.mpepil.com)

Greenfield J (1989) The return of cultural treasures. Cambridge University Press, Cambridge

Hafner G (2009) Some thoughts on the state-oriented and individual-oriented approaches in international law. Austrian Rev Int Eur Law 14:27–39

Hodgson D (2003) Individual duty within a human rights discourse. Ashgate, Aldershot

Kim J (2013) International cooperation to prevent trafficking and facilitate restitution of cultural property: evolving normative frameworks. Master of International Studies, Graduate School of International Studies, Seoul National University

Kowalski WA (1998) Art treasures and war: a study on the restitution of looted cultural property, pursuant to public international law. Institute of Art and Law, Leicester

Langfield M, Logan WS, Craith MN (eds) (2009) Cultural diversity, heritage and human rights: intersections in theory and practice. Routledge, London

Lenzerini F (2013) The role of international and mixed criminal courts in the enforcement of international norms concerning the protection of cultural heritage. In: Francioni F, Gordley J (eds) Enforcing international cultural heritage law. Oxford University Press, Oxford

Lindblom A-K (2005) Non-governmental organisations in international law. Cambridge University Press, Cambridge

Lostal M (2015) Syria's world cultural heritage and individual criminal responsibility. Int Rev Law 3:1–17

Nijman JE (2004) The concept of international legal personality: an inquiry into the history and theory of international law. T.M.C. Asser Press, The Hague

Nowlan J (1993) Cultural property and the Nuremberg war crimes trial. Humanitäres Völkerrecht 6(4):221–223

O'Keefe R (1999) The meaning of 'cultural property' under the 1954 hague convention. Netherlands Int Law Rev 46(1):26–56

O'Keefe R (2010) Protection of cultural property under international criminal law. Melborne Journal of International Law 11:339–392

Orakhelashvili A (2001) The position of the individual in international law. California Western Int Law J 31(2):241–276

Parlett K (2011) The individual in the international legal system: continuity and change in international law. Cambridge University Press, Cambridge

Peters A (2016) Beyond human rights: the legal status of the individual in international law. Cambridge University Press, Cambridge
Peters A, Koechilin L, Till TF, Zinkernagel GF (eds) (2009) Non-state actors as stand-ard setters. Cambridge University Press, Cambridge
Posey DA, Dutfield G (1997) Beyond intellectual property: towards traditional resource rights for indigenous peoples and local communities. IDRC, Ottawa
Prott LV, O'Keefe PJ (1992) 'Cultural heritage' or 'cultural property'? Int J Cult Prop 1(2):307–320
Prott LV (1997) Commentary on the UNIDROIT convention. Institute of Art and Law, Leicester
Randelzhofer A (1999) The legal position of the individual under present international law. In: Randelzhofer A, Tomuschat C (eds) State responsibility and the individual: reparation in instances of grace violations of human rights. Martinus Nijhoff, The Hague
Shelton D, Nmehielle VO, Cerone J (2006) Status of the individual in international law. Am Soc Int Law 100:249–277
Stamatopoulou E (2007) Cultural rights in international law: article 27 of the universal declaration of human rights and beyond. Brill, Leiden
Stephens B (2002) Individuals enforcing international law: the comparative and historical context. DePaul Law Rev 52(2):433–472
Thürer D (2005) The emergence of non-governmental organizations and transnational enterprises in international law and the changing role of the state. In: Hofmann R (ed) Non-state actors as new subjects of international law. Duncker & Humblot, Berlin
Tomuschat C (2003) Human rights: between idealism and realism. Oxford University Press, Oxford
Tomuschat C (2010) The responsibility of other entities: private individuals. In: Crawford J, Pellet A, Olleson S (eds) The law of international responsibility. Oxford University Press, Oxford
Vicuña FO (2003) Regulatory authority and legitimate expectations: balancing the rights of the state and the individual under international law in a global society. Int Law FORUM Du Droit Int 5(3):188–197
Yusuf AA (2008) Article 1-definition of cultural heritage. In: Francioni F (ed) The 1972 world heritage convention: a commentary. Oxford University Press, Oxford

Chapter 2
The Protection of Cultural Property in Armed Conflict

A blue and white shield is the symbol of the Hague Convention for the Protection of Cultural Property in the Event of Armed Conflict (1954; hereinafter, '1954 Convention'). This first international legal instrument is intended as a 'shield' for the protection of cultural property that may be damaged in war zones.

Since the adoption of the 1954 Convention and its two Protocols in 1954 and 1999, Contracting States as well as NSAs have participated in their implementation. In particular, various NSAs ranging from UNESCO, experts, and NGOs to individuals have shown various statuses and roles that have been altered as the provisions of the Convention and its Protocols have adapted to changing global environments. Indeed, the development of the Guidelines for the Implementation of the Second Protocol (hereinafter, 'Guidelines') since their introduction in 2009 demonstrates that there have been considerable changes in terms of the status and roles of NSAs with time. Cases of NSA participation in the implementation of the Convention and Protocols support this interpretation, with additional differences according to the various NSA categories.

After introducing the background and key contents of the 1954 Convention and its two Protocols, this chapter will analyze their legal texts related to the status and roles of different NSAs. Then it will examine several cases to evaluate those NSAs' participation in the implementation of the Convention's provisions.

J. Kim, *Non-State Actors in the Protection of Cultural Heritage*, Creativity, Heritage and the City 3, https://doi.org/10.1007/978-981-16-6659-9_2

2.1 Introduction of the Legal Protection of Cultural Property in the Event of Armed Conflict

2.1.1 History of the Adoption of the 1954 Convention and its Key Contents

Following up on the Lieber Code (1863) of the United States, which sought to limit the destruction of cultural property during wartime (Articles 34–36), the 1899 Hague Convention (II) with respect to the Laws and Customs of War on Land (para. 9 of the Preamble, Articles 46, 53, 55, and 56) and the 1907 Hague Convention (IV) respecting the Laws and Customs of War on Land (Articles 23, 25, 27, 28, 46, 47, 53, 55, and 56) developed provisions to protect cultural property in the context of civilian property during land warfare. The Roerich Pact, signed by the United States and 20 Latin American countries in 1935,[1] took a more advanced approach with respect to "cultural treasure of peoples" in times of both peace and war (Preamble). A draft convention for the entire international community was prepared and submitted to the League of Nations in April 1938, with the active support of the government of the Netherlands (O'Keefe and Prott 2011, p. 16), but the outbreak of the Second World War prevented further steps.

In light of the widespread and extensive damage to cultural heritage properties that occurred during that war, many countries became determined to create an international legal instrument to prohibit and/or punish such destruction. Three years after being established as the only United Nations organization with a mandate for culture, UNESCO provided a suitable and effective platform for the difficult negotiations, which had to compromise between the humanitarian and military requirements of different nations. At the same time, the 1949 Geneva Conventions, especially the Fourth Convention relative to the Protection of Civilian Persons in Time of War, exercised a fundamental influence on the draft of the new Convention (Chamberlain 2013, p. 20). In particular, Article 53 of the Fourth Convention explicitly prohibited the destruction of cultural property by an Occupying Power except where such act is made absolutely necessary by military operations.

Based on comprehensive studies led by UNESCO in cooperation with the International Council of Museums (ICOM) and consultations with Member States of UNESCO at its General Conference (Toman 1996, pp. 21 et seq.), the final draft of the 1954 Hague Convention was adopted at the Diplomatic Conference with the

[1] Treaty on the Protection of Artistic and Scientific Institutions and Historic Monuments (Roerich Pact). The former Soviet Union signed the Pact in 1954, making it the only non-American party to do so.

participation of fifty-six Member States on May 14, 1954, in The Hague, the Netherlands.[2] Since its entry into force on 7 August 1956, the Convention has been ratified by 133 States.[3]

The 1954 Convention is the first legally binding international instrument that focuses solely on the protection of cultural property during armed conflict and occupation. As stated in the Preamble, the basic principles of the Convention are that "damage to cultural property belonging to any people whatsoever means damage to the cultural heritage of all mankind, since each people makes its contribution to the culture of the world" (para. 2) and that "this heritage should receive international protection" (para. 3). Hereafter, these became the founding principles for the development of all international heritage laws (O'Keefe and Prott 2011, p. 16).

The objects of the 1954 Convention are both movable and immovable cultural properties with great importance, buildings holding those properties, or centers containing monuments (Article 1). Upon ratification of the Convention, States Parties are requested to respect and safeguard cultural property (Articles 2 to 4). Particularly, Article 4(2) states that this duty "may be waived only in cases where military necessity imperatively requires such a waiver." Another duty of States Parties in that regard is to train their respective militaries in the principles of the Convention (Article 7). For an occupying power, a special series of duties are set out as well, such as supporting the local authorities' safeguarding and preservation of cultural property and cooperating with them if they are unable to take necessary measures (Article 5).

A distinctive label and symbol for cultural property (Articles 6, 16 and 17), a blue and white shield, was developed with the intention of performing the same role for cultural property as did the Red Cross and Red Crescent for the protection of people by the Geneva Conventions. Similarly, there exists a mechanism of 'Special Protection' under the Convention (Articles 8 to 11) that grants special protection to sites or 'refuges' of the cultural property inscribed on the list maintained by UNESCO, but it has been very little used. Later, this system was improved by the Second Protocol of the 1954 Convention adopted in 1999.

The Convention is annexed by the Regulations for the Execution of the Convention that include 21 Articles divided into four chapters dealing with Control (Articles 1 to 10), Special Protection (Articles 11 to 16), Transport of Cultural Property (Articles 17 to 19) and Distinctive Emblem (Articles 20 and 21). There is no particular reason why the Convention is divided into two parts, Convention and Regulations; it is said to have been an historical accident without any intentionality for the latter having a lower status than the Convention (Chamberlain 2013, p. 75). Basically, the Regulations facilitate the implementation of the Convention, just as the Operational Guidelines do for the 1972 World Heritage Convention and the Operational Directives do for the 2003 Intangible Cultural Heritage Convention. The Second Protocol of the 1954

[2] Pursuant to Article 33 of the 1954 Convention, it entered into force on 7 August 1956.

[3] As of 30 November 2020. Israel and the United States of America ratified the Convention in 1957 and 2009 respectively, but they left UNESCO as of 31 December 2018. However, their withdrawal from the Organization does not imply denunciation.

Convention also has its Guidelines for implementation. However, the Regulations being a part of the Convention have not been revised, unlike those other Conventions' Guidelines or Directives, which have been regularly updated in response to changing cultural heritage protection environments.

2.1.2 *First Protocol to the 1954 Convention*

The 1954 Convention could not address the issue of large-scale looting and illicit export of cultural property from occupied territories, such as what had happened during the Second World War. This was mainly due to the complexities related to the pertinent private law issues, such as the burden of proof of *bona fide* acquirers and the limitation period for restitution claims. Many delegations attending the negotiations for the 1954 Convention were not prepared to accede to the draft provisions related to these issues (O'Keefe and Prott 2011, p. 18). As a result, the relevant original provisions of the draft Convention were incorporated into a separate Protocol, namely the Protocol to the Convention for the Protection of Cultural Property in the Event of Armed Conflict 1954 (hereinafter, 'First Protocol'). Nonetheless, nine States attending the Conference in 1954 signed the Convention but refused to sign the Protocol,[4] and a Resolution was adopted by the Conference to express the hope that the Director-General of UNESCO would convene a meeting of the High Contracting Parties as soon as possible, aiming at enabling the Parties to proceed with further study on the issue of the return of cultural property (Toman 1996, p. 343).

The First Protocol, which interested States may join separately from the 1954 Convention itself, consists of three Parts. Part I (paras. 1 to 4) is related to the return of cultural property exported from a territory under occupation. In detail, a State Party that occupies a territory during armed conflict shall prevent the export of cultural property from that territory (para. 1). Furthermore, if the occupying State Party discovers any cultural property that has been illegally imported from the occupied territory, the State Party is obliged to seize it (para. 2) and return it to the competent authorities of the original territory after the hostilities have ended (para. 3), along with an indemnity to the rightful holders in good faith (*bona fide*) of the property (para. 4). Part II (para. 5) concerns the return of property coming from the territory of one Contracting Party and deposited in that of another party for protection. Lastly, Part III (paras. 6 to 15) includes the final provisions. When joining the First Protocol, states have the option of accepting the Protocol in its entirety or opting to accept either Part I or II (para. 9).

[4] Andorra, Australia, Hungary, Ireland, Israel, New Zealand, Portugal, Romania, the United Kingdom and the United States of America.

The First Protocol has been ratified by 110 Member States of UNESCO.[5] However, it has hardly ever been applied, and almost no States Parties have specific legislation related to it, simply because more comprehensive conventions have since come into being, such as the 1970 UNESCO Convention on the Means of Prohibiting and Preventing the Illicit Import, Export and Transfer of Ownership of Cultural Property (O'Keefe and Prott 2011, p. 37). However, the First Protocol retains great significance as the first international legal instrument to address the illegal export of cultural objects.

2.1.3 Second Protocol to the 1954 Convention Adopted in 1999

The 1954 Convention gained additional international recognition through the 1977 Protocols I and II additional to the 1949 Geneva Conventions.[6] Article 53 of Protocol I and Article 16 of Protocol II recognized that the 1954 Convention and its Protocol constitute an instrument of paramount importance for the international protection of the cultural heritage of all mankind against the effects of armed conflict and that the application of the Convention will in no way be prejudiced by the adoption of the Articles [Article 53 of Protocol I and Article 16 of Protocol II] (Toman 1996, p. 379). Moreover, the Statute of the International Tribunal for the Prosecution of Persons Responsible for Serious Violations of International Humanitarian Law Committed in the Territory of Former Yugoslavia since 1991 (ICTY), which was established under United Nations Security Council Resolution 827 in 1993, declared, in Article 3(d), that "seizure of, destruction or willful damage done to institutions dedicated to religion, charity and education, the arts and sciences, historic monuments and works of art and science." Moreover, the Rome Statute of the International Criminal Court (ICC), drafted in 1998, also defined as 'war crimes,' "intentional attacks against buildings dedicated to religion, education, art, science or charitable purposes, as well as historic monuments, in both international and non-international armed conflicts" (Articles 2(b)(ix) and (e)(iv)), which move reflected the awareness-raising of the international community concerning the subject matter to that point.

In the meantime, the effectiveness of the 1954 Convention had become an issue of general concern to the international community during the conflicts in Iran, Iraq, Kuwait and the former Yugoslavia in the 1980s and 1990s. Recognizing the insufficiency of the 1954 Convention as a regime to protect cultural heritage during armed conflict, the Government of the Netherlands and UNESCO jointly commissioned

[5] As of 30 November 2020.

[6] Protocol Additional to the Geneva Conventions of 12 August 1949, and relating to the Protection of Victims of International Armed Conflicts (Protocol I), 8 June 1977 and Protocol Additional to the Geneva Conventions of 12 August 1949, and relating to the Protection of Victims of Non-International Armed Conflicts (Protocol II), 8 June 1977. As of 30 May 2021, 174 States are Parties to Protocol I, and 169 States are Parties to Protocol II.

a review of the 1954 Convention and its Protocol (Boylan 1993), and began the process of supplementation, which came to be embodied in another Protocol. The five main areas that the draft of the Second Protocol focused on were the exception of military necessity; precautionary measures; the system of special protection; individual criminal responsibility, and institutional aspects (Chamberlain 2013, p. 123). The Diplomatic Conference was held in The Hague again, in March 1999, and on the 26th of March, the Second Protocol to the Hague Convention of 1954 for the Protection of Cultural Property in the Event of Armed Conflict (hereinafter, 'Second Protocol') was adopted by consensus.[7] Unlike the First Protocol that has independent standing, the Second Protocol is additional to the 1954 Convention (Article 2), which means that a State can become a Party to the Second Protocol only if it is a Party to the 1954 Convention (Articles 40 to 42). So far, 84 States have become Parties to the Second Protocol.[8]

The Protocol consists of 47 Articles, divided into nine chapters. After the introduction in Chap. 1 (Articles 1 to 4), general provisions regarding protection (Articles 5 to 9) follow in Chap. 2. It is significant that a more precise definition of "military necessity" (Article 6) was included in this chapter. More details on precautions to be taken to limit damage to cultural property in the event of attack (Article 7) were specified, with the principle of "proportionality," for the first time,[9] as well as those to be taken against the effects of hostilities (Article 8).

In Chap. 3, a new regime of 'enhanced protection' that replaces the 'special protection' of the 1954 Convention was introduced. Bearing in mind that entry in the International Register of Cultural Property under Special Protection was conditional on the property being situated at an adequate distance from any large industrial center or from any important military objective, which was almost impossible to fulfil for many cultural property located in a city center or area surrounded by potential military objectives, the Second Protocol eliminated the distance criterion and introduced new conditions (Article 10). In addition, decisions on the management of the List of Cultural Property under Enhanced Protection became the authority of the Committee for the Protection of Cultural Property in the Event of Armed Conflict (Articles 11 and 14), established under Article 24 of the Second Protocol.

According to Chap. 4 on criminal responsibility and jurisdiction, States Parties shall prosecute and penalize violation of the provisions of the Convention or the Second Protocol. It defines 'serious violation' and asks the States to adopt necessary legislative measures in their national criminal law for punishment (Article 15). Articles 16 to 18 enable a State to prosecute or extradite those accused of serious violations and expand its jurisdiction wherein the alleged offender is found or where the offence occurred on its territory or where the alleged offender is a national of

---

[7] The Second Protocol entered into force on 9 March 2004.

[8] As of 30 November 2020.

[9] Article 7(d) reads: "cancel or suspend an attack if it becomes apparent: (…) (ii) that the attack may be expected to cause incidental damage to cultural property protected under Article 4 of the Convention which would be excessive in relation to the concrete and direct military advantage anticipated."

that State. In addition, Article 21 specifically calls for a State to adopt legislative and administrative or disciplinary measure to suppress any illicit export or other removal or transfer of ownership of cultural property from occupied territory.

Article 22 of Chap. 5 confirms the principle of the application of the Second Protocol both in civil and international conflicts. This provision stems from the case of Yugoslavia, where a State was divided and some of its former parts were recognized as independent States by different States, which made enforcement difficult once the conflict became an international one (O'Keefe and Prott 2011, p. 45). A similar problem arose concerning the recognition of Croatia as an independent State.

Lastly, the establishment of an intergovernmental committee to supervise the implementation of conventions, part of an existing trend in UNESCO, was an effective mechanism by which to follow up the implementation of multilateral treaties with the involvement of States Parties in the 1990s (O'Keefe and Prott 2011, pp. 43–44). The Committee created under the Second Protocol was an institutional response to enhance the effectiveness of the Protocol (Articles 24 to 28) as well. The creation of the Fund for the Protection of Cultural Property in the Event of Armed Conflict (hereinafter, 'Fund') to provide for collective international assistance in support of preparatory or emergent measures to be taken to protect cultural property during periods of armed conflict, was another new institutional aspect of the Second Protocol (Article 29).

2.2 NSAs in the 1954 Convention and its Two Protocols

As noted above, States Parties shall protect and respect cultural property by taking necessary measures. Concerning the transportation of cultural property, the two Protocols impose additional duties of return of illicitly trafficked instances to the States Parties. They also apply for international lists, appropriate training and education of military and civil society, respectively, and periodical submission of reports to UNESCO.[10] The Meeting of States Parties and Intergovernmental Committee functions to deal with general matters of the Convention and the Protocols in their implementation in addition to the management of the List in the case of the Intergovernmental Committee under the Second Protocol.

[10] Periodic reports on the 1954 Convention and its Protocols have not been regularly submitted. Since the entry into force of the 1954 Convention in 1956, the Director-General of UNESCO received national reports in 1962, 1965–1966, 1969–1970, 1977–1978, 1984, 1989, 1995 and 1998. In 2007, the Director-General reminded all Contracting Parties that the submission of the report was a statutory mandate for State Parties, and in 2010, he received 42 national reports for the period 2005–2010. Another submission was made in 2013 with 27 reports for the 2010–2012 cycle. The most recent periodic reporting was conducted in 2017, with 38 reports for the 2013–2016 cycle. Periodic reports submitted by States Parties are available at http://www.unesco.org/new/en/culture/themes/armed-conflict-and-heritage/convention-and-protocols/periodic-reporting/ (accessed 30 May 2021).

Compared with the States Parties, whose status and roles are well stipulated in the provisions, those of NSAs, as mentioned in the Convention and its two Protocols, are of only limited scope. For example, there are several provisions directly addressing UNESCO as a coordinator, supervisor, and service provider of the Convention and two Protocols, but sometimes an extended role is assigned as a conciliator or mediator in the absence of Protecting Powers. Meanwhile, individuals are referred to in rather indirect ways. Those with expertise can be appointed as a Commissioner-General for Cultural Property by relevant States once they are on the international list of persons managed by UNESCO, and play a series of roles in the course of the protection of the cultural property at issue. Similarly, NGOs specialized in this subject also are invited to serve specific roles, sometimes active ones, such as submitting a property for possible Enhanced Protection. The individuals who commit wrongdoing against the Convention and its two Protocols are subject to punishment. The *bona fide* possessors of the cultural property in question are the subjects of indemnity in the process of the return of the property to the country of origin. The different status and roles of each stakeholder of the 1954 Convention and its two Protocols can be summarized in Table 2.1, and those of the NSAs will further analyzed below in the next section.

2.2.1 NSAs in the Text of the 1954 Convention and its Regulations

UNESCO

Among the NSAs mentioned in the text of the 1954 Convention, UNESCO has the most explicit roles. Under Article 23(1), UNESCO is called to provide technical assistance to the States Parties in organizing the protection of their cultural property. Also, as a manager of the Convention, like many other Secretariats of international conventions, UNESCO convenes meetings of States Parties of the Convention to study problems concerning its application and execution of its Regulations, or undertake revisions of the Convention or Regulations (Article 27). UNESCO is also entitled to maintain the Convention's Register of Cultural Property under Special Protection (Article 12 of the Regulations). The Regulations demonstrate these roles in detail, from the receipt of application for registration (Article 13) and the handling of related objections (Article 14) to management of the Register (Articles 15 and 16). On another list under the Convention, the International List of Persons for Commissioner-General for Cultural Property, UNESCO compiles all persons nominated by the States Parties as qualified to carry out the functions of Commissioner-General and revises it periodically (Article 1 of the Regulations).

Further to UNESCO's roles as a Secretariat of the Convention, the 1954 Convention gives it more room to exert its own expertise and mandate according to its Constitution.[11] When there exists disagreement between Parties to the conflict as

[11] Article 1(2)(c) of the UNESCO Constitution: "Maintain, increase and diffuse knowledge: By assuring the conservation and protection of the world's inheritance of books, works of art and

Table 2.1 Stakeholders of the 1954 convention and its two protocols and their status and roles

Stakeholders		Status and roles			Goal
		1954 convention	1st protocol (1954)	2nd protocol (1999)	
States	States parties	Safeguarding and respecting cultural property	Preventing the export of cultural property and returning it	Safeguarding and respecting cultural property, Suppressing illicit export of cultural property	Protection of cultural property in the event of armed conflict Protection of cultural property in the event of armed conflict
		Application of the special protection register	–	Application of the enhanced protection list	
		Appointing a special representative for cultural property, training military, dissemination of the convention, reporting	–	Including experts in delegation, training for military and civilians, dissemination of the protocol, reporting	
		Criminal Sanctions upon persons breaching the convention	Indemnity to the holders in good faith when returning	Criminal sanctions, prosecution, extradition upon persons breaching the convention and protocol	
		–	–	International cooperation, request of onternational assistance	
	Inter-governmental committee	–	–	Managing the enhanced protection list, developing guidelines for the protocol, monitoring the implementation, use of the fund	
				Cooperation with NGOs	

(continued)

Table 2.1 (continued)

Stakeholders		Status and roles			Goal
		1954 convention	1st protocol (1954)	2nd protocol (1999)	
	Meeting of the parties	Studying problems of the convention	–	Election of the committee, discussing problems of the protocol	
NSAs	UNESCO	Compiling the international list of commissioner-general for cultural property	–	–	
		Managing the special protection register		Managing the enhanced protection list	
		Invitation to the meeting of states parties		Invitation to the meeting of states parties, assisting the committee	
		Conciliation for disputes		Conciliation for disputes (incl. acting power)	
		Technical assistance to the states parties (incl. own initiatives)		Technical assistance to the states parties (incl. own initiatives)	
	NGOs	–	–	Application of the enhanced protection list	
		Providing advice to UNESCO for the register		Cooperation with the states parties and committee	

(continued)

Table 2.1 (continued)

Stakeholders		Status and roles			Goal
		1954 convention	1st protocol (1954)	2nd protocol (1999)	
	Experts (e.g. commissioner-general, inspectors, etc.)	(Commissioner-general) engaged in the protection activities (incl. acting power)	–	–	
		Providing advice to UNESCO for the special protection register		Providing advice to the committee for the enhanced protection list	
		–		Participation in the committee	
	Individuals (e.g. property holders, criminals, etc.)	Receipt of sanctions for infringement of the convention	Eligibility for an indemnity as a holder in good faith	Receipt of sanctions for infringement of the convention and protocol	

Source Author (based on the 1954 Convention and its two Protocols)

to the application or interpretation of the Convention or Regulations, UNESCO can invite the Parties concerned for a meeting, and can nominate a chair of the meeting as well (Article 22(2)). It is indeed noteworthy that UNESCO is entitled to invite conflicting Parties to a meeting. Compared with many other conventions including the Geneva Conventions, which leave the initiative for such a meeting only to the Parties concerned, the 1954 Convention lends more active roles to UNESCO (Toman 1996, p. 253). Furthermore, Article 23(2) enables UNESCO to make proposals on its own initiative concerning matters related to the execution of the Convention and its Regulations to the States Parties. Similarly, Article 19(3) enables UNESCO to offer its services to parties to conflicts that are not of an international character. It was the intention of the authors of the Convention to base their work on the examples of the Red Cross and the Geneva Convention, their wish being for UNESCO to play a role as a "Red Cross of Cultural Property" (Toman 1996, p. 256). The United Kingdom asked for the deletion of this article, arguing that UNESCO should act only when requested to do so by a Contracting Party and that this paragraph might interfere with the sovereignty of States, but this proposal was not supported by others, who wanted to confer upon UNESCO more than a passive role in this matter (Chamberlain 2013, p. 59). Indeed, UNESCO has played an active role in taking initiatives in conflicts risking cultural properties, and examples will be shown in Sect. 2.3.1 below.

Along with UNESCO, another International Organization, the International Court of Justice (ICJ), is mentioned twice in the Regulations as a decision-maker when disagreement occurs in choosing personnel between the Parties concerned. In the case of failure to reach consensus in appointing the Commissioner-General for Cultural Property between the Party to which he or she will be accredited and the Protecting Powers acting on behalf of the opposing Parties, the ICJ can intervene to appoint the person upon the request of Parties (Article 4(2)). However, the person appointed cannot take up the duties without the approval of the Party to which he or she is accredited, and therefore, it can be said that the impact of the ICJ's engagement is not that of assistance (Chamberlain 2013, p. 78). On the contrary, when disagreement between two parties occurs regarding an objection to a registration of cultural property for Special Protection, the ICJ's intervention in appointing a chief arbitrator becomes final (Article 14(7)). This provision can be understood in the light of the authority and expertise of the ICJ in arbitration.

Experts

As an individual expert, the Commissioner-General for Cultural Property is explicitly mentioned with specific roles in the provisions of the Regulations.[12] As soon as any State Party enters into a situation of armed conflict, the Commissioner-Generals

monuments of history and science, and recommending to the nations concerned the necessary international conventions."

[12] Although individuals engaged in the protection of cultural property are mentioned in Article 15 as 'personnel,' it is not clear whether 'personnel' means military or civilians, or both, and therefore, this article was not a subject of the analysis on the status of NSAs. Toman 1996, p. 256) argues the 'personnel' indicates both military and civilians, as this article was modeled on the First Geneva Convention, while Chamberlain (2013, p. 46) points that there are no definitions and that the rules applied to military and civilians are different.

should be appointed by joint agreement between the Parties concerned (Articles 2(c) and 4). His or her functions, which are substantive and broad, are well stipulated in Article 6. As a person dealing with all matters in connection with the application of the Convention, the Commissioner-General has powers of decision and appointment (Articles 6(1) and 6(2)). For example, he or she has the authority to grant the distinctive emblem of the Convention to an improvised refuge for its Special Protection, and to request the Director-General of UNESCO to enter the refuge in the Register of Cultural Property under Special Protection (Article 11). The Commissioner-General also can make any representations to the Parties concerned regarding the application of the Convention and can draw up such reports to the Parties (Articles 6(4) and 6(5)).

The decision-making power of the Commissioner-General extends to matters of immunity. The request to obtain immunity for transportation of cultural property should be directed to the Commissioner-General, and he or she can decide whether such transfer is justified or not (Articles 17(1) and 17(2)). Here, the decision lies solely with the Commissioner-General, as the Parties concerned are required to be consulted only on measures for carrying out the transfer. With respect to a transfer in occupied territory, the decision is made by the Commissioner-General whether the transfer is necessary and the usual custodians, those having responsibility for the safety of the property at issue, are invited for consultation only (Article 19). The Regulations even confer the functions of a Protecting Power on the Commissioner-General, in the absence of a proper Power (Article 6(6)). Considering the technical roles of the Commissioner-General, this provision seems extraordinary, and may be controversial in that there could be conflicts of interests between the impartiality of the Commissioner-General and the interests of the Parties (Chamberlain 2013, p. 80).

However, the right of the Commissioner-General is ultimately limited in that the order of investigation (Article 6(3)) or the appointment of inspectors and experts (Article 7) must obtain the approval of the Party to which he or she is accredited. Most of all, the mandates of the Commissioner-General (as well as delegates, inspectors and experts) should take account of the security needs of the Party (Article 8), and this fundamentally limits the powers granted to the Commissioner-General. The original draft of this Article stipulated both that the Party's security requirements be respected and that their activities could be restricted only on grounds of 'imperative military necessity,' but it was replaced by the United States (Chamberlain 2013, p. 81). As a result, not to mention the fact that the rights and duties of the Commissioner-Generals can be conferred only by States Parties, their actions are also subject to restriction in the name of 'military situation' as defined by States Parties.

As an expert in the field, individuals can be invited to deliver advisory services to UNESCO concerning objections to the registration of specific cultural property on the International Register of Cultural Property under Special Protection addressed to UNESCO. According to the Regulation, the Director-General of UNESCO, if necessary, may seek the advice of the International Committee on Monuments, Artistic and Historical Sites and Archaeological Excavations[13] and any competent organization or person (Article 14(3)). Both individuals and NGOs can function only on the invitation of the Director General, and therefore, UNESCO has a leadership role in mobilizing the expertise of these entities.

Individuals

The status of individuals involved in matters of cultural property protection during armed conflict can be inferred through the duties of States Parties. However, in terms of the legal premise for individuals' obligations, the ground of the States Parties' sanction on individuals in other words, is set out directly in the Preamble of the Convention. In paragraph 3, the Convention emphasizes that "the preservation of the cultural heritage is of great importance for all peoples of the world" and justifies the necessity of its international protection (para. 4). When considering the authors' intention to change the usual term 'international community of States' to 'all peoples of the world,' it can be interpreted that the duty for the protection of cultural heritage is to be imposed on all people in the world without this necessarily having to be done through the conventional government regimes (Toman 1996, p. 42).

Individuals' obligations towards all (*erga omnes*) becomes more concrete in Article 28, where they become subjects of criminal sanctions for breaching the provisions of the Convention. This Article followed the tradition of the 1907 Hague Regulations[14] and the 1936 Preliminary Draft Convention of the International Museums Office,[15] leaving the prosecution of offenders to the States. Although the Convention does not contain any list of possible breaches, mainly due to the different criminal systems among States Parties, it does contain several provisions whose breach may entail the criminal responsibility of individuals as well as those who order such actions to be committed. These include attacks on cultural property under general protection without justification of military necessity (Article 4(1)), theft, pillage or misappropriation of, and acts of vandalism committed against, cultural property (Article 4(3)), attacks on cultural property under Special Protection without justification by unavoidable military necessity (Article 9), attacks against transport of cultural property under Special Protection (Article 12), attacks on personnel engaged in the protection (Article 15), and the misuse, of the emblem of the Convention (Article 17). Other than these breaches, the Convention asks the States Parties to take their own actions, as the breach is the responsibility only of the Parties concerned (Chamberlain 2013, p. 65).

Another aspect of this criminal responsibility of individuals is that it does not establish universal jurisdiction. Article 28 enables the States Parties to impose sanctions on persons who commit breaches "whatever their nationality," but "within the

---

[13] Statutes of the International Committee on Monuments, Artistic and Historical Sites and Archaeological Excavations were drafted in 1951, and the final statues were adopted in 1959 with amendments.

[14] Article 56 reads: "...all seizure of, destruction or willful damage done to historic monuments, works of art and science, is forbidden, and should be made the subject of legal proceedings."

[15] Article 3(3) requires Contracting States "to take steps to punish in time of war any person looting or damaging monuments and works of art."

framework of their ordinary criminal jurisdiction." Therefore, individuals can be subject to punishment by States only when there exists a nexus between the two with regard to territory or nationality. The difference between the criminal responsibility of individuals under the 1954 Convention and that under the Second Protocol that establishes universal jurisdiction lies here.

2.2.2 NSAs in the Text of the First Protocol

The only NSAs that are set out in the provisions of the First Protocol are individuals as holders of cultural property in good faith.[16] In paragraph 4, States Parties shall pay an indemnity to the *bona fide* acquirer of cultural property that has to be returned to the territory previously occupied. This functions as a sanction on any Parties that failed to fulfil the mandate, under paragraph 1, for prevention of the exportation of cultural property from a territory occupied. In other words, this implies the upholding of the right of individuals, who may have acquired the property not knowing that it had been illegally exported, for just compensation from the State concerned. This is to protect the contractual right of the good-faith acquirer, whose ownership would undoubtedly constitute a 'possession' for the purposes of Article 1 of the First Protocol to the European Convention on Human Rights (ECHR), and therefore, a Party taking the property into custody without paying any compensation would breach Article 1 (Chamberlain 2013, p. 105).

However, the First Protocol does not go further into this issue of indemnity for holders in good faith. For example, there is no time limit as to how long ago the property at issue should have been illicitly exported.[17] At the same time, no definition of 'good faith' was provided either.[18] And, it was not mentioned how indemnification

---

[16] UNESCO is also mentioned as a depository of the Protocol dealing with accession, denunciation, and meetings of States Parties, but this will not be discussed here, as those roles are ordinary and basic mandates of any international organization for the management of its multilateral treaties.

[17] Later, the 1995 UNIDROIT Convention on Stolen or Illegally Exported Cultural Objects, which was formulated by UNIDROIT with the close cooperation of UNESCO to address the issue of return of cultural property in international private law, set a limitation on claiming restitution or return of 50 years from the date of theft (to be extended up to 75 years for objects belonging to a public collection), or within three years from the time when the claimant learns the location of the cultural objects (Article 3).

[18] The 1995 UNIDROIT Convention has several provisions addressing this issue as well. Article 4(1) says that "the possessor of a stolen cultural object required to return it shall be entitled to payment of fair and reasonable compensation provided that the possessor neither knew nor ought reasonably to have known that the object was stolen and can prove that it exercised due diligence when acquiring the object." The due diligence test may include review of "the character of the parties, the price paid, whether accessible registers of stolen cultural objects and other relevant documentation were consulted, and whether accessible agencies were consulted (Article 4(4)). The possessors of illegally exported cultural objects are entitled to fair and reasonable compensation by the requesting State (Article 6). These issues will be further analyzed in the following Chap. 3.

by the Occupying State would proceed.[19] These questions were considered as matters of private law, regarding which, each country has different definitions and practices. As a result, due to the vagueness of the provision, the rights of individuals in the First Protocol became merely declaratory and difficult to pursue.

2.2.3 NSAs in the Text of the Second Protocol

UNESCO

UNESCO has two independent Articles in the Second Protocol that explicitly addresses its functions. The first concerns its function as an assistant to the Committee for the Protection of Cultural Property in the Event of Armed Conflict (hereinafter, 'Committee') (Article 28), and the other, as a provider of technical assistance to States Parties in organizing the protection of their cultural property (Article 33(1)). The former is related to the institutional function of UNESCO as a Secretariat of the Second Protocol, and the power of convening meetings of States Parties regularly as well as Extraordinary Meetings is understood in the same vein (Articles 23(1) and 23(4)). In addition, as it did for the Register of Cultural Property under Special Protection of the 1954 Convention, but in a rather limited way yielding most of the roles to the Committee, UNESCO contributes to the maintenance of the List of Cultural Property under Enhanced Protection by notifying any decision of the Committee related to the List to the United Nations and all States Parties (Articles 11(11) and 14(3)).

The latter is same as the mandates of UNESCO stipulated in Article 23(2) of the 1954 Convention, including the paragraph authorizing UNESCO to make proposals on these matters on its own initiative (Article 33(3)). This discretionary power of UNESCO to act independently with its expertise is set out in Article 22(7) as well, where UNESCO may offer its services to the parties to non-international conflicts, which power was already recognized in Article 19(3) of the 1954 Convention. In addition, the role of UNESCO as a neutral body with expertise goes further in the conciliation process. As under the 1954 Convention, UNESCO can propose a meeting to the Parties in disagreement as to the application or interpretation of the Second Protocol and present a person as a chair as well (Article 35(2)); however, the Second Protocol even lends the role of conciliator or mediator to UNESCO in the absence of Protecting Powers (Article 36(1)).[20] There exists a similar clause in the 1954 Convention (Article 6(6)), wherein the Commissioner-General functions as the Protecting

[19] At the Diplomatic Conference, the delegate of Greece argued that an occupied country, sometimes perhaps ruined, could not be asked to bear the cost of indemnification, and therefore that it ought to be borne by the occupying Power. After the vote, the final text of the Protocol imposed the obligation of the payment of an indemnity only on the occupying Party and not on the Parties into whose territory the property was imported or on the authorities of the territory previously occupied (Toman 1996, p. 347).

[20] This will be the case where the armed conflict is non-international (Chamberlain 2013, p. 169).

Power in the absence of a proper Power, but the role of UNESCO here in the Second Protocol is neutral in terms of 'good offices'; it does not carry any certain Power. This can be considered further recognition for UNESCO's ability take the initiative to resolve conflicts.

NGOs

In terms of NGOs, their roles seem to be expanded in the Second Protocol compared with the 1954 Convention, wherein they provide advice to UNESCO by invitation regarding objections to the registration of certain cultural properties on the International Register of Cultural Property under Special Protection (Article 14(3) of the 1954 Convention). A similar advice-giving role is performed by NGOs for the Committee under the Second Protocol (Article 27(3)), and this kind of cooperation extends to that with the States Parties as well, where they are asked to be engaged in developing and implementing peacetime training and educational programs (Article 30(3)(b)).

Further involvement of NGOs can be observed in the Articles related to the List of Cultural Property under Enhanced Protection. Article 11(3) enables NGOs with relevant expertise, including the International Committee of the Blue Shield (ICBS), to recommend specific cultural properties to the Committee for their inclusion on the List. The Committee may invite the concerned Party to request inclusion of such properties, but the term 'may invite' implies that is there is no obligation for the State to make such a request (Chamberlain 2013, p. 144). This means that NGOs can make a recommendation regardless of the approval of the concerned State Party, but that inclusion on the List is in the hands of the Committee (Articles 11(5) and 27(1)(b)). However, it is important to note that the Committee should ask for the advice of NGOs, as well as governmental organizations and individual experts, in making their decision on a request (Article 11(6)). The 'should' there shows the irreplaceable status of the NGOs.

Experts

Compared with the role of NGOs, which was extended and rendered in greater specificity in the Second Protocol, those of individuals with expertise went in the opposite direction. As mentioned above, Article 11(6) enables individual experts, together with NGOs and governmental organizations, to deliver advice to the Committee concerning the request for inclusion of certain cultural properties on the List, and this shows the established roles of experts. In addition, experts can become a part of a delegation of States Parties to the Committee to ensure that the Committee as a whole contains adequate expertise in the fields of cultural heritage and laws (Article 24(4)). It seems that the active roles of experts engaged in the protective activities of States Parties under the 1954 Convention, in particular as a Commissioner-General, have been converged and confined to those two roles in the Second Protocol.

Individuals

When it comes to the status and roles of individuals, the obligation to protect cultural property under the provisions of the 1954 Convention or the Second Protocol has been strengthened with a detailed list of violations. Moving forward from the provision of the 1954 Convention that stipulated the duty of the States Parties to take necessary steps to prosecute and impose penal or disciplinary sanctions (Article 28 of the 1954 Convention), the Second Protocol suggests a list of acts that breach the Convention and the Second Protocol, and which are therefore subject to punishment,. Compared with the 'grave breach' in Additional Protocol I[21] and the 'war crime' of the Statute of the ICC,[22] the serious violations under the Second Protocol are wider and clearer with respect to cultural property (Article 15(1)) (Chamberlain 2013, p. 152). Moreover, the objects of sanction extend to the persons involved, who aid and abet the offence, or who order the offence, which persons would include co-conspirators, etc. This provision is a restatement of Articles 25(3) and 28 of the Statute of the ICC (Chamberlain 2013, p. 154).

It is noteworthy that the Second Protocol establishes a so-called universal jurisdiction for the offences listed in Article 15(1)(a) to (c). Paragraph (a) deals with attacks on cultural property under enhanced protection whereas (b) refers to the usage of such property for military action. Paragraph (c) is directed to cultural property under general protection, but the term 'extensive' was attached to meet the criteria of a serious violation. According to Article 16(1)(c), these three become offences that are subject to legislative actions of the States Parties of the Second Protocol. In other words, a State Party can establish its jurisdiction even when the offence is committed abroad by a non-national and the offender is present in that State's territory. For any other violations that are committed intentionally, including the illicit export, removal, or transfer of ownership of the cultural property from occupied territory, are included as subjects of sanction by States Parties (Article 21). Although there exists an Article guaranteeing a fair-treatment trial as a tool for the protection of the rights of offenders (Article 17(2)), there is no doubt that these new provisions of the Second Protocol concerning criminal sanctions on individuals exemplify a further strengthened legal mechanism requiring a greater obligation on the part of individuals for protection of cultural property during armed conflict.

---

[21] Article 85(4) of the Additional Protocol I reads: "In addition to the grave breaches defined in the preceding paragraphs and in the Conventions, the following shall be regarded as grave breaches of this Protocol, when committed will fully and in violation of the Conventions of the Protocol:…(d) making the clearly-recognised historic monuments, works of art or places of worship which constitute the cultural or spiritual heritage of peoples and to which special protection has been given by special arrangement, for example within the framework of a competent international organisation, the object of attack, causing as a result extensive destruction thereof, where there is no evidence of the violation by the adverse Party of Article 53, sub-paragraph (b), and when such historic monuments, works of art and places of worship are not located in the immediate proximity of military objectives."

[22] Article 8(2)(b)(ix) of the Statute of the International Criminal Court reads: "Intentionally directing attacks against buildings dedicated to religion, education, art, science or charitable purposes, historic monuments, hospitals and places where the sick and wounded are collected, provided they are not military objectives."

2.2.4 NSAs in the Guidelines of the Second Protocol

Unlike the 1954 Convention and the First Protocol, the Second Protocol has its own Guidelines to facilitate its implementation by the key actors: States Parties, the Meeting of the Parties, its Committee, and UNESCO (para. 1). With a detailed explanation on the Articles of the Second Protocol, the Guidelines also attempt to embody best practices in the Protocol's implementation (para. 2), and therefore add more details concerning the interpretation of the provisions of the Second Protocol. Compared with the Convention, which requires unanimous support by all Contracting Parties for revisions (Article 39), the Guidelines are developed by the Committee, subsequently endorsed by the Meeting of the Parties, and can be revised to reflect recommendations and decisions adopted by the Committee and the Meeting (para. 3).[23] Therefore, the Guidelines can be a good source for observation of the changing status and roles of NSAs in the course of the Second Protocol's implementation.

First of all, the roles of UNESCO become more solidified and expanded. A separate annex to the Guidelines illustrates the possible measures of technical assistance provided by UNESCO under Article 33 of the Second Protocol (Annex III). This includes both expert advice and operational activities that UNESCO can take on its own initiative. In addition, in 2019, a new role for UNESCO was added to the Guidelines, that of assisting the monitoring of the implementation of the International Assistance provided the Committee (paras. 140 and 141). This enables UNESCO to have an extended role in the part of monitoring the implementation of the Protocol, by checking the report of the recipient States of the International Assistance.

NGOs also receive further recognition in the Guidelines. Departing from Article 27(3) of the Second Protocol, whereby NGOs were invited to the Committee only in their advisory capacity, in the Guidelines, they are mentioned as a partner of the Committee and UNESCO for proper handling of requests for different categories of International Assistance, as well as of the Bureau for consultation concerning evaluations of requests (paras. 155, 165 and 173). It is important to note also that the Guidelines have a paragraph encouraging States Parties to cooperate with NGOs in general (para. 28).

As for individuals, the relevant provisions of the Second Protocol already demonstrated their obligation for the protection of cultural property by suggesting the list of offences that are subject to sanctions by States Parties.[24] Indeed, the Guidelines do not go further on this issue, but there was one addition in 2015 when a distinctive emblem was created for the exclusive marking of cultural property under Enhanced Protection. In paragraph 98, it is said that the use of the emblem intends to ensure legal certainty with regard to criminal responsibility of belligerents. Therefore, this new emblem can become evidence of 'intention' of offence by individuals violating the Convention or the Protocol, and has the effect of reminding and strengthening, thereby, the duty of individuals to this end.

---

[23] Indeed, the Guidelines have been revised five times since their first adoption in 2009. The current version was adopted in December 2019.

[24] Article 15.

The provisions of the 1954 Convention, its two Protocols, and the Guidelines of the Second Protocol concerning the rights, duties and roles of NSAs that have been analyzed so far are summarized in Table 2.2. The table traces the changing status and roles of NSAs with the addition or deletion of the relevant provisions of each legal instrument. As this shows, the provisions of the 1954 Convention, the First and Second Protocols, and the Guidelines for the Second Protocol effected gradual increments or decrements to the status and roles of NSAs. While UNESCO's active

Table 2.2 Provisions of the 1954 convention, its two protocols and guidelines of the second protocol concerning the status and roles of NSAs

NSAs	Roles	1954 Convention (Art.)	First protocol (Art.)	Second protocol (Art.)	Guidelines for the second protocol (Para.)
UNESCO	Managing the list	(R) 1 (commissioner-general), 12–16	–	11(11), 14(3)	45–46, 69, 79, 90
	Invitation to the meeting of the state parties	27		23(1), 23(4)	18
	Assisting the committee	–		20	25
	Technical service to the state parties	23(1)		33(1)	26, 140–141**, 152–154, 173
	Conciliation***	**22(2)**		**35(2), 36(1)**	–
	Initiative for proposal and service	**19(3), 23(2)**		**22(7), 33(3)**	
NGOs	Advice for the list	((R) 14(3))	–	27(3)	24
	Advice for international assistance	-		–	155, 165, 173
	Application of the list			**11(3), 11(6)**	**47, 51**
	Cooperation with the state parties			30(3)(b)	13, 28, 115
Experts	**Engagement in protection activities (commissioner-general)**	**(R) 6–7, 11, 17, 19**	–	–	–
	Advice for the list	((R) 14(3))			
	Participation as the state party delegation	–		24(4)	21
Individuals	**Receipt of sanctions for offences**	**(28)**	–	**15(1), 17(2), (21)**	**98***

(continued)

Table 2.2 (continued)

NSAs	Roles	1954 Convention (Art.)	First protocol (Art.)	Second protocol (Art.)	Guidelines for the second protocol (Para.)
	Right to request an indemnity as a good-faith acquirer	–	**(4)**	–	–

Note 1 Status and roles in bold are those considered important, from the author's perspective, in the evaluation of the status and roles of the NSAs in these provisions
Note 2 Articles or paragraphs in () connote the status and roles of each stakeholder. (R) represents Regulations of the 1954 Convention
Note 3 Paragraphs of the Guidelines with * are those added in 2015, and ** in 2019. The First draft of the Guidelines was adopted in 2009
Note 4 Conciliation functions of UNESCO with *** can be fulfilled by the International Court of Justice (ICJ) as well. It can appoint the Commissioner-General in cases of disagreement of Parties concerned (Article 4(2)) and appoint a chief arbitrator (Article 14(7)) under the 1954 Convention
Source Author (based on the 1954 Convention, its two Protocols and the Guidelines of the Second Protocol)

role in conciliation and initiatives for proposals and services has continued, new attention to NGOs has been added by the Second Protocol of 1999 and its Guidelines adopted in 2009.

More provisions for criminal responsibility, for example, have been added with respect to individuals in the Second Protocol and its Guidelines relative to the main Convention. By contrast, the role of experts has been diminished relatively, from active engagement in the course of heritage protection as a Commissioner-General to a mere advisor capacity in the delegation of States Parties to statutory meetings.

2.3 NSAs in the Implementation of the 1954 Convention and its Two Protocols

The provisions on the status and roles of NSAs can be observed through different cases in practice. However, not each and every role mentioned in Table 2.2 can find relevant cases. For example, Articles 11(3) and 11(6) enable the NGOs to submit an application for the List of Cultural Property under Enhanced Protection, but there has been no such case so far. Lack of information also deters observation on the specific roles of NSAs. This is the case for the NGOs again, in terms of their advice-giving function regarding the International Register of Cultural Property under Special Protection of the 1954 Convention and the List of Cultural Property under Enhanced Protection of the Second Protocol, because it is difficult to find cases without detailed meeting minutes open to the public or records of behind-the-scenes consultations.

Therefore, the analysis on the operation of the provisions related to NSAs in this chapter will be confined to and based on the information available to date.

2.3.1 UNESCO

UNESCO has played its basic roles as a Secretariat of the legal instruments in charge, such as the organization of the statutory meetings of States Parties or the Committee, and the management of the Lists under the 1954 Convention and the Second Protocol.[25]

UNESCO's exercise of discretionary power for its technical services can be observed in many examples. It has developed various manuals and organized many capacity-building programs such as workshops for the development of legal or administrative measures and awareness-raising programs for the relevant stakeholders for protection of cultural property (McGuire et al. 2018, pp. 54–93; UNESCO 2019a). The form of technical support includes advice for the States Parties. For example, UNESCO gave advice for the inclusion of Vatican City in the Register of Cultural Property under Special Protection and facilitated the agreement between Vatican City and Italy concerning the use of the Via Aurelia (Chamberlain 2013, p. 59). Missions have been dispatched as well at the request of the States Parties. In 1982, the Lebanese government requested UNESCO to visit the archaeological site of Tyre, which was then occupied by the Israeli army.[26]

If UNESCO had gone further by suggesting a meeting of the two States Parties concerned, Lebanon and Israel in the above case, its role in facilitating good offices could have been executed as well. However, there has been no such a case of UNESCO's being deeply involved in the conciliation process. This can be understood as being owed to the basic difficulties in bringing Parties in conflict to the negotiation table for matters related to cultural property, as well as UNESCO's cautious approach in dealing with possible political negotiation with concerned Parties.

UNESCO has been most active in terms of its own initiatives in matters related to the protection of cultural property that became endangered due to armed conflicts. Not to mention its overtures to States Parties of the Convention, it has appealed to non-Parties as well to request them to ensure the protection of cultural property in hostile situations by joining the Convention.[27] Many UNESCO missions, moreover, have been undertaken on its own initiative. Two personal representatives were sent to Iran and Iraq in 1985 and 1986 to visit affected areas of cultural property from the conflict, who successfully held talks with the authorities of both sides and facilitated

---

[25] The International Register of Cultural Property under Special Protection under the 1954 Convention and the List of Cultural Property under Enhanced Protection of the Second Protocol.

[26] The mission was impeded in the absence of Lebanese archaeologists, although approaches were made to both Lebanese and Israeli authorities (Toman 1996, p. 265).

[27] In 1969, when armed conflict broke out between Honduras and El Salvador, the Director-General of UNESCO sent his appeal to those Member States to become Parties to the 1954 Convention.

their appointment of Commissioners-General for Cultural Property under the 1954 Convention.[28] During the conflict in the Gulf, UNESCO asked both Iraq and Kuwait to comply with their obligations under the 1954 Convention and its First Protocol through a number of appeals issued in 1990 and 1991.[29] When the war broke out in Yugoslavia in 1991, UNESCO sent several missions to Belgrade, Dubrovnik, Ljubljana, Split and Zagreb and the Director-General's special envoys to meet the authorities and initiate technical cooperation with the local people for the protection cultural property under threat of armed conflict. Two permanent observers were dispatched as well.[30]

More recently, with more frequent conflicts in various parts of the world, UNESCO has played a more active role in addressing the importance of protection of cultural property from any intentional and unintentional harm. Examples are countless, from the Giant Buddhas of Bamiyan in Afghanistan that were destroyed deliberately by the Taliban in 2001, the City of Palmyra that was fortified and later destroyed during the 2012 civil war in Libya, to Timbuktu, the World Heritage Site in Mali that was destroyed by the Malian jihadist tied to al Qaeda in 2012. UNESCO moved forward to strengthen its appeal to the international community, and backed the adoption of UN Security Council Resolution 2199 in 2015, which prohibited the illicit trafficking of cultural property from Iraq and Syria. In 2017, thanks to the efforts of UNESCO to raise awareness on the issue of destruction of cultural heritage and illicit trafficking of cultural property, Resolution 2347, which focuses solely on the protection of heritage according to the 1954 Convention, was adopted by the Security Council.

2.3.2 NGOs

There was only one NGO mentioned in the 1954 Convention: the International Committee on Monuments, Artistic and Historical Sites and Archaeological Excavations (Article 14(3) of the Regulation). The NGO list was expanded in the Second Protocol to include those having official relationships with UNESCO, such as the International Committee of the Blue Shield (ICBS), the International Centre for the Study of the Preservation and Restoration of Cultural Property (ICCROM), the International Committee of the Red Cross (ICRC); also, the Guidelines of the Second Protocol specify the constituent bodies of the ICBS as the Co-ordinating Council of Audiovisual Archives Association (CCAAA), the International Council on Archives (ICA), the International Council of Museums (ICOM), the International Council on

[28] However, the war between the Islamic Republic of Iran and Iraq ended before they actually appointed their Commissioners-General (Toman 1996, pp. 265–266).

[29] All appeals made by the Director-General of UNESCO are available at https://en.unesco.org/pressroom/search (accessed 30 May 2021).

[30] The two permanent observers witnessed the bombing of the Old City of Dubrovnik by the Yugoslav military, which was made in error, and UNESCO offered its services for the restoration of the cultural heritage in the City afterwards (Toman 1996, pp. 266–267).

Monuments and Sites (ICOMOS), and the International Federation of Library Associations and Institutions (IFLA) (Article 27(3) of the Second Protocol and para. 24 of its Guidelines). Many of these NGOs as well as others not listed in the provisions have participated in statutory meetings of the Convention and its two Protocols and have taken the floor from time to time as an observer of meetings. However, it is not clear whether their attendance in any such situations was directly related to their advisory service for the Lists or International Assistance. As mentioned earlier, there are no detailed meeting minutes produced after statutory meetings.

However, at the national level, there are many cases of NGO involvement in the implementation of the 1954 Convention and its two Protocols, in particular in post-conflict areas, and sometimes in projects supported by the Fund of the Second Protocol. In Lebanon, the recently established Blue Shield Lebanon developed a list of properties within Lebanon that need to be protected, and another NGO named BILADI created a game to teach young people about the importance of cultural property as provisioned in the Convention and Protocols (McGuire et al. 2018, pp. 71–72). In Mali, NGOs received technical support as well as seed money from UNESCO to support the preservation and restoration of cultural property in Timbuktu (McGuire et al. 2018, p. 78). NGOs also participate in national advisory groups for the protection of cultural property in relation to the implementation of the 1954 Convention, as seen in the example of the United Kingdom, where a cross-jurisdictional Cultural Protection Property Working group was created in 2014, consisting of military and government officials, academics, NGOs, custodians of cultural property, police and experts (McGuire et al. 2018, p. 95).

Lastly, there has as yet been no case of any NGO applications concerning the List of Cultural Property under Enhanced Protection under the Second Protocol.

2.3.3 Experts

The representative role of experts under the 1954 Convention is that of the Commissioner-General for Cultural Property nominated by the States Parties.[31] According to the provisions of the Regulations of the 1954 Convention, the Commissioner-General performs many functions for the protection of cultural property during armed conflict. However, those functions have been conducted only once in practice (Chamberlain 2013, p. 78): during the Arab-Israel conflict of 1967 (The Six-Day War). During the Iran-Iraq War of 1980–88, under the active consultation of the personal representatives of the Director-General of UNESCO, the two belligerent governments examined the possibility of appointing the Commissioners-General, but the war ended before their actual action (Toman 1996, pp. 266–267). In no other case has it yet been possible to reach agreement on the appointment of the Commissioners-General (Boylan 1993, p. 87).

[31] There is no regulation respecting the nationality of persons nominated for Commissioner-General by each State Party.

Where experts have provided advice to the Register of the International Register of Cultural Property under Special Protection is not clear, as there are no detailed records of relevant meetings or possible behind-the-scenes discussions. However, as there is no case of objections on the registration of cultural property on the Register, it is logical to conclude that this advisory role of individual experts has not been fully exercised. Nonetheless, as demonstrated above in the case of UNESCO's missions to emergency areas, individuals have actively cooperated with UNESCO in their own respective capacities.

As regards the participation of delegations of States Parties, many States indeed have appointed experts in cultural property, international law, or other related areas as their representatives to statutory meetings of the Convention and its two Protocols.[32] These experts have actively participated in the meetings in delivering their expertise for both States Parties and the meeting as a whole. Other individual experts also have attended meetings, but they have been mostly quiet, as they had been admitted only as observers. At the national level, as the example of Mali shows, experts are invited to serve as facilitators of workshops in training relevant military and government officers, NGOs, and other civilians (McGuire et al. 2018, p. 77), and to a national advisory body as in the UK case above.

2.3.4 *Individuals*

Article 28 of the 1954 Convention asks States Parties to undertake all necessary measures to prosecute and impose penal or other sanctions upon those persons who commit or order to be committed a breach of the Convention, and the Second Protocol takes further steps on this issue by suggesting specified list of offences and extending the responsibility of States to exercise their jurisdictions (Articles 15–21). There are two representative cases that show the practical application of these provisions at the international level.

The first case is that of prosecutions made by the ICTY. As mentioned earlier, the destruction of cultural property is declared a war crime in Article 3(d) of the Statute, and several judgements have been made based on this provision.[33] However, there are two arguments of interpretation as to how this provision is applied in practice. The first is that many of the prosecutions are only indirectly applied to cultural property, because they put more weight on the crime of persecution of a people on the grounds of their race, religion or politics than on damage to civilian property (Abtahi 2001,

[32] The lists of participants referred to in this book are those of the 9th, 10th and 11th Meeting of the High Contracting Parties of the 1954 Convention (UNESCO 2012a, 2014a, 2016a).

[33] *Prosecutor v. Tihomir Blaškić*, IT-95-14-T, Trial Judgement, 3 March 2000; *Prosecutor v. Biljana Plavšić*, IT-00-39&40/1-S, Sentencing Judgement, 27 February 2003; *Prosecutor v. Mladen Naletilic & Vinko Martinovic*, IT-98-34-T, Judgement, 31 March 2003; *Prosecutor v. Pavle Strugar*, IT-01-42-T, Judgement, 31 January 2005; *Prosecutor v. Miodrag Jokić*, IT-01-42/1-S, Sentencing Judgment, 18 March 2004; *Prosecutor v. Radoslav Brdanin*, IT-99-36-T, Judgement, 1 September 2004.

p. 13). In other words, the destruction of civilian property, which might also have historical and cultural value, was considered to have been indirect persecution of the people associated with that property (Forrest 2010, p. 128).

The second argument is whether the 1954 Convention is one of the sources of customary international law underpinning the ICTY's Statute, which does not mention the Convention explicitly. Indeed, in *Prosecutor v. Pavle Struger*, the ICTY upheld the conviction of Pavle Struger in relation to the operational command of the destruction of the Old Town of Dubrovnik based only on Articles 51 and 52 of Additional Protocol I and Article 13 of Additional Protocol II. In *Prosecutor v. Duško Tadić*,[34] the ICTY concluded that Article 19 of the 1954 Convention, which applies the 1954 Convention to the event of an armed conflict not of an international character as well, reflected customary international law (Keane 2005, p. 21). In the recent declaration of the ICTY Trial Chamber in *Prosecutor v. Jadranko Prlić* et al.,[35] the chamber declared that "the 1954 Hague Convention is regarded as an integral part of customary international law (Lostal 2017, pp. 40–41)." Although this is an argument that the Trial Chamber gave no justification such as existence of *opinion juris* and state practice (Lostal 2017, p. 41), the cases of ICTY are the practice of executing one of the core obligations of the 1954 Convention, which puts criminal responsibility for the destruction of cultural property onto individuals. Even though those applications were imperfect and showed some evolving aspects of the application of the 1954 Convention, they are important evidence of the criminal responsibility of individuals under international law.

The case that marked the first time a war crime was charged for the destruction of cultural property as the primary charge was the *Al Mahdi* case, which came only recently before the ICC, in 2016.[36] Ahmad Al Faqi Al Mahdi was a member of Ansar Dine, an armed Islamist group whose aim is to impose sharia law throughout Mali, and he was involved in preparations for and ensuring the execution of the planned attacks to destroy a series of historic and religious buildings and monuments in Timbuktu.[37] In connection with these actions, Al Mahdi was charged with the war crimes of intentionally directing attacks against buildings dedicated to religion as well as historic monuments that were not legitimate military objectives, as stipulated in Article 8(2)(e)(iv) of the Statute of ICC.

In bringing this case, ICC Prosecutor Fatou Bensouda stressed the importance of such properties in Timbuktu to the community's identity, arguing that "[t]he charges we have brought against Ahmad al-Faqi al-Mahdi involve most serious crimes…They are about the destruction of irreplaceable historic monuments, and they are about a callous assault on the dignity and identity of entire populations, and their religious

[34] *Prosecutor v. Duško Tadić*, IT-94-1-AR72, Appeals Chamber, Decision, 2 October 1995.

[35] *Prosecutor v. Jadranko Prlić* et al., IT-04-74-T, Judgement, 29 May 2013.

[36] *Prosecutor v. Ahmad Al Faqi Al Mahdi*, ICC-01/12-01/15, Judgement and Sentence, 27 September 2016.

[37] *Charge brought by the Prosecution against Ahmad Al Faqi Al Mahdi*, ICC-01/12-01/15-70-AnxA, Office of the Prosecutor, 17 December 2015 (Charges), Section 3.

and historical roots."[38] The *Al Mahdi* Trial Chamber reinforced this link between the demolished sites and the local people, pointing out that the sites "constitute a common heritage for the community" and described them as "an integral part of the religious life of [Timbuktu's] inhabitants."[39] In addition, the Trial Chamber used the status of nine of the targeted buildings as UNESCO World Heritage Sites, which "reflects their special importance to international cultural heritage," as evidence of their qualification as religious buildings and historical monuments according to Article 8.2(e)(iv) of the ICC Statute.[40] This shows the difference between the cases under ICTY and the *Al Mahdi* case, in that the latter articulated a more universalist perspective than a relativist approach (Casaly 2016, p. 1214). The Trial Chamber stated that "the wide diffusion of culture, and the education of humanity for justice and liberty and peace are indispensable to the dignity of man and constitute a sacred duty which all the nations must fulfill in a spirit of mutual assistance and concern," and pointed out that Al Mahdi's attacks on the cultural properties in question were "clearly an affront to these values (*Al Mahdi* Judgement 2016, Section 46)." The Trial Chamber sentenced him to nine years of imprisonment. Another trial case on the destruction of Timbuktu, the *Al Hassan* case, which opened in July 2020, is currently ongoing before the ICC.[41]

Alongside this criminal responsibility imposed on individuals who commit the offences of damaging cultural property during armed conflict, there exists a provision in the First Protocol that protects the rights of individuals as *bona fide* acquirers of cultural property exported from an occupied territory. However, as discussed earlier, Article 4 of the First Protocol does not provide any detailed criteria or process for individuals to request an indemnity to the occupying State Party whose obligation was to prevent the export of the property from the territory under its occupation. In addition, this is not easy if the State to which the property was returned is not the former Occupying Power, and if the Occupying Power is not a Party to the Protocol (Chamberlain 2013, p. 106). No individuals have insisted on their rights as a holder of specific cultural property in good faith in asking indemnity from a State. In other words, no State has been successful in returning cultural property exported from an occupied territory that came into the possession of the *bona fide* acquirer. As seen in the *Autocephalous Greek Orthodox Church in Cyprus v. William O.A. Lans* case,[42] the Netherlands courts failed to seize and return four icons illegally exported from

---

[38] Office of the Prosecutor (OTP), Statement of the Prosecutor of the International Criminal Court, Fatou Bensouda, at the opening of the confirmation of charges hearing in the case against Mr. Ahmad Al-Faqi Al Mahdi, 1 March 2016, available at https://www.icc-cpi.int/PAges/item.aspx?name=otp-stat-01-03-16 (accessed 30 May 2021).

[39] *Prosecutor v. Ahmad Al Faqi Al Mahdi*, ICC-01/12-01/15, Judgement and Sentence, 27 September 2016, Section 34.

[40] *Ibid.*, Section 46. In addition, the Guidelines of the Second Protocol presume that cultural property inscribed on the World Heritage List satisfies the condition of greatest importance for humanity (para. 36).

[41] *Prosecutor v. Al Hassan Ag Abdoul Aziz Ag Mohamed Ag Mahmoud*, ICC-01/12-01/18. More details are available at https://www.icc-cpi.int/mali/al-hassan#_blank (accessed 30 May 2021).

[42] The *Autocephalous Greek Orthodox Church in Cyprus v. William O.A. Lans*, District Court of Rotterdam, Case n. 44053, 4 February 1999; confirmed in Appeal, Hof Den Haag, 99/693, 7 March 2002 (O'Keefe 2004, p. 110).

Turkish-occupied North Cyprus, which shows the difficulty of implementing this provision in practice.[43]

2.4 Main Findings

As the first legal instrument that solely focused on the protection of cultural property in the event of armed conflict, the 1954 Convention has played an important role in raising awareness among the States. Together with the Convention, its Protocol adopted in 1954 (First Protocol) touched upon the issue of the illicit export of cultural property from occupied territories, and the one adopted in 1999 (Second Protocol) further developed the tendency of the 1954 Convention by providing more detailed explanations for the exception of military necessity, precautionary measures and individual criminal responsibility, while reflecting changes in the characteristics of wars and the development of relevant issues in international law.

From the very first legal instruments addressing the protection of cultural property, the 1954 Convention and the following two Protocols rendered specific status and roles to NSAs. Apart from the basic functions of th1999/xlink

NGOs were mentioned only once in the 1954 Convention for their possible advice concerning objections to the registration of specific cultural property on the International Register of Cultural Property under Special Protection addressed to UNESCO, but they find more room for action under the Second Protocol. They can give advice to the Committee as well as to States Parties. This is a reflection of the growth of specialized NGOs both at the international and local levels. Although the participation of NGOs in Committee meetings could be read as rather symbolic, they have been actively involved in many local projects for the protection of cultural property in practice, as the Guideline of the Second Protocol encouraged the States Parties to cooperate with NGOs. The provision of the Second Protocol even gives an opportunity to NGOs to recommend specific cultural properties to the Committee for their inclusion on the List of Cultural Property under Enhanced Protection, which is remarkable, in that application to the List can be considered as the sole authority of States Parties. Nonetheless, no proposals from NGOs have been made so far.

The 1954 Convention introduced a system of appointing a Commissioner-General for Cultural Property. As an expert on cultural property, he or she has a series of explicit rights and duties in acting for the protection of cultural property during armed conflict. For example, he or she has powers of decision, such as on matters of immunity for transportation of cultural property, and can register a cultural property refuge for Special Protection. Although there has been only one case of appointing a Commissioner-General, it is important to note that considerable roles were given to experts appointed as Commissioners-General under the Convention. Other experts also can be invited to deliver advisory service to UNESCO concerning the Special

[43] However, since that case, legislation has been passed to rectify the situation (O'Keefe and Prott 2011, p. 37).

Protection Register of the 1954 Convention as well as to the Committee concerning the Enhanced Protection List under the Second Protocol. Although States Parties are requested to include experts in their delegation to the Committee to ensure the competence of the Committee as a whole, it seems that the role of individual experts, including that of the Commissioner-General, have gradually given way to specialized NGOs.

One of the most striking areas of considerable growth of the status of NSAs is the criminal responsibility of individuals. Although the 1954 Convention addresses the *erga omnes* obligation of individuals for the protection of cultural property in its Preamble and requests the State Parties to undertake criminal sanctions upon individuals who commit breaches of the Convention, the Second Protocol further imposes further obligations to individuals. With the wider and clearer lists of serious violations, the Protocol even establishes a universal jurisdiction for specific offences. Any other violations committed by individuals, including the illicit export, removal, or transfer of ownership of cultural property, also have become subject to punishment. Although it is arguable whether the 1954 Convention or its two Protocols were directly applied or not, the cases of ICTY and the ICC have fortified the customary rule applying stronger responsibility to individuals for their crimes in making damage to cultural property.

The rights of individuals as holders of cultural property in good faith are stipulated in the provisions of the First Protocol. It is important to note that the Protocol provides latitude for individuals to request indemnity to the Occupying State regarding property, but there exists no concrete process or guidelines within the Protocol. Indeed, there have been no cases where an individual quoted the First Protocol in requesting indemnity of his or her property to another State. Whereas criminal responsibility could have been dealt with effectively as a war crime under the 1954 Convention and the Second Protocol, which have many aspects of international humanitarian law, the issue of individual property rights has been relatively ignored, as it is bound up with complex issues of private law.

Last but not least, it is worth emphasizing that the 1954 Convention and its two Protocols are facing a new challenge in dealing with new and very active NSAs in matters involving protection of cultural property during armed conflict: non-State armed groups. Although this category of NSA was never mentioned in the provisions, concerns are growing with respect to how to deal with such entities. Their activities in destroying cultural property have been witnessed in many places, from Afghanistan to Mali, but the perspective taken on them has been punitive only. However, there is an argument as to whether these armed groups should be effectively engaged via activities of awareness-raising for the Convention or not. UNESCO may play a role to bring them to the table to talk about cooperation for the protection of cultural property in their activities, based on Article 19(3) of the Convention, which enables UNESCO to offer its services to the parties to non-international conflict.[44] At the

[44] UNESCO financed a study on the potential of the engagement of armed non-state groups for the protection of cultural heritage, and the study was undertaken by an NGO called Geneva Call. The result, 'Culture under Fire: Armed Non-State Actors and Cultural Heritage in Wartime,' presented various recommendations on how to encourage non-state actors to respect international rules of law, including the 1954 Convention and its two Protocols (Geneva Call 2018).

same time, there exists an opposite opinion as well, which argues that only indirect solutions should be pursued so as not to engage with these non-state armed groups, and to leave them in the hands of the respective national courts or the ICC (McGuire et al. 2018, p. 34).

This is an important issue to address, but at the same time is very sensitive, requiring a process whereby all relevant stakeholders and experts can be brought together to consider it. Indeed, the Meeting of the High Contracting Parties of the 1954 Convention held in 2019 could not find any adequate solution to the problem of engagement with non-state armed groups, and in fact, their resolution recommended that UNESCO's Internal Oversight Service (IOS) not engage non-State armed groups (UNESCO 2019b). A consent-based approach to make them declare unilateral status or enter bilateral agreements could be possible (Ryngaert 2011, pp. 289–291), but it is difficult to expect such groups to respect cultural heritage of origins differing from their own. The Committee of the Second Protocol decided to discuss this issue continuously (UNESCO 2018a, 2020a). Upon its decision, more roles will be assigned to NSAs ranging from UNESCO, relevant NGOs and experts to individuals as well as this new entity known as non-State armed groups. The 1954 Convention and its two Protocols evidently have momentum to move forward for further involvement of NSAs to secure the protection of cultural property during armed conflict.

References

Abtahi H (2001) The protection of cultural property in times of armed conflict: the practice of the International Criminal Tribunal for the former Yugoslavia. Har Hum Rights J 14(1):1–32

Boylan PJ (1993) Review of the convention for the protection of cultural property in the event of armed conflict. UNESCO Doc. CLT-93/WS/12, 1993. https://unesdoc.unesco.org/ark:/48223/pf0000100159. Accessed 30 May 2021

Casaly P (2016) Al Mahdi before the ICC: cultural property and world heritage in international criminal law. J Int Crim Justice 14:1199–1220

Chamberlain K (2013) War and cultural heritage: a commentary on the hague convention 1954 and its two protocols. Institute of Art and Law, Builth Wells

Forrest C (2010) International law and the protection of cultural heritage. Routledge, London

Geneva Call (2018) Culture under fire: armed non-state actors and cultural heritage in wartime. Online Publication: Geneva Call. https://www.genevacall.org/wp-content/uploads/2019/02/Cultural_Heritage_Study_Final_HIGHRES.pdf. Accessed 30 May 2021

Keane D (2005) The failure to protect cultual property in wartime. De Paul J Arts Technol Intellect Prop Law 14(1):1–38

Lostal M (2017) International cultural heritage law in armed conflict: case-studies of Syria, Libya, Mali, the Invasion of Iraq, and the Buddhas of Bamiyan. Cambridge University Press, Cambridge

McGuire M, Koren G, Djiam SEY, Yip C (2018) Evaluation of UNESCO's standard-setting work of the culture sector: Part V – 1954 convention for the protection of cultural property in the event of armed conflict and its two protocols (1954 and 1999). UNESCO, Online Publication

O'Keefe PJ (2004) The first protocol to the hague convention fifty years on. Art Antiq Law 9(2):99–116

O'Keefe PJ, Prott LV (eds) (2011) Cultural heritage conventions and other instruments: a compendium with commentaries. Institute of Art and Law, Builth Wells

Ryngaert C (2011) Non-state actors in international humanitarian law. In: d'Aspremont J (ed) Participants in the international legal system: multiple perspectives on non-state actors in international law. Routledge, Abingdon

Toman J (1996) The protection of cultural property in the event of armed conflict. UNESCO, Paris

UNESCO (2012a) CLT-11/CONF/209/2. The ninth meeting of the high contracting parties to the 1954 Hague convention for the protection of cultural property in the event of armed conflict. Paris, 12 December 2011

UNESCO (2014a) CLT-13/10.HCP/CONF.201/INF.1. The tenth meeting of the high contract-ing parties to the 1954 hague convention for the protection of cultural property in the event of armed conflict. Paris, 16 December 2013

UNESCO (2016a) CLT-15/11.HCP/CONF.201/INF.1. The eleventh meeting of the high con-tracting parties to the 1954 hague convention for the protection of cultural property in the event of armed conflict. Paris, 8 December 2015

UNESCO (2018a) Decision 13.COM 15. The 13th meeting of the committee for the protection of cultural property in the event of armed conflict. Paris, 6–7 December 2018

UNESCO (2019a) C54/19/14.COM/4. The 14th meeting of the committee for the protection of cultural property in the event of armed conflict. Paris, 5–6 December 2019

UNESCO (2019b) Resolution 13.HCP 6. The 13th meeting of the high contracting parties to the 1954 Hague convention. Paris, 2 December 2019

UNESCO (2020a) Decision 15.COM 13. The 15th meeting of the committee for the protection of cultural property in the event of armed conflict. Paris, 10–11 December 2020

Chapter 3
The Restitution of Cultural Property

States cannot perfectly control the import and export of cultural property, especially when its transportation is made clandestinely. This happens during peacetime using loopholes in different legal systems among countries, not to mention during the chaos of war. Transportation advances and the development of internet transactions, moreover, have aggravated the issue of illicit trafficking of cultural property and made its restitution even more difficult than before.

The UNESCO Convention on the Means of Prohibiting and Preventing the Illicit Import, Export and Transfer of Ownership of Cultural Property (1970; hereinafter, '1970 Convention') and the UNIDROIT Convention on Stolen or Illegally Exported Cultural Objects (1995; hereinafter, '1995 Convention') are endeavors of the international community to tackle this issue of the illegal import and export of cultural property. Additional efforts in this respect are the creation of the relevant intergovernmental committees and the introduction of the Operational Guidelines for the implementation of the 1970 Convention (hereinafter, 'Operational Guidelines').

These 1970 and 1995 Conventions impose various duties on States Parties and NSAs while ensuring certain rights as well. In particular, the importance of the participation of the different NSAs has been recognized in many legal and operational texts as well as in actual practice. In this chapter, after the introduction of the 1970 and 1995 Conventions, an analysis of the provisions related to the status and roles of NSAs will be presented. Several cases involving NSAs will support ideas on their changing status and roles in the field of illicit trafficking of cultural property and its restitution.

J. Kim, *Non-State Actors in the Protection of Cultural Heritage*, Creativity, Heritage and the City 3, https://doi.org/10.1007/978-981-16-6659-9_3

3.1 Introduction of the Legal Mechanisms to Prevent Illicit Movement of Cultural Property and Promote Its Restitution[1]

3.1.1 History of the Adoption of the 1970 Convention and Its Key Contents

Immediately after the First World War, the League of Nations discussed the problem of illicit trafficking of cultural property. In cooperation with the Office International des Musees (OIM), a draft Convention regarding the Repatriation of Objects of Artistic, Historical or Scientific Interest, which have been Lost, Stolen or Unlawfully Alienated or Exported was prepared for negotiations in 1933.[2] However, the work was not further developed, due to the Second World War in 1939 and UNESCO's subsequent preoccupation with the 1954 Hague Convention for the Protection of Cultural Property in the Event of Armed Conflict (hereinafter, '1954 Convention') and its Protocol (hereinafter, 'First Protocol'), both reviewed in Chap. 2 of this book.

With the increasing participation, at that time, of newly independent states and the Eastern bloc states, for which pilfered cultural property and its return were special concerns, new ideas began to take root. In particular, Mexico and Peru raised the problem of the illicit export, import and transfer of ownership of cultural property in 1960, pointing out that the issue had not been comprehensively covered by the First Protocol of the 1954 Convention.[3] Hence, UNESCO adopted the Recommendation on the Means of Prohibiting and Preventing the Illicit Export, Import and Transfer of Ownership of Cultural Property in 1964, as a preliminary step toward a new convention (O'Keefe 2000, p. 12). In 1968, a draft convention was circulated for Member States' comments, and finally, the 1970 Convention was adopted at the 16th General Conference of UNESCO. The Convention entered into force on 24 April 1972.[4]

---

[1] Some parts of Sect. 3.1 have been extracted from the earlier publication of the author (Kim 2013, pp. 15–24), with several revisions to complement original contents and reflect up-to-date information.

[2] The draft was not adopted due to criticism from the Netherlands, United Kingdom and the United States. The second draft was submitted to the League of Nations in 1936 but again was deferred for further study. OIM wanted to ensure broad participation of States to adopt the third draft in 1939, but its hopes were not met, due to the worsening world political situation that would lead to the Second World War (O'Keefe 2000, pp. 2–3).

[3] According to the First Protocol, a State Party that occupies a territory during armed conflict should prevent the export of cultural property from that territory (para. 1). If the occupying State Party discovers any cultural property that has been illegally imported from the occupied territory, the State Party is obliged to seize that property (para. 2) and return it to the competent authorities of the original territory after the hostilities have ended (para. 3), along with an indemnity to the rightful holders in good faith (*bona fide*) of the property (para. 4). The property coming from the territory of one Contracting Party and deposited in that of another party for its protection has to be returned at the end of hostilities (para. 5).

[4] Pursuant to Article 21 of the 1970 Convention.

The negotiation surrounding the Convention was quite difficult, due to countries' conflicting interests. Whereas those countries that had suffered from illicit trafficking of cultural property asked for stricter international obligations, many market States were reluctant to participate in the drafting process itself.[5] Issues such as retroactivity and import controls were particularly thorny.[6] However, given that cooperation between countries was (and is) absolutely essential to prevent the illegal import and export of cultural property, a compromise had to be reached.[7]

The 1970 Convention addresses the illicit trafficking of cultural property through a trifold structure, providing its States Parties with measures to prevent trafficking, provisions for restitution, and a framework for international cooperation. The objective scope of the 1970 Convention, i.e. the characterization of which cultural properties are protected, is quite exhaustive, in that it requires specific designations by each State (Article 1) (Prott and O'Keefe 1989, p. 729.).

Unlike the UNIDROIT Convention on Stolen or Illegally Exported Cultural Objects of 1995, to be introduced in the next section, the 1970 Convention includes extensive provisions on preventive measures, most of which are addressed to the source nations (Kono and Wrbka 2010, p. 470). Each State Party is requested to establish national inventories of protected property and to introduce special export certificates (Articles 5 and 6). Pursuant to Article 7(a) of the Convention, importing States Parties must also take necessary measures, consistent with national legislation, to prevent museums and similar institutions within their territories from illegally importing cultural property from another State Party after the Convention has taken effect in the concerned States. States Parties also shall impose penal or administrative sanctions in cases of illicit export or import of cultural property (Article 8).

Per Article 7(b)(ii) of the Convention, States Parties undertake, "at the request of the State Party of origin, to take appropriate steps to recover and return any such cultural property imported after the entry into force of the Convention in both States concerned, provided, however, that the requesting State shall pay just compensation to an innocent purchaser or to a person who has valid title to that property." Notably, however, this important provision covers only inventoried objects stolen from a museum, religious or secular public monument or similar institution; it does not cover objects taken from a clandestine excavation or stolen from private owners. The need to address such situations led to the introduction of the 1995 UNIDROIT

---

[5] The States included Austria, France, Germany, Japan, the United Kingdom and the United States, all of which expressed reservations and objections during the second meeting for the draft convention held in April 1970. In particular, the United States submitted a long objection to almost all of the articles of the draft convention (O'Keefe 2017, pp. 22–23). Switzerland, one of the representative market countries, did not participate in the discussion of the draft convention.

[6] For details on the preliminary issues, see e.g. O'Keefe (2017), pp. 14 et seq.

[7] In particular, the US remained uninterested until the last Expert Committee in 1970, when they presented a significantly revised version of the draft Convention. However, the global political climate of the late 1960s favored increased US participation in international organizations and the pursuit of better relationships with them; accordingly, at the Convention, there was a clear desire to include the US in the negotiations, and in fact, the US delegation exerted considerable influence on the final text of the Convention (Forrest 2010, p. 167).

Convention. Article 13 of the 1970 Convention outlines further steps on restitution and cooperation, more indirectly and subject to domestic legislation.

Lastly, the 1970 Convention provides the States Parties with a framework for international cooperation. Article 9 provides the possibility for more specific activities, such as a call for import and export controls in cases where cultural heritage is in jeopardy. This Article, for instance, has been used by the many States Parties, in particular United States and Switzerland, as their basis to conclude certain bilateral treaties (Prott and O'Keefe 1989, p. 66).

Thus far, the implementation of the 1970 Convention has been reviewed by periodic reporting, which has been conducted about every six years.[8] Through the monitoring process, the relevant practices of the States Parties' can be usefully reviewed and referenced against one another. In addition to its pioneering status as the first international convention dedicated to tackling the illicit trafficking of cultural property, the 1970 Convention is also the most widely ratified international Convention in the field, having been ratified by 141 Member States of UNESCO.[9]

3.1.2 Adoption of the 1995 Convention and Its Key Contents

Even after the successful introduction of the 1970 Convention by UNESCO, illicit trafficking remained a persistent problem, in part because vast discrepancies in national laws provided relatively wide loopholes that enabled illegally acquired cultural properties to be transferred into the legal market (Prott and O'Keefe 1989, p. 110). In particular, two of the main aspects of private law under contention were the statute of limitations on claims and the status of a good faith acquirer. In addition, the 1970 Convention was criticized for failing to provide adequate protection for artifacts from archaeological sites. To address these issues, in 1983, experts recommended UNESCO to consult with an organization specialized in the harmonization of private laws (Prott and O'Keefe 1983), and the International Institute for the Unification of Private Law (UNIDROIT) was commissioned to draft a preliminary text for a new convention.[10]

In the process of producing the draft Convention, UNIDROIT commissioned two expert studies and convened two meetings in 1988 and 1989, and then consulted with experts nominated by each government. Opinions were widely divided among several different interest groups. The first and largest group was made up primarily

[8] The monitoring mechanism has been strengthened since the formation of the subsidiary intergovernmental committee under the Meetings of States Parties of the 1970 Convention in 2013.

[9] As of 17 March 2021.

[10] The UNIDROIT (International Institute for the Unification of Private Law), with its seat in Rome, was set up in 1926 as an auxiliary organ of the League of Nations, and re-established in 1940 on the basis of a multilateral agreement, the UNIDROIT Statute, following the demise of the League. Its purposes are to study needs and methods for modernizing, harmonizing and coordinating private and in particular commercial law as between States and groups of States and to formulate uniform law instruments, principles and rules to achieve those objectives.

of countries in Latin America, Africa and Asia, who had lost significant amounts of cultural property due to illegal trade. The second group, consisting mainly of European nations and the United States, were countries that were often the destination for illegally trafficked cultural objects. Lastly, the smallest group was represented by Australia and Canada, who wished to emphasize the protection of indigenous artifacts (Prott and O'Keefe 1989, pp. 110–111). Thus, pragmatic compromise was necessary to make the Convention acceptable to as many nations as possible. After four sessions of considerable negotiations and amendments (Prott 1997, pp. 12–14), the final text for the 1995 Convention was adopted by a Diplomatic Conference in Rome on 24 June 1995.[11]

Unlike the 1970 Convention, which provided a minimal framework for international public law for the issue of illicit trafficking of cultural property in general, the 1995 Convention put greater emphasis on the issues of return and restitution of cultural property by covering aspects of private law. In this respect, the 1995 Convention complemented, rather than replaced, the 1970 Convention (Prott 1997, p. 15). Specifically, the 1995 Convention attempts to use private international law to resolve international claims demanding the restitution of stolen cultural objects and the return of illegally exported objects by allowing private parties to bring suit in courts (Olivier 1996, p. 656).

As for the objective scope of its application, the 1995 Convention covers all stolen or illicitly exported cultural objects, not just inventoried objects, under Article 7(b)(ii) of the 1970 Convention, as pursuant to Article 2 for stolen cultural property and Article 5(3) for illicitly exported property, respectively.[12] Therefore, cultural objects that have been unlawfully excavated are to be considered stolen and protected, so long as that is consistent with the law of the State where the excavation took place. Moreover, per the personal scope of application of the 1995 Convention, not only the States Parties but also the (original) owners of stolen cultural objects may make claims directly through national courts (or other competent authorities) of States Parties (Article 5(1)). In the case of theft, claimants may be individuals, entities, or States Parties, while only States Parties may be claimants in cases of illicit export. Statutes of limitations for claiming restitution or return were set: 50 years from the date of theft (to be extended up to 75 years or such longer period as is provided in the law for the objects belonging to a public collection), and within three years from the time when the claimant learns the location of the cultural objects or without time limitation with regard to cultural objects forming an integral part of an identified archaeological site or public collection (Article 3).

[11] Pursuant to Article 12 of the 1995 Convention, it entered into force on 1 July 1998.

[12] The expansive scope in terms of stolen cultural objects is justified by the fact that the theft of movables per se is considered illegal all over the world, irrespective of its classification. The limitation with respect to illegal export, on the other hand, is explained by the wish that States Parties should not be bound by the stricter export regulations of other states (Thorn 2005, pp. 90 et seq., cited in Kono and Wrbka 2010, pp. 497–498).

The 1995 Convention goes further than the First Protocol of the 1954 Convention as well as the 1970 Convention regarding the issue of *bona fide* acquirers,[13] by moralizing trade on cultural objects, with conditional compensation only with the evidence of due diligence. Article 4(1) reads that "the possessor of a stolen cultural object who is required to return it shall be entitled, at the time of its restitution, to payment of fair and reasonable compensation provided that the possessor neither knew nor ought reasonably to have known that the object was stolen and can prove that it exercised due diligence when acquiring the object." This due diligence test may include a review of the character of the parties, the price paid, whether accessible registers of stolen cultural objects and other relevant documentation were consulted, and whether accessible agencies were consulted (Article 4(4)). The *bona fide* possessors who pass the due diligence check successfully are entitled to fair and reasonable compensation for his or her cultural objects from the requesting State (Article 6).

In spite of the fact that only 51 countries have joined the 1995 Convention so far,[14] its importance as the first international private law Convention providing concrete standards to combat the theft and illegal export of cultural property cannot be underestimated.[15] Indeed, many provisions of the 1995 Convention have influenced the implementation of the 1970 Convention, and they were duly included in the Operational Guidelines of the 1970 Convention as well. This is why the 1995 Convention deserves as much attention as the 1970 Convention. Further details on the influence of the 1995 Convention will be addressed later in this chapter.

3.1.3 Work of the Intergovernmental Committee

Although it is not an international legal instrument regarding the issue of restitution of cultural property, the work of the Intergovernmental Committee for Promoting the Return of Cultural Property to its Countries of Origin or its Restitution in Case of Illicit Appropriation (hereinafter, 'ICPRCP') is worth mentioning, as it works as a complementary mechanism to deal with the complex issue of the retroactivity of the return of cultural property. The lack of retroactivity of the 1970 Convention led Member States of UNESCO to create an intergovernmental body to address cases of illicit trafficking of cultural property that had occurred, mainly under foreign or colonial occupation, before 1970. Following the recommendation of the meeting of experts in 1976, the General Conference of UNESCO created ICPRCP in 1978 as a

[13] Under para. 4 of the First Protocol to the 1954 Hague Convention, indemnity is to be paid to "holders in good faith," and pursuant to Article 7(b)(ii) of the 1970 Convention "just compensation" is to be paid to the "innocent purchaser or person who has valid title."

[14] As of 3 September 2021.

[15] Although the actual text of the 1995 Convention does not refer to the issue of its 'self-executing' power in the States Parties, the Convention is definitely not self-executing, in that it proclaims legal principles by setting a legal framework that clearly relies on the implementation of national legislation (Aust 2007, p. 183, cited in Kono and Wrbka 2010, p. 499).

permanent intergovernmental body (UNESCO 1978). The Committee is composed of 22 Member States elected for four-year terms at the General Conference of UNESCO, and they convene the meeting every two years.

The ICPRCP mediates conflicts among States related to the return of or restitution for cultural property in cases where the provisions of the 1970 Convention cannot apply. The ICPRCP has no legal authority to decide cases, but it nonetheless provides a unique framework for discussion and facilitates bilateral negotiations for restitution of cultural objects.[16] In 2010, upon a resolution adopted by the General Conference of UNESCO (UNESCO 2005), the Committee reviewed and adopted the Rules of Procedure for Mediation and Conciliation suggested by the subcommittee of the ICPRCP (UNESCO 2010a).

The Committee has also helped to develop many useful legal and practical tools to facilitate restitution for cultural property. In particular, ICPRCP recently encouraged UNESCO and UNIDROIT to create a committee of independent experts to draft model legislative provisions defining State ownership of cultural properties, especially archaeological heritage, which may form a basis for drafting national legislation and promoting uniformity of cultural terminology.[17] As a result, a Model Provisions on State Ownership of Undiscovered Cultural Objects (hereinafter, 'Model Provisions') was introduced in 2011, to ensure that all States are equipped with sufficiently explicit legal principles to guarantee their ownership of undiscovered antiquities (UNESCO 2011a). Although the Model Provisions do not constitute a binding legal instrument, they represent a notable response to the increasing need to standardize the definition of State ownership of undiscovered archaeological objects, which are particularly vulnerable to illicit trafficking. The six relatively brief provisions are clear enough to be enforced both domestically and internationally to protect undiscovered cultural objects against theft and ensure restitution should such theft occur.[18] The Model Provisions extend the principle of inalienability to all cultural property, both known and undiscovered, through authorized excavation and otherwise.[19] As a practical tool for guidance, the Model Provisions facilitate the application of both the 1970 and 1995 Conventions.

In spite of all of these efforts, ICPRCP has created confusion for the many States Parties of the 1970 Convention due to its lack of statutory linkage with the Convention, and therefore has had legal limitations in addressing fundamental questions of the Convention itself. This was particularly pointed out at the 40th anniversary of the 1970 Convention in 2011, when States Parties were discussing the adoption of an Action Plan to strengthen the implementation of the Convention (UNESCO

---

[16] Information on successful cases under the aegis of the Intergovernmental Committee is available at http://www.unesco.org/new/en/culture/themes/restitution-of-cultural-property/return-or-restitution-cases/ (accessed 30 May 2021).

[17] In an extraordinary session of the ICPRCP (Seoul, 25–28 November 2008), in celebration of the 30th Anniversary of the Committee, legislation on undiscovered antiquities was one of the major issues discussed, since many states had encountered numerous legal obstacles when requesting restitution of such objects found in another country.

[18] Provision 6 of the Model Provisions.

[19] *Ibid.*, Provisions 5 and 4, respectively.

2012b, para. 17).[20] This led the second meeting of States Parties to the Convention in the following year, where the creation of the Subsidiary Committee of the Meeting of States Parties (hereinafter, 'Subsidiary Body') was decided. In 2013, eighteen States Parties were elected for the Subsidiary Body at the extraordinary meeting of the States Parties for four-year terms and became responsible for monitoring of the national implementation of the Convention and addressing difficulties resulting from the implementation. One of the most important mandates of the Subsidiary Body at its beginning was the drafting of the Operational Guidelines for the implementation of the 1970 Convention, which was adopted by the third Meeting of States Parties in 2015. In addition, the Subsidiary Body focuses on emergency action to tackle illicit trafficking of cultural property in armed conflict, as it relates to the Resolutions of the UN Security Council.[21]

3.2 NSAs in the 1970 and 1995 Conventions

As international public law, the 1970 Convention imposes duties to prohibit the illicit import, export and transfer of ownership of cultural property *mainly on States Parties*, while the 1995 Convention imposes them on *both States Parties and NSAs* as a matter of international private law. To be specific, States Parties of the 1970 Convention are responsible for implementing most provisions of the Convention, from export control of their own cultural property to restitution of illegally imported cultural property from other Contracting Parties.

Museums, institutions, and antique dealers have become subject to the actions taken by the States Parties, or in other words, are obliged to fulfill statutory duties such as not acquiring cultural properties illegally exported from other countries, and maintaining a register of records on the origin of cultural properties. As for the Secretariat of the Convention, UNESCO is included in the text of the 1970 Convention as an organ for technical assistance and research. Moreover, UNESCO extends its role to good offices to settle the disputes over implementation of the Convention by the States Parties and cooperation with NGOs.

According to the characteristics of private law mentioned above, the 1995 Convention stipulated the rights and duties of both States and NSAs. All entities with rights over stolen or illegally exported cultural objects as defined by the Convention can bring a claim to the court or other competent authorities of another Contracting State to return the objects. Innocent possessors of those cultural objects can request fair and reasonable compensation as well, provided that they exercised due diligence when purchasing the objects. This means that those individuals, museums, or institutions who acquire cultural objects have a duty to check all circumstances of the acquisition. The different status and roles of each of the stakeholders of the two Conventions can be summarized in Table 3.1, and those of NSAs will be further analyzed in this section.

---

[20] The 1970 Convention does not have any provision concerning creation and/or operation of the intergovernmental committee under the Convention.

[21] These include S/RES/2199 (2015), S/RES/2253 (2015) and S/RES/2347 (2017).

Table 3.1 Stakeholders of the 1970 and 1995 conventions and their status and roles

Stakeholders		Status and roles		Goal
		1970 convention	1995 convention	
States	States parties	Establishment of specialized national service, introduction of export certificate for cultural property, prevention of illicit acquisition, imposition of penalties or sanctions on responsible actors, public education	Request for return of illegally exported cultural objects, giving compensation to an innocent possessor of illegally exported objects	Restitution of cultural property and prevention of its illicit trafficking
		International cooperation for restitution of cultural property and prevention of illicit trade, giving compensation to an innocent purchaser, admission of actions for recovery of cultural property brought by rightful owners, periodic reporting on the implementation of the convention	Bringing a claim for the return of illegally exported cultural objects	
NSAs	UNESCO	Technical assistance for states parties, conduct of research, proposals concerning the implementation of the convention to states parties	–	
		Good offices for dispute resolution		
		Cooperation with NGOs		
	UNIDROIT	–	Convening a special committee to review the practical operation of the convention	

(continued)

Table 3.1 (continued)

Stakeholders		Status and roles		Goal
		1970 convention	1995 convention	
	Individuals (incl. museums, institutions, antique dealers)	No acquisition of cultural property illegally, maintenance of object ID register	Return of stolen cultural objects, exercise of due diligence in acquisition	
		Receipt of sanctions for the infringement of relevant rules	–	
		Bringing actions for recovery of lost or stolen items, request of compensation from the requesting state	Bringing a claim for the restitution of stolen cultural objects, requesting compensation	

Source Author (based on the 1970 and 1995 Conventions and Operational Guidelines of the 1970 Convention)

3.2.1 NSAs in the Text of the 1970 Convention

UNESCO

Under the 1970 Convention, UNESCO is the only NSA that has an explicit Article addressing its roles and functions. As in the other conventions reviewed in this book,[22] UNESCO mainly provides to the States Parties, upon their request, technical assistance regarding information and education; consultation and expert advice; and coordination and good offices (Article 17(1)). Moreover, it can conduct research and publish studies on the issues of illicit trafficking of cultural property and make its own proposals to States Parties concerning the implementation of the Convention (Articles 17(2) and 17(4)).

The latter role of UNESCO is noteworthy, in that it has the authority to initiate its own projects under the Convention, without request or approval of States Parties.[23] The difference of these activities of UNESCO compared with those stipulated in other conventions discussed in this book is connected to the fact that UNESCO is not specifically appointed as a Secretariat of the 1970 Convention. In other words, the 1970 Convention provides more latitude for UNESCO to apply its expertise on its own initiative. For example, the work of UNESCO, such as publishing violations of the Convention, can bring pressure to responsible States Parties (Abramson and Huttler 1973, p. 963). It is also important to see that NGOs are empowered by the Convention to cooperate with UNESCO for research and publications, upon the

[22] Except the 1995 Convention developed at UNIDROIT.

[23] A similar provision enabling UNESCO to make its own proposals is set out in Article 23(2) of the 1954 Convention on the Protection of Cultural Property in the Event of Armed Conflict.

latter's request (Article 17(3)). This provision becomes concrete in the Operational Guidelines in terms of the partners and the contents of collaboration.

A similar conception of UNESCO as a manager of the Convention with own expertise is set out in Article 17(5), where the Convention commissions UNESCO to function in its good offices to settle disputes over the implementation of the Convention among States Parties. However, this role can be performed only at the request of at least two State Parties engaged in the disputes.

Individuals

There is no Article in the 1970 Convention that directly stipulates rights, duties, and roles directly to individuals. However, in its preamble, the Convention explicitly calls on cultural institutions, museums, and other relevant depositories of cultural property to ensure that their collections are built up based on the universally recognized moral principles (para. 6 of the Preamble). The Convention further sets out the responsibilities of the States Parties in their relations with individuals, including museums, institutions, and antique dealers. Speaking reversely, these can be interpreted as indirect duties and rights of those individuals concerned who would act in conformity with relevant provisions.

First of all, Articles 7(a) and (b)(i) stipulate that States Parties are to undertake the necessary measures to prevent museums and similar institutions from acquiring or importing illegally exported cultural property. Moreover, antique dealers are obliged to maintain a register of records on the origin of cultural properties under Article 10(a). When individuals do not comply with the export and import regulations stipulated in Articles 6(b) and 7(b), they become subject to penalties or administrative sanctions under Article 8.

With these duties, individuals are entitled to bring actions for recovery of lost or stolen cultural property, which right to legal restitution is ensured by the States Parties under Article 13(c). The 1970 Convention also protects the right of an innocent purchaser or a person who has valid title to a property by requiring just compensation by the state requesting its restitution under Article 7(b)(ii). The expenses incident to the return are also borne by the requesting State.

3.2.2 NSAs in the Text of the 1995 Convention

UNIDROIT

Unlike the 1970 Convention, which renders specialized roles for UNESCO to support States Parties or initiate its own proposals, the 1995 Convention does not confer any similar status to UNIDROIT. In fact, the depositary of the 1995 Convention is not UNIDORIT, but the Government of the Italian Republic, from which UNIDROIT merely receives information (Article 21).

However, per Article 20, the President of UNIDROIT can exert its authority to regularly hold a special committee with a view to reviewing the operation of the

Convention.[24] This is noteworthy in that approval or request of the States Parties is not mandatory for UNIDROIT to convene a meeting. The meetings of the 1954 Convention, for example, required the approval of the Executive Board and at least one-fifth of the Contracting Parties' request (Article 27(1)). Although the power of organizing a meeting of States Parties cannot be considered to be a sufficient reason to see UNIDROIT as a proactive NSA in the 1995 Convention (as this can be considered to be merely a customary function of depositaries of international conventions), it is nonetheless comparable to the active role of UNESCO in tabling its own proposals in the 1970 Convention.

Individuals

It should be noted that the rights and duties of individuals deriving from the 1970 Convention are still in the hands of states, and are realized by the actions of the States Parties, in particular through domestic measures taken by each State. This means it is actually difficult to say that individuals have full legal status under the 1970 Convention. By contrast, however, the 1995 Convention imposes and confers direct duties and rights, respectively, on individuals.

In particular, Article 3(1) clearly states that the obligation of the possessor of a stolen cultural object is to return it to the original owner. In order for the possessor to be entitled to fair and reasonable compensation (Articles 4(1) and 6(1)), he or she is required to prove that due diligence was exercised when acquiring the object. Articles 4(4) and 6(2) specifically list several conditions determinative of whether the possessor is a *bona fide* acquirer. In other words, these are some of the legal actions that individuals including museums, institutions, and antique dealers need to take when they transact cultural property.

In addition to rights to compensation, the 1995 Convention secures for individuals the rights to claim for restitution of cultural objects by providing specific time limits that vary according to the characteristics of the objects (Articles 3(2)–(5)). Special attention to the tribal or indigenous communities can be observed with respect to the time limitation on claims for their stolen cultural objects: more than 75 years, like those accorded to public collections (Article 3(8)). Similarly, Article 7(2) deems an object illegally exported during the lifetime of the person who created it or within a period of fifty years following his or her death to be the subject of restitution as well, if it has traditional or ritual attachment with the given community. This kind of provision protecting the rights of indigenous groups or local communities regarding restitution of cultural property is absent from the 1970 Convention, and its presence in the 1995 Convention tells of their strengthened status in that legal instrument. Several relevant cases will be considered when discussing the implementations of the two Conventions in the next section.

---

[24] Or at any time at the request of five Contracting States.

3.2.3 NSAs in the Operational Guidelines of the 1970 Convention

The Operational Guidelines for the implementation of the 1970 Convention were adopted at the third Meeting of States Parties in 2015, after two years of discussion at the Subsidiary Committee of the Convention and consultation with States Parties. They aim to strengthen and facilitate the implementation of the 1970 Convention through shared understanding and experience of it. Compared with, *inter alia*, other Operational Guidelines or Directives of international cultural heritage laws analyzed in this book, Operational Guidelines of the 1972 World Heritage Convention adopted in 1978 and Operational Directives of the 2003 Intangible Cultural Heritage Convention adopted in 2008, the Operational Guidelines of the 1970 Convention are more descriptive and informative than regulatory. Indeed, this question of the legal status and objectives of the Operational Guidelines was one of the recurrent topics at the meeting of the Subsidiary Committee in 2013.[25] The informative characteristic of the Operational Guidelines seems to derive from their ambition to accommodate all developments since the adoption of the 1970 Convention, such as sales on the internet or at auction houses and the evolving legal practices facilitating restitution of cultural property.

UNESCO

The only NSA that has a role solely dedicated to itself in the Operational Guidelines is, again, UNESCO, but this time as a Secretariat of the Convention (para. 123), unlike the 1970 Convention where there was no such specific assignment. The tasks of appointing the Secretary and of assisting States Parties, Meetings of States Parties and the Subsidiary Committee are similar to those conducted by the Secretariats of the other UNESCO cultural heritage conventions (paras. 119–120). Together with dissemination of information through its homepage, creation of a communication channel to assist States Parties' cooperation with art markets has been added to the Operational Guidelines as another concreted mandate for UNESCO (para. 121). The list of these kinds of tasks of UNESCO is not exclusive, in that a new provision enabling UNESCO to take its own initiative to conduct research and publications, call on cooperation with any competent body, and make proposals for States Parties, has been added to the Operational Guidelines (para. 124).

Its role to provide good offices to deal with controversies on the implementation of the Convention became more descriptive than the relevant provisions in the 1970 Convention, such as technical assistance, negotiations, checking due diligence, etc. In addition, this service has been extended to NSAs such as auction houses and e-commerce sponsors to enhance cooperation with art markets and effectively fight against illicit trafficking of cultural property thereby (para. 122). Furthermore,

---

[25] Concerning this question, Lyndel V. Prott, who drafted the Operational Guidelines, recalled that the conventions and recommendations are the only two ways of setting up legal standards in UNESCO; she further pointed out that the guidelines also could be very useful tools regardless of their legal implications (UNESCO 2014b, pp. 12–13).

UNESCO became eligible to intervene in controversial auctions by issuing, upon the petition of the affected States, a public statement emphasizing the negative effects of such practices on the spirit of the Convention (para. 71). Good offices can be extended to the issue of the non-retroactivity of the Convention, wherefrom States Parties find difficulties in concluding agreements for items illegally exported and imported before the entry into force of the Convention (para. 103).

Efforts to address pillage of archaeological and ethnological materials under Article 9 of the Convention became another duty of the Secretariat to conduct under the Operational Guidelines. Upon the request of a State Party whose cultural property is in jeopardy, UNESCO is encouraged to respond expeditiously, including in cases of clandestine excavations, natural disasters, and conflict (paras. 105, 106, and 109). When doing so, UNESCO cooperates with other partners, as mentioned in Article 17(3). The Operational Guidelines include specific provisions about these partners in paras. 129–131. They can be intergovernmental organizations or NGOs such as INTERPOL, UNIDROIT, UNODC, WCO, and ICOM,[26] whose detailed ways of collaborating with UNESCO are demonstrated in the Annex of the Operational Guidelines. ICOMOS, ICCROM, Europol and national specialized bodies are also mentioned as international, regional and local partners of UNESCO.[27] These partner organizations are new NSAs that came to have a section in the Operational Guidelines for their specific roles independent of the Secretariat.

Individuals

More concrete rules regarding imposition of obligations on individuals, including museums, institutions, or antique dealers, have been developed in the Operational Guidelines. For example, paras. 64 to 66 mention the penalties or administrative sanctions, under Articles 8, on individuals responsible for illegal movement of cultural property referred to under Articles 6(b) and 7(b). In doing so, consideration for other international instruments developed by UNODC was added as well.[28] More duties of individuals are requested for maintaining their register of cultural properties, in Article 10(a). And for the first time, curators of museums or institutions are mentioned as being subject to application of the same constraints in the forms of legislative or ethical rules as collectors and dealers already had been subject to (para. 73). Indeed, under the policy- and regulation-strengthened supervision of the States Parties, dealers and museums lost their power to exhibit or keep any cultural property without clear provenance (paras. 77 and 81).

The new phenomenon of internet auctions served to extend the duties of individuals as well. The dramatic growth of internet usage has aggravated illicit trafficking of stolen and clandestinely excavated archaeological objects, and therefore, individual activities on the internet became subject to supervision by the relevant States Parties (paras. 68 and 69). In the process of screening websites used for cultural property

---

[26] ICOM has maintained formal relationships with UNESCO since 1946, and holds associate status.

[27] ICOMOS and ICCROM are the Advisory Bodies of the 1972 Convention Concerning the Protection of the World Cultural and Natural Heritage.

[28] UN Convention against Transnational Organized Crime (UNTOC), adopted on 15 November 2000.

marketing, cooperation with individuals was mentioned for the first time. In para. 69 of the Operational Guidelines, online monitoring to verify the nature and importance of related cultural objects, either by specialists or interested individuals who can work with public administrations, has been offered as an example of exemplary action for States Parties to take.

In the meantime, it is noteworthy that incentive regimes have been introduced to encourage institutions to take appropriate steps not to acquire illegally imported cultural property (para. 75). Benefits such as tax incentives or government subsidies have been suggested as means of promoting concerted efforts against illicit trafficking of cultural property by individuals.

Together with more academic means of awareness raising for local communities and the public in general with respect to the threat of theft, clandestine excavations and illicit import and export of cultural property, practical capacity-building and training programs for all related officials and individuals working in the field, including legal and customs officers, police, museums, or institutions, have been introduced as examples of measures for States Parties to take (paras. 52 and 53). This is an area where individuals become the beneficiaries, under the Convention and Operational Guidelines, of their right to education.

However, the most important rights of individuals that have been protected in the course of restitution of stolen or illegally exported cultural items hint at a changing environment in which additional countervailing obligations are being imposed. For example, the compensation, which is paid to innocent purchasers in the course of the recovery of stolen or illegally exported items (para. 82), has come to be predicated on a due diligence check necessary to be eligible for it. The rules relating to this have been developed, significantly, in the Operational Guidelines (para. 93) rather than in the text of the 1970 Convention (Article 7(b)(ii)). Article 4(1) of the 1995 Convention stipulates the criteria for qualifying as a *bona fide* acquirer, and in fact, para. 94 of the Operational Guidelines indicates that the duties of individuals in the art trade have become more numerous and onerous than before. This means, simply, that the burden of proof for individuals' exercising of due diligence has increased, and that due diligence, as already alluded to above, is the duty that individuals must serve before they may call for their rights to just compensation as innocent acquirers.

In spite of these changes requiring more obligations on the parts of individuals, the procedural rights of individuals are still well emphasized and well protected in the Operational Guidelines. Under Article 13(c) of the 1970 Convention, the States Parties are requested to admit actions brought by individuals to recover cultural property. The Operational Guidelines go further, asking States Parties to confirm that there exists sufficient legal standing for individuals to proceed, and if there is none such, to find some (para. 99). By incorporating this legal information into the UNESCO database, the Operational Guidelines pressures States Parties to certify individual rights to claim of ownership of lost or stolen cultural property.

The provisions in the 1970 and 1995 Conventions and the Operational Guidelines of the 1970 Convention concerning the rights, obligations and roles of NSAs that have been analyzed thus far are summarized in Table 3.2. The table shows that

Table 3.2 Provisions of the 1970 and 1995 conventions and operational guidelines of the 1970 convention concerning the status and roles of NSAs

NSAs	Status and roles	1970 convention (Art.)	1995 convention (Art.)	Operational guidelines of the 1970 convention (Para.)
UNESCO	Technical assistance for states parties	17(1)	–	105–106, 109, 119–121, 123–124
	Taking own initiative for research, cooperation, or making proposals for States Parties	**17(2), 17(4)**		**124**
	Good offices for dispute resolution	**17(5)**		**103, 122**
	Requesting NGOs to cooperate	**17(3)**		**129–131**
	Intervention on auctions	–		**71**
UNIDROIT	**Convening a special meeting of States Parties**	–	**20**	-
Individuals (Museums, institutions, auction houses, dealers, general public)	Duty of no acquisition of cultural property illegally	Para. 4 of Preamble, (7(a), 7(b)(i))	–	(72–78, 81)
	Duty of maintaining object ID register	(10(a))		(72)
	Receipt of sanctions for the infringement of relevant rules	**8**		**64–66**
	Duty of exercising due diligence in acquisition	–	**4(4), 6(2)**	**94**
	Right of requesting compensation	**(7(b)(ii))**	**4(1), 6(1)**	**82, 93**

(continued)

Table 3.2 (continued)

NSAs	Status and roles	1970 convention (Art.)	1995 convention (Art.)	Operational guidelines of the 1970 convention (Para.)
	Right of bringing actions for recovery	**(13(c))**	**3(1)–(5), <u>3(8), 7(2)</u>**	**83, 99**
	Beneficiary of the education	(10(b))		(52–53)
	Cooperation with administration on internet	–	–	69

Note 1 Status and Roles in bold are those considered important from the author's perspective in the evaluation of the status and roles of the NSAs in these provisions
Note 2 Convention Articles with underlining are those with special relevance to indigenous people in the Convention
Note 3 Articles or paragraphs in () connote the status and roles of each stakeholder
Source Author (1970 and 1995 Conventions and the Operational Guidelines of the 1970 Convention adopted in 2015)

since the adoption of the 1970 Convention, several roles of NSAs have been added through the introduction of the 1995 Convention and the Operational Guidelines of the 1970 Convention adopted in 2015. By comparing the provisions of those two Conventions and Operational Guidelines in chronological way, strengthened or weakened rights and duties of individuals can be observed.[29] UNESCO, an active NSA in the text of the 1970 Convention from the beginning, is well recognized in the Operational Guidelines. And with respect to individuals generally, the table shows that their obligations as well as rights in transactions have become more concrete and reinforced with time.

3.3 NSAs in the Implementation of the 1970 and 1995 Conventions

The NSAs participating in the implementation of the 1970 and 1995 Conventions are generally divided into two categories: UNESCO as a Secretariat of the 1970 Convention, and individuals working at museums, institutions, or as independent antique dealers or buyers. The partner IGOs and NGOs of UNESCO can be addressed together with UNESCO.

Unlike the 1972 Convention and 2003 Conventions, which have a strong intergovernmental committee deciding key issues of implementation such as the annual

[29] The two Conventions and the Operational Guidelines of the 1970 Convention were introduced in 1970, 1995, and 2015, respectively.

update of its international List(s) and the revision of its Operational Guidelines or Directives, the 1970 and 1995 Conventions do not have their own intergovernmental committees.[30] Even the Meetings of States Parties of the 1970 Convention have been held just occasionally, and have become regular only recently.[31] This different pace of the development of governance and operational mechanisms concerning the 1970 and 1995 Conventions relative to other international cultural heritage laws limits the capacity of an international forum to observe their implementation.

Moreover, the state-centric approach of the 1970 Convention has brought the issue of preventing illicit trafficking of cultural property mainly to the national arena (Vrdoljak 2006, p. 209), which of course makes analysis of the status of NSAs under the international convention more difficult. The 1970 Convention is not self-executing; it needs the States Parties to adopt necessary national legislation for its implementation (Chechi 2014, p. 101). Moreover, the intergovernmental nature of restitution claims under the 1970 Convention, meaning that they can be made only through diplomatic channels under Article 7(b)(ii), also shrinks the arena in which the rights, obligations and roles of NSAs are exercised.

Meanwhile, the 1995 Convention complements the 1970 Convention by addressing complex private law issues to tackle the illegal import and export of cultural property. In spite of its low ratification rate, the 1995 Convention has influenced national legislation of many countries via what is called the '1970 UNESCO Convention plus option (Schneider 2013, p. 129).' The Netherlands, for example, accepted the 1970 UNESCO Convention in 2009, and implemented it based on additional elements from Article 4(4) of the 1995 Convention (Van der Horst 2010, pp. 261–273). Regionally, the 1995 Convention has been influential on the introduction of Council Directive 93/7/ECC on the return of cultural objects that have been unlawfully removed from the territory of a Member State (Schneider 2013, p. 131). However, again, this tendency added more weight to dispute resolution by the States, and facilitated diplomatic cooperation before the Parties concerned pursue the case at court and apply the Conventions.

In this vein, observation of NSAs in the restitution of cultural property can be done in two aspects. First, the activities of UNESCO will be reviewed concerning its roles stipulated in the 1970 Convention and its Operational Guidelines, including its cooperation with several IGOs and NGOs. The meetings convened by UNIDROIT will be mentioned as well, though briefly. Secondly, practices involving individuals including museums, institutions, or antique dealers or buyers will be analyzed to observe their participation in the issue of restitution of illegally exported objects.

[30] The Subsidiary Committee of the 1970 Convention was under the Meeting of the States Parties, not directly under the Convention. The Intergovernmental Committee for Promoting the Return of Cultural Property to its Countries of Origin or its Restitution in Case of Illicit Appropriation (ICPRCP) stands independently from the 1970 Convention.

[31] The first meeting was held in 2003, the second in 2012, and the third in 2013, at which it was declared that the Meeting would be held every two years afterwards. The event commemorating the 40th anniversary of the Convention held in 2011 infused vitality into the Convention, which led to the creation of the Subsidiary Committee of the Meeting of States Parties of the 1970 Convention and development of the Operational Guidelines of the 1970 Convention.

Several cases related to operational issues of the 1970 and 1995 Conventions will be dealt with as well, even though those legal instruments are not directly quoted in the cases.

3.3.1 UNESCO and UNIDROIT

UNESCO conducts its role as a Secretariat of the 1970 Convention in various ways, from supporting States Parties through meetings of States Parties and the Subsidiary Committee. In particular, UNESCO provides capacity-building programs for the States Parties so that they can develop their own capacities and establish appropriate measures regarding the prevention of illicit trafficking of cultural property and facilitation of their restitution. For example, in the 2012–2013 biennium only, UNESCO held 17 training workshops with more than 600 participants from 78 countries, and the number of events was increased dramatically compared to the previous biennium (Torggler et al. 2014, p. 59). These workshops typically involve representatives of partner organizations of UNESCO. In particular, UNESCO concluded a MOU with several organizations including ICOM, UNIDROIT, INTERPOL, and WCO to invite their staffs as speakers or trainers to its events and exchange information concerning stolen objects.

Moreover, UNESCO has cooperated with these organizations to develop many practical instruments to support the implementation of 1970 Convention. These were developed through joint research or projects, and disseminated to the States Parties. UNESCO also promotes partner organizations' own tools as well, for example, the ICOM Code of Ethics for Museums and its Red Lists. All measures related to the issue of illicit trafficking of cultural property and its restitution are listed in Table 3.3, and they have been widely used by the States Parties. In particular, the ICOM Code of Ethics for Museums, Object ID Standard, Basic Actions Concerning Cultural Items Offered for Sale on the Internets, and UNESCO Database of National Cultural Heritage Legislation have been perceived to be beneficial to the implementation of the 1970 Convention by States Parties and other stakeholders in the art market, whereas the UNESCO International Code of Ethics for Cultural Property Dealers has not yet been widely adopted by dealers (Torggler et al. 2014, pp. 64–65).

Other than these initiatives with partner organizations, UNESCO also promotes its own campaigns calling for stopping the looting of cultural property, and especially addresses emergencies in conflict and post-conflict areas such as Egypt, Haiti, Iraq, Libya, Mali and Syria. Press releases and video clips have been distributed to the public as well as emergency missions of experts to assess existing loss of cultural property and develop strategies with local partners.[32] For example, as soon as the looting happened in the Malawi National Museum in Egypt in August 2013,

[32] For further information on the emergency actions of UNESCO in Egypt, Haiti, Iraq, Libya, Mali and Syria, see http://www.unesco.org/new/en/culture/themes/illicit-trafficking-of-cultural-property/emergency-actions/ (accessed 30 May 2021).

Table 3.3 Legal and practical instruments developed by UNESCO and its partners

Name	Description	Organizations involved	Year
Object-ID	Standardized international description of cultural property	J. Paul Getty Trust, ICOM, UNESCO	1997
UNESCO international code of ethics for cultural property dealers	Serves to harmonize professional practices and establish more ethical behavior in transactions	UNESCO	1999
ICOM red lists	Categories of cultural property that are particularly in danger in certain countries or regions (for example following a conflict or natural disaster), with a view to preventing such property from being sold and illegally exported	ICOM	2000 (ongoing)
ICOM code of ethics for museums	Sets minimum standards of professional practice and performance for museums and their staff	ICOM	1986 (revised in 2004)
UNESCO database of national cultural heritage legislation	Database containing over 2,650 texts from 181 countries related to national cultural heritage laws	UNESCO	2005 (ongoing)
Basic actions concerning cultural items offered for sale on the internets	Measures to improve the monitoring of property circulating through online sales platforms, cooperation with foreign and international police and the possibility of seizing property	UNESCO, INTERPOL, ICOM	2007
Model export certificate for cultural objects	Model export certificate that States that State Parties can partially or completely adopt	UNESCO, WCO	2007

(continued)

Table 3.3 (continued)

Name	Description	Organizations involved	Year
Witnesses to history (documents and writings on the return of cultural objects)	A compendium giving an outline of the legal, historical, philosophical, ethical and practical aspects of the return of cultural objects	Prof. Lyndel V. Prott (ed.)	2010
Model provisions on state ownership of undiscovered cultural objects	Six provisions articulating legal status of undiscovered cultural property	UNESCO, UNIDROIT	2011
Mediation and conciliation procedures	Tool to facilitate bilateral negotiations through the intermediary of the ICPRCP	UNESCO	2011

Source Torggler et al. (2014, pp. 63–64) and UNESCO (2012c, pp. 6–7)

UNESCO quickly communicated with the Egyptian authorities to disseminate the museum inventory, which contributed to coverage by the media and facilitated actions by Member States of the UNESCO, resulting in more than half of the stolen objects being recovered by the end of September 2013 (UNESCO 2013a).

Concerning UNESCO's good offices role in facilitating disputes over the implementation of the Convention, it has never been called on to do so, although there have been several occasions on which such a dispute could be detected.[33] This is mainly because UNESCO can offer the service only at the request of at least two States Parties that are engaged in a dispute. This confines the expertise of UNESCO when considering that there are no other specialized mechanisms to address disputes over illicit movement of cultural property, and indeed, this has been pointed out as one of the major defects of the Convention (Prunty 1983–1984, pp. 1167–72). ICPRCP has tried to complement this by introducing the Rules of Procedure for Mediation and Conciliation, but the mechanism is different in that it occurs under the Intergovernmental Committee, elected by the Member States of UNESCO. In the recent meeting of the Subsidiary Committee, several countries including Turkey, Ecuador, and Greece suggested adding a mediation role to the Subsidiary Committee of the 1970 Convention as well, but it has been decided instead to explore synergy between the two Committees for efficient mediation (UNESCO 2018b, para. 5).

As for the intervention of UNESCO in controversial auctions, no pertinent cases are yet available, which seems to be due mainly to the fact that this mandate was

[33] Mexico rejected the form of the US implementation of the Convention, and Canada presented a different opinion from that of the US as to the application of the Convention to pillaged objects (O'Keefe 2000, p. 108).

newly included in the Operational Guidelines of the 1970 Convention as late as 2015 (para. 122). However, this role will more likely be performed, as UNESCO has been increasing its efforts to engage the art market in the legal frame of the 1970 Convention through various meetings.[34]

Several special meetings have been held by UNIDORIT as well, starting with the first meeting in 2012 to review the practical operation of the 1995 Convention in conjunction with the Meeting of States Parties to the 1970 Convention and the ICPRCP. Recently, UNIDROIT has organized or supported more and more conferences, seminars and workshops in cooperation with UNESCO, UNODC, INTERPOL and other non-government entities to raise awareness of the 1995 Convention and support States' capacity building.[35]

3.3.2 *Individuals*

According to a UNESCO survey of the States Parties of the 1970 Convention in 2013–14,[36] about 89% of respondents answered that their countries imposed criminal and/or administrative sanctions for activities related to the illegal transfer of cultural property, according to the provisions of Article 8 of the Convention (Torggler et al. 2014, p. 30). Non-legal instruments are widely adopted by museums and institutions, in line with the principles of the 1970 Convention. In particular, as mentioned above, with the promotion by UNESCO and its partners, the ICOM Code of Ethics for Museums came to be embraced by the museum community. Now, some countries such as the Netherlands ask all museums registered in the national association to apply the ICOM Code of Ethics (Torggler et al. 2014, p. 46).

Indeed, acquisition practices by museums show considerable changes of attitude. Many museums have adopted the policies that use 1970 as a baseline date,[37] although it does not have any real legal basis in their national legislation.[38] In addition, many of them have started to return cultural properties without sufficient provenance to the country of origin upon request. For example, the Louvre returned five fragments

[34] One of the representative meetings is the one organized at UNESCO in March 2018 under the theme, "Engaging the European Art Market in the fight against the illicit trafficking of cultural property."

[35] The list of these events is available at https://www.unidroit.org/conferences-and-seminars/previous-years (accessed 30 May 2021).

[36] 66 states responded (response rate: 53%).

[37] For example, the Association of Art Museum Directors (AAMD) representing museums in the US, Canada and Mexico adopted the Guidelines on the Acquisition of Archaeological Materials and Ancient Art in 2013, stating that "Member museums should normally not acquire a Work unless provenance research substantiates that the Work was outside of its country of probable modern discovery before 1970 or was legally exported from its probable country of modern discovery after 1970."

[38] In fact, the legality of export of cultural property is determined by national legislation, not the 1970 Convention itself.

of an ancient wall painting that it had purchased between 2000 and 2003, after they were stolen in the 1980s from Egypt (AFP 2009). It is said that this kind of case is the influence of the requirement of due diligence checking stipulated in the 1995 Convention.[39]

Museums have become more active in communication with entities of civil society calling for the return of museum collections. Without the direct intervention of the government entities of each of the parties, museums and groups of civil society, often represented by NGOs or experts, can participate in discussions for restitution with more flexibility. For example, between South Korean and Japan, who have experienced political and historical difficulties in dealing with the restitution of cultural property displaced during the Japanese colonial time (1910–1945) (Kim 2013, pp. 72–84), there has been some progress made, thanks to the efforts of NSAs. For example, in 2015, as a result of a Korean expert's role, seven traditional gowns of the last princess of Korea's Joseon Dynasty (1392–1910) were donated to the National Palace Museum of Korea (Jang 2015). Sunao Onuma, the chairman of Bunak Gakuen Costum Museum in Japan, was persuaded by her long-time acquaintance, Sun-hee Kim, the head of Chojun Textile and Quilt Art Museum in Korea, who had worked together for exchange exhibitions. It was a particularly meaningful donation in that cooperation at the non-state level facilitated the restitution of cultural property that could not be handled legally and politically by two governments.

Large international auction houses have shown meaningful shifts as well. Like many museums mentioned above, they set the date of 1970 as a norm for acquisition of cultural property, which means that sellers have to establish provenance dating back to at least this date. Participants of the art market are demanding more provenance for cultural objects, and provenance came to be considered crucial for confirmation of the legitimacy and value of cultural objects, with the recognition that it will support long-term sustainability of the market (Levine 2009, pp. 224–225). Internet market providers, in particular eBay, has made known its efforts to conduct duties under the 1970 and 1995 Conventions though various initiatives. For example, it established an interface to search for stolen cultural goods in France (Planche 2010), and forbad the sale of cultural property without proof of legality issued by the Swiss or relevant countries' competent authority (Boz 2018, p. 81). A similar provision was adopted in Germany concerning proof of origin in 2008 (Kreder and Nintrup 2014, pp. 156–157).

However, in terms of individual dealers, only 52% of the States Parties responding to the 2013–14 UNESCO survey of the States Parties of the 1970 Convention reported that antique dealers were obliged to register sales in their countries as requested under Article 10(a) of the Convention. This can be interpreted as implying that adequate sanctions did not exist in other 48% of the States Parties.[40] And most likely, a similar situation of lacking both object ID registration and punitive measures would be

[39] The influence of the 1995 Convention can be witnessed in many other examples, although France has still not ratified it after its signing (Carpentier 2014).

[40] This surmise is supported by the national reports submitted for the 2015 periodic reporting cycle of the 1970 Convention, in which several states were not able to provide reliable data on their domestic market or only presented information concerning the numbers of auction houses, galleries, antique dealers, and their turnovers (UNESCO 2015a, p. 11).

found in even more States Parties. In particular, for unlawful excavation of cultural property, it was reported in 2009 that only three Member States of UNODC provided their data on the related crimes (UNODC 2009). This means while proper national administrative and legal measures are not in place, individual dealers are not fulfilling their obligations under the 1970 and 1995 Conventions. One study on antiquities dealers in the UK showed that half of the survey respondents sensed no change in market behavior after the adoption of relevant legal measures (Mackenzie and Green 2000).

Against this slow sympathizing of art dealers, the courts have been consistent to limit their right in line with the 1970 Convention. In the United States, the Ancient Coin Collectors Guild (ACCG) attempted to challenge import regulations of the State under the 1970 Convention when their importation of 23 ancient coins was seized by customs officials (Spence et al. 2019). ACCG filed a suit against the State Department, but the courts have consistently decided in favor of the US Government.[41] This consistency could be found in the *Shultz* case as well, wherein two *amicus curiae* briefs were submitted to uphold the ability of the legitimate collectors to do business in support of the defendant, Frederick Schultz.[42] Their argument was dismissed by the Court of Appeals,[43] which judged that the illegality of international smuggling of cultural property does not limit lawful importation by innocent art dealers (Gerstenblith 2009, pp. 27–32).

The lack of due diligence by art dealers also has resulted in their loss of ownership. Although the 1970 Convention was not cited, in the *Autocephalous Greek Orthodox Church of Cyprus v. Goldberg and Feldman Fine Arts, Inc.* case, the U.S. Court of Appeal affirmed the decision of the District Court that the cultural properties at issue should be returned to the original owner because the purchaser had behaved in a bad faith (Van Pelt 1990, pp. 441–464).[44] The Church of the Panagia Kanakaria learned that their four mosaics stolen in 1976 following the Turkish military intervention in Cyprus were in Indianapolis in Peg Goldberg's possession. The court concluded that the defendant could have known that the objects came from an immovable property of unique cultural and economic value located in the occupied territory, and could suspected the uprightness of salesman Dikman and other intermediaries who suggested the low purchase price relative to the market price, or made inquiries to the

---

41 *Ancient Coin Collectors Guild v. US Customs and Border Protection, Department of Homeland Security*, et al., 801 F. Supp. 2d 383 (D. Maryland 2011) and *Ancient Coin Collectors Guild v. US Customs and Border Protection*, 698 F.3d 171 (4th Cir. 2012).

42 The first brief was submitted by the National Association of Dealers in Ancient, Oriental and Primitive Art et al., and the second brief was submitted by a group called Citizens for a Balanced Policy with Regard to the Importation of Cultural Property, which consists of politicians, academics, and art collectors.

43 *United States v. Frederick Schultz*, 333 F.3d 393 (2nd Cir. 2003), para. 84.

44 *Autocephalous Greek-Orthodox Church of Cyprus v. Goldberg and Feldman Fine Arts, Inc.*, 717 F.Supp. 1374 (S.D. Ind. 1989) and *Autocephalous Greek-Orthodox Church of Cyprus v. Goldberg and Feldman Fine Arts, Inc.*, 917 F.2d 278 (7th Cir. 1990).

Cyprus authorities. Due to these reasons, Goldberg could not have acquired a valid title for the mosaics, and therefore, they were returned to Cyprus in 1991 (Contel et al. 2012).

By contrast, however, the right of the individual is strongly protected by international law sometimes when it is connected with a human rights issue, and if the person holds a valid title. In the *Beyeler v. Italy* case,[45] the European Court of Human Rights judged that Italy had violated Byeler's right to peaceful enjoyment of his possession by using its preemption right for public interest (Rudolf 2000, pp. 736–740). Under Italian law in 1939, any transaction transferring title or possession of a work of historic or artistic interest should be declared to the Ministry of Cultural Heritage. Ernst Beyeler, a Swiss art collector, had bought *Portrait of a Young Peasant* by Vincent van Gogh, which was subject to Italian law, through an intermediary, and declared it to the Ministry with the name of the intermediary in 1977. In 1986, several months after giving its permission to Beyeler to move the painting to Italy to sell it to the Peggy Guggenheim Collection in Venice, the Ministry exercised its right of preemption, citing uncertainty of ownership.[46] It was eventually sold to the Guggenheim Collection in 1988, and both Beyeler and Guggenheim declared the contract to the Ministry, but the Ministry declined their assent, claiming that the vendor did not have a valid title to the painting. After exhausting all domestic measures to challenge the preemption order of the Ministry, in 1996, Beyeler applied to the European Court of Human Rights arguing that the Ministry had violated Article 1 of Protocol No. 1 of the European Convention on Human Rights.[47] According to the court, the protection of cultural property should be considered to be a general public interest, and as such, States were allowed to interfere with the art market with legal measures and proper compensation for the acquirer; however, it also deemed that the Ministry had failed to prove this (Velioglu et al. 2013). It thus ordered the Italian State to compensate Beyeler in consideration of the painting's market value and costs incurred before presenting at the domestic courts.

There is another case of the support of strengthened rights of individuals in recovery of their cultural objects, though it did not refer to the 1970 or 1995 Convention explicitly. As Articles 3(8) and 7(2) of the 1995 Convention have recognized, action of recovery for cultural objects related to the rights of indigenous people can be made. Since the 1980s, the Tasmanian Aboriginal community had made

---

[45] *Beyeler v. Italy*, Application No. 33202/96, European Court of Human Rights, Judgement of 5 January 2000.

[46] While the dispute became prolonged concerning Beyeler's right of access to the painting, the Ministry expressed an interest in purchasing the painting, which was not successful due to a shortage of funds.

[47] Council of Europe, Protocol 1 to the European Convention for the Protection of Human Rights and Fundamental Freedoms, 20 March 1952, which reads: "Every natural or legal person is entitled to the peaceful enjoyment of his possessions. No one shall be deprived of his possessions except in the public interest and subject to the conditions provided for by law and by the general principles of international law. The preceding provisions shall not, however, in any way impair the right of a State to enforce such laws as it deems necessary to control the use of property in accordance with the general interest or to secure the payment of taxes or other contributions or penalties."

several requests to the Natural History Museum in London for the repatriation of the human remains of 17 Tasmanian Aboriginals held in the Museum, which requests were refused. After a 2000 agreement between the UK and Australia concerning the repatriation of the remains (Howard 2000), but before actually returning them to Tasmania, the Museum attempted to perform several invasive scientific tests (Gallagher 2010, p. 69). The Tasmanian Aboriginal Centre, representing the community, protested these examinations for violations of customary aboriginal rights, and filed an application for an injunction in the Administrative jurisdiction of the High Court in London in 2006 to prevent the tests. The Court's judge suggested mediation,[48] and the dispute was ultimately settled by compromise that permitted scientific investigations for the benefit of the Tasmanian society as well. The remains were returned to Tasmania in 2007 (Prott 2009, pp. 401–404).

Last but not least, concerning the public's benefits from education, which was implied in the 1970 Convention and its Operational Guidelines, a survey conducted for the evaluation of the Convention determined that it is well addressed by many State Parties in general, through public awareness campaigns, educational programs developed in cooperation with museums, or promotional publications for potential buyers or deals in the art market (Torggler et al. 2014, pp. 48–50). While the general public's access to education is well protected by the States Parties, local communities' engagement, young people's volunteerism, or market participants' enhanced attention to the public education have been observed as well (Torggler et al. 2014, p. 51).

3.4 Main Findings

Movable cultural properties have long been subject to illegal export during wartime as well as peacetime. The 1970 Convention was the first international legal instrument to provide measures to prevent the illicit trafficking of cultural property and make provisions for their restitution and framework for international collaboration. However, the Convention could not address persistent issues mainly demanded by the source countries, such as the lack of retroactivity for cases occurring before the entry into force of the Convention and the limitations on claims. The former was addressed with the creation of the ICPRCP in 1978. Although it has no legal authority to decide cases, the ICPRCP functions as a unique platform for discussion of cases to which the 1970 Convention cannot be applied.[49]

[48] *In re An Application by the Tasmanian Aboriginal Centre Inc* [2007] TASSC 5.

[49] One of the representative cases that has been discussed for a long time on the ICPRCP is that of the Parthenon Sculptures ('Elgin Marble') currently held in the British Museum. The Greek Government requested both the UK Government and the Board of Trustees of the British Museum in 2013 to proceed with mediation by the ICPRCP, but their request was rejected in 2015. However, Greece declared that it would continuously strive for the sculptures' return (Andreadaki Vlazaki 2018).

The latter issue, related to limitations on claims, is related to private law issues that relate to the status of *bona fide* acquirers of claimed cultural objects. The 1995 Convention was the result of another difficult negotiation among countries to resolve these issues related to the restitution of stolen or illegally exported cultural objects. To complement the 1970 Convention with elements of international private law, the 1995 Convention furthered the status of *bona fide* acquirers with due diligence requirements, set a time limitation for claims, and enabled individual owners to make claims directly to the court.

Under these two Conventions, NSAs find their rights, obligations and roles in various aspects. According to the provisions of the 1970 Convention, UNESCO plays not only its basic functions of assisting States Parties technically, but also takes its own initiatives to conduct activities related to the Convention. In doing so, UNESCO has cooperated with many NGOs for the development of practical tools to facilitate effective implementation of the Convention, produced various publications for awareness raising, and organized workshops for capacity building of Convention stakeholders.

There exist provisions both in the 1970 Convention and the Operational Guidelines that enable UNESCO to provide good offices for disputes between States Parties, but they have not been operationalized so far. This is not because of the lack of power or authority of UNESCO to moderate the relevant cases; rather, it is due to the sensitive characteristics of cases that usually are connected to historical or political issues of concerned Parties, and bilateral negotiations, sometimes at high level, are much faster or effective means of breaking through the deadlock. Considering the needs of interventions to auction houses, a new role for UNESCO, that of issuing public statements concerning arguable or questionable sales in auctions, was newly added when the Operational Guidelines were adopted in 2015; however, this tool has not yet been operationalized either. Nonetheless, UNESCO recently has enlarged its cooperation with auctions, and this new situation needs to be observed over a longer term. In the 1995 Convention, there exist no roles addressed to UNIDROIT as a depository of the Convention other than to convene review meetings of the Convention with its own authority, which function seems to have become active recently.

The duties of individuals seem to have been expanded with the development of more concrete legal instruments. From the 1970 Convention's newly adopted Operational Guidelines' request for museums and institutions to obey universal moral principles in building their collections, the duty for relevant participants of the art market to follow the measures taken by States Parties became more concrete. Sanctions imposed on individuals for infringing the prohibitions referred to in the Convention also have been extended to curators of museums or institutions through the Operational Guidelines, specifically with regard to the maintenance of the register of cultural properties. The other international legal instrument, UN Convention against Transnational Organized Crime (UNTOC), developed by United Nations Office on Drugs and Crime (UNODC), was added to cover new aspects of the illicit trafficking of cultural property as well.

Stronger duties required for the participants in the art market, from museums to individual collectors, are mentioned in the 1995 Convention's provisions related to due diligence checking. Unlike the 1970 Convention, wherein the right of individual *bona fide* acquirers for compensation was merely stated as the duty of the States Parties, the 1995 Convention goes further in that it requests those individuals to demonstrate evidence of having exercised due diligence. The criteria of due diligence in the provisions of the 1995 Convention are supported by the Operational Guidelines of the 1970 Convention.

In practice, it has been observed that there have been considerable changes in the purchases made by museums and institutions. A more 'moralized' or 'ethical' market is emerging in the wake of the stipulations of the new norms in the 1970 and 1995 Conventions. Although their spread is rather slow among the individual dealers and buyers, the importance of exercising good faith in the art market has been upheld in many relevant court judgements.

The right to take action for recovery of lost or stolen cultural property has long been supported by the two Conventions. The 1970 Convention asks the States Parties to admit the rightful owners' claims to bring their cultural properties back, and the Operational Guidelines of the Convention even ask the States Parties to create relevant legal proceedings if there are none in their legal system. The 1995 Convention reinforced this right of individuals to make a claim for recovery of their cultural objects, especially when they are members of tribal or indigenous communities. As the cases show, the protection of the right of ownership of individuals has also been strengthened when it is connected with human rights issues.

More public campaigns and educational programs have been organized in many parts of the world, by States Parties as well as NSAs such as UNESCO, NGOs, and cultural institutions, and actors in the art market and the general public are benefiting from them. This will help to ensure the achievements of the goals of the 1970 and 1995 Conventions: prevention of illicit importing and exporting of cultural property, and facilitation of restitution of illegally transported property.

However, the export market for cultural objects is continuously increasing, from US$ 2.56 billion in 2004 to 3.73 billion in 2013 (UNESCO UIS 2016, p. 130); moreover, the dramatic increase in individual online transactions is hard to capture in the internet age (UNESCO UIS 2016, p. 87). Another challenge is the illicit trade of cultural property for financial resources by terrorist groups such as Al-Qaida, the Islamic State in Iraq and the Levant (ISIL, also known as Daesh), and the Al-Nusrah Front (ANF).[50] All of these issues pose the question of how to further engage various NSAs in the legal frameworks of the 1970 and 1995 Conventions.

[50] The UN Security Council has adopted Resolutions 2199, 2253 and 2347 to address this issue and asked UNESCO to follow-up.

References

Abramson RD, Huttler SB (1973) The legal response to the illicit movement of cultural property. Law Polit Int Bus 5:932–970

AFP (2009, 9 October) France to return stolen relics to Egypt. Daily News Egypt. https://dailynewsegypt.com/2009/10/09/france-to-return-stolen-relics-to-egypt/. Accessed 30 May 2021

Andreadaki–Vlazaki M (2018) 21st session of the intergovernmental committee for promoting the return of cultural property to its countries of origin or its restitution in case of illicit appropriation. (Paris, 30–31 May 2018). http://www.unesco.org/new/fileadmin/MULTIMEDIA/HQ/CLT/movable/pdf/Greece_21stICPRCPfinaltel.pdf. Accessed 30 May 2021

Aust A (2007) Modern treaty law and practice. Cambridge University Press, Cambridge

Boz Z (2018) Fighting the illicit trafficking of cultural property: a toolkit for European judiciary and law enforcement. UNESCO, Paris

Carpentier L (2014, 3 November) French museums face a cultural change over restitution of colonial objects. The Guardian. https://www.theguardian.com/world/2014/nov/03/france-museums-restitution-colonial-objects. Accessed 30 May 2021

Chechi A (2014) The settlement of international cultural heritage disputes. Oxford University Press, Oxford

Contel R, Chechi A, Renold M-A (2012) Case Kanakaria Mosaics – Autocephalous Greek Orthodox Church of Cyprus and Cyprus v. Goldberg. Platform ArThemis (http://unige.ch/art-adr), Art-Law Centre, University of Geneva. https://plone.unige.ch/art-adr/cases-affaires/kanakaria-mosaics-2013-autocephalous-greek-orthodox-church-of-cyprus-and-cyprus-v-goldberg/case-note-2013-kanakaria-mosaics-2013-autocephalous-greek-orthodox-church-of-cyprus-and-cyprus-v-goldberg. Accessed 30 May 2021

Forrest C (2010) International law and the protection of cultural heritage. Routledge, London

Gallagher S (2010) Museums and the return of human remains: an equitable solution? Int J Cult Prop 17(1):65–86

Gerstenblith P (2009) Schultz and Barakat: universal recognition of national ownership of antiquities. Art Antiq Law 1:21–48

Howard J (2000, 4 July) Joint statement with tony blair on aboriginal remains. Prime Minister of Australia Media Releases. https://plone.unige.ch/art-adr/cases-affaires/17-tasmanian-human-remains-2013-tasmanian-aboriginal-centre-and-natural-history-museum-london/john-howard-media-release-joint-statement-with-tony-blair-on-aboriginal-remains-4-july-2000/view. Accessed 30 May 2021

Jang W (2015, 25 June) Princess Deokhye's belongings return to Korea. The Dong-A Ilbo. https://www.donga.com/en/article/all/20150625/410957/1/Princess-Deokhye-s-belongings-return-to-Korea. Accessed 30 May 2021

Kim J (2013) International cooperation to prevent trafficking and facilitate restitution of cultural property: evolving normative frameworks. Graduate School of International Studies, Seoul National University, Master of International Studies

Kreder JA, Nintrup J (2014) Antiquity meets the modern age: ebay's potential criminal liability for counterfeit and stolen international antiquity sales. J Law Technol Internet 5:143–178

Kono T, Wrbka S (2010) The impact of uniform laws on the protection of cultural heritage and the preservation of cultural heritage in the 21st century. In: Sánchez-Cordero Dávila JA (ed) The impact of uniform law on national law: limits and possibilities. Instituto de Investigaciones Jurídicas, Ciudad Universitaria

Levine JA (2009) The importance of provenance documentation in the market for ancient art and artifacts: the future of the market may depend on documenting the past. DePaul J Art Technol Intellect Prop Law 19(2):219–233

Mackenzie S, Green P (2000) Criminalizing the market in illicit antiquities: an evaluation of the dealing in cultural objects (offences) act 2003 in England and Wales. In: Mackenzie S, Green P (eds) Criminology an archeology: studies in looted antiquities. Hart, Oxford

Olivier M (1996) The UNIDROIT convention: attempting to regulate the international trade and traffic of cultural property. Golden State Univ Law Rev 26(3):627–673
O'Keefe PJ (2000) Commentary on the UNESCO 1970 Convention on Illicit Traffic. Institute of Art and Law, Leicester
O'Keefe PJ (2017) Protecting cultural objects: before and after 1970. Institute of Art and Law, Builth Wells
Planche E (2010, 19 February) Fighting against illicit trafficking of cultural goods in the Internet: UNESCO and its partners' response. CITES World Official Newsletter for the Parties. https://www.cites.org/eng/news/world/19/5.php. Accessed 30 May 2021
Prott LV, O'Keefe PJ (1983) National legal control of illicit traffic in cultural property. UNESCO Doc. CLT/83/WS/16, 1983. http://unesdoc.unesco.org/images/0005/000548/054854Eo.pdf. Accessed 30 May 2021
Prott LV, O'Keefe PJ (1989) Law and the cultural heritage: vol. 3 – movement. Butterworths, London
Prott LV (1997) Commentary on the UNIDROIT convention. Institute of Art and Law, Leicester
Prott LV (2009) Return of the Remains of Seventeen Tasmanian Aboriginals. In: Prott LV (ed) Witness to history. UNESCO, Paris
Prunty A (1983–1984) Toward establishing an international tribunal for the settlement of cultural property disputes: how to keep Greece from losing its marbles. Georget Law J 72:1155–1182
Rudolf B (2000) Beyeler v. Italy. Application No. 33202. Am J Int Law 94(4):736–740
Schneider M (2013) Protection and return of cultural objects: the interplay of law and ethics. In: Prott LV, Redmond-Cooper R, Urice S (eds) Realising cultural heritage law: Festschrift for Patrick O'Keefe. Institute of Art and Law, Leicester
Spence A, Chechi A, Renold M-A (2019) Case ancient coins – ancient coin collectors Guild v. United States. Platform ArThemis (http://unige.ch/art-adr), Art-Law Centre, University of Geneva. https://plone.unige.ch/art-adr/cases-affaires/case-ancient-coins-2013-ancient-coin-collectors-guild-v-united-states/case-note-2013-accg-v-united-states/view. Accessed 30 May 2021
Thorn B (2005) Internationaler Kulturgüterschutz nach der UNIDROIT-Konvention (International protection of cultural property after the UNIDROIT convention). De Gruyter Rechtswissenschaften Verlags-GmbH, Berlin
Torggler B, Abakova M, Rubin A, Vrdoljak AF (2014) Evaluation of UNESCO's standard-setting work of the culture sector: Part II – 1970 convention on the means of prohibiting and preventing the illicit import, export and transfer of ownership of cultural property. UNESCO, Online Publication
UNESCO (1978) 20 C/resolution 4/7.6/5. The 20th session of the general conference of UNESCO. Paris, 24 October–28 November 1978
UNESCO (2005) 33 C/resolution 44. The 33rd session of the general conference of UNESCO. Paris, 3–21 October 2005
UNESCO (2010a) CLT-2010/CCONF.203/COM.16/7. The 16th session of the ICPRCP. Paris, 21–23 September 2010
UNESCO (2011a) CLT-2011/CONF.208/COM.17/5. The 17th session of the ICPRCP. Paris, 30 June–1 July 2011
UNESCO (2012b) CLT/2011/CONF.207/8REV. The fight against the illicit traffic of cultural property: the 1970 convention: past and future. Paris, 15–16 March 2011
UNESCO (2012c) C70/12/2.MSP/INF.2. The second meeting of states parties to the convention on the means of prohibiting and preventing the illicit import, export and transfer of ownership of cultural property. Paris, 20–21 June 2012
UNESCO (2013a) Warning: looting of the Mallawi National Museum in the upper Egypt city of Minya. UNESCO Press Release. https://en.unesco.org/news/warning-looting-mallawi-national-museum-upper-egypt-city-minya-0. Accessed 30 May 2021
UNESCO (2014b) C70/14/2.SC/2. The second session of the subsidiary committee of the 1970 convention. Paris, 30 June-2 July 2014
UNESCO (2015a) C70/15/3.SC/6. The third session of the subsidiary committee of the 1970 convention. Paris, 28–30 September 2015

UNESCO Institute for Statistics (UIS) (2016) The globalization of cultural trade: a shift in consumption—international flows of cultural goods and services 2004–2013. UNESCO UIS, Montreal

UNESCO (2018b) C70/18/6.SC/Dec.6. The sixth session of the subsidiary committee of the 1970 convention. Paris, 28–29 May 2018

UNODC (2009) Overview of statistics on illicit trafficking in cultural property. http://www.unodc.org/documents/treaties/organized_crime/SASS_Illicit_trafficking_in_cultural_property.pdf. Accessed 30 May 2021

Van der Horst NM (2010) The Dutch ratification of UNESCO: implementation acts and the protection of cultural property. Art Antiqu Law 15(3):261–274

Van Pelt M (1990) Autocephalous Greek Orthodox Church of Cyprus v. Goldberg and Feldman Fine Arts, Inc.: a case for the use of civil remedies in effecting the return of stolen art. Penn State Int Law Rev 8(3):441–464

Velioglu E, Chechi A, Renold M-A (2013) Case Portrait of a Young Peasant – Beyeler v. Italy. Platform ArThemis (http://unige.ch/art-adr), Art-Law Centre, University of Geneva. https://plone.unige.ch/art-adr/cases-affaires/portrait-of-a-young-peasant-2013-beyeler-v-italy/case-note-2013-portrait-of-a-young-peasant-2013-beyeler-v-italy. Accessed 30 May 2021

Vrdoljak AF (2006) International law, museums and the return of cultural objects. Cambridge University Press, Cambridge

Chapter 4
The Protection of World Heritage

'World Heritage' is well-known as a flagship program of UNESCO, inscribing cultural and natural heritage of outstanding universal value on its international 'World Heritage List.' The List, created under the Convention Concerning the Protection of the World Cultural and Natural Heritage (1972; hereinafter, '1972 Convention'), functions as a pivotal mechanism of the Convention to protect heritage of important value for the international community, and invites both States and NSAs to collaborate on its managing and updating.

The 1972 Convention stipulates the status and roles of several NSAs in the implementation of the Convention, which roles have been expanded with the development of the Operational Guidelines for the Implementation of the World Heritage Convention (hereinafter, 'Operational Guidelines'). Those changes in the status and roles of NSAs in practice can be seen in the work of the 1972 Convention's intergovernmental committee known as the 'World Heritage Committee.' However, disjunctions between the Convention' text and its Operational Guidelines and practice implies challenges for further promotion of the participation of NSAs in its implementation process.

After introducing the history and key contents of the Convention as well as the provisions related to NSAs, this chapter will deal with several practical cases in order to demonstrate the changing status and roles of NSAs.

4.1 Introduction of the Legal Protection for Cultural and Natural Heritage of Outstanding Universal Value

4.1.1 History of the Adoption of the 1972 Convention

International initiatives for the protection of 'heritage of universal value' commenced in two similar but distinct areas: natural heritage and cultural heritage (Cameron and

J. Kim, *Non-State Actors in the Protection of Cultural Heritage*, Creativity, Heritage and the City 3, https://doi.org/10.1007/978-981-16-6659-9_4

Rössler 2016, p. 17). Natural heritage encompasses the efforts of the International Union for Conservation of Nature (IUCN) as well as the mid-1960s proposal by the United States for a 'World Heritage Trust' (Redgwell 2007, pp. 268–270). Cultural heritage is entailed in the 1960s UNESCO-led international campaigns to rescue great treasures of civilization along with the work of the International Council on Monuments and Sites (ICOMOS). These actions were a global response not only to the unprecedented destruction of heritage during the two World Wars but also as a remedy to the rising challenges of rapid industrialization and development.[1]

The idea of World Heritage was introduced to the IUCN General Assembly in 1966, inspired by the proposal of Joseph Fisher for a uniform definition as well as international action regarding World Heritage at a White House Conference in the previous year (Cameron and Rössler 2016, p. 18).[2] A Swedish offer to the UN General Assembly to host the Stockholm Conference on the Human Environment in 1972 was the catalyst for the movement. The 1972 Stockholm Conference ended up becoming the avenue where the natural and cultural threads regarding the protection of heritage were brought together (UN 1972). In addition to the IUCN, which submitted a Draft Convention for the Conservation of the World's Heritage (Stott 2011, p. 284), UNESCO submitted a proposal titled 'International Protection of Monuments, Groups of Building and Sites of Universal Value' (UNESCO 1966). The UNESCO draft drew from its early legal achievements in developing international conventions in the field of cultural heritage,[3] and several successful campaigns such as preserving Nubian monuments in Abu Simbel and Philae, Egypt, from the construction of the Aswan Dam in 1959 and rescuing Venice and Florence from catastrophic flooding in 1966. These actions undertaken by UNESCO began the practice of facilitating shared international responsibility in the protection of heritage. It also further defined the concept of common heritage that was first invoked by the 1964 International Charter for the Conservation and Restoration of Monuments and Sites (known as the Venice Charter).[4]

Both proposals from the IUCN and UNESCO were considered by the International Working Group for the 1972 Stockholm Conference, but there were concerns regarding the UNESCO proposal, due to its imbalanced approach to protection between cultural and natural heritage (Yusuf 2008, p. 26). While referring to

[1] The 1972 Convention Concerning the Protection of the World Cultural and Natural Heritage recognizes these phenomena in its Preamble at para. 1.

[2] Fisher proposed two lists (IUCN 1967, p. 71), a basic list of areas and sites that might be of international concern and a selection of a few areas and sites that meet the high standards, and called for international cooperation to raise funds and provide technical assistance.

[3] These include the Convention for the Protection of Cultural Property in the Event of Armed Conflict in 1954, the first international convention solely dedicated to the protection of cultural heritage, and the Recommendation on International Principles applicable to Archaeological Excavations in 1956.

[4] The Venice Charter has become a part of the fundamental ethical guidelines of the ICOMOS (UNESCO 2007a, p. 28).

'heritage' in the limited context of wildlife and its habitats,[5] the Stockholm Conference recommended to the UNESCO General Conference to examine the proposals of the working group with a view of adopting them (UN 1972, Recommendation 98 and 99). UNESCO then hosted a committee of government experts, where the American delegation submitted their own proposal that put more emphasis on natural heritage compared with the original UNESCO proposal, and ultimately many articles of the IUCN proposal were incorporated into the UNESCO proposal (Cameron and Rössler 2016, p. 30). Finally, with an additional few amendments on funding mechanisms,[6] the 17th session of the General Conference held in October–November 1972 adopted the first international instrument for protecting the common heritage of humanity: the 1972 Convention.[7] So far, 194 States have joined the Convention, which can be considered to be almost universal participation.[8]

4.1.2 Key Contents of the 1972 Convention

The 1972 Convention consists of 38 Articles divided into eight Chapters. Chapter I (Articles 1 to 3) defines the objects of the Convention, cultural and natural heritage, followed by Chapter II (Articles 4 to 7), arguably the most important chapter, as it sets out the international obligations for the protection of cultural and natural heritage. Chapter III (Articles 8 to 14) stipulates the establishment of the Intergovernmental Committee of the Convention and its operation; Chapter IV (Articles 15 to 18), the establishment of the international fund for the protection of cultural and natural heritage, called the 'World Heritage Fund'; and Chapter V (Articles 19 to 26), the conditions and arrangements for international assistance in the protection of World Heritage Sites. The obligations of the States Parties for educational programs are addressed in Chapter VI (Articles 27 to 28), while those for national reporting concerning the implementation of the Convention are found in Chapter VII (Articles 29). Lastly, Chapter VIII (Articles 30 to 38) consists of the final clauses of the Convention.

The Preamble introduces the fundamental principles and purposes of the Convention: participation of the international community as a whole in the protection of the cultural and natural heritage of outstanding universal value.[9] The objects of the Convention, cultural and natural heritage, are defined under Articles 1 and 2. For 'cultural heritage,' the Convention defines as follows:

---

[5] Principle 4 of the 1972 Stockholm Declaration of the UN Conference on the Human Environment states that "[m]an has a special responsibility to safeguard and wisely manage the heritage of wildlife and its habitat […]."

[6] The most significant amendment was concerning the system of compulsory and voluntary contributions (Lenzerini 2008, pp. 269–287).

[7] Adopted by the General Conference of UNESCO at its seventeenth session in Paris on 16 November 1972 and entered into force on 17 December 1975.

[8] As of 23 October 2020.

[9] Para. 7 of the Preamble of the 1972 Convention.

monuments: architectural works, works of monumental sculpture and painting, elements or structures of an archaeological nature, inscriptions, cave dwellings and combinations of features, which are of outstanding universal value from the point of view of history, art or science;

groups of buildings: groups of separate or connected buildings which, because of their architecture, their homogeneity or their place in the landscape, are of outstanding universal value from the point of view of history, art or science;

sites: works of man or the combined works of nature and man, and areas including archaeological sites which are of outstanding universal value from the historical, aesthetic, ethnological or anthropological point of view (Article 1.).

Meanwhile, 'natural heritage' is defined as follows:

natural features consisting of physical and biological formations or groups of such formations, which are of outstanding universal value from the aesthetic or scientific point of view;

geological and physiographical formations and precisely delineated areas which constitute the habitat of threatened species of animals and plants of outstanding universal value from the point of view of science or conservation;

natural sites or precisely delineated natural areas of outstanding universal value from the point of view of science, conservation or natural beauty (Article 2).

Some of these categories are interrelated and partially overlapping as well, which has been a subject of criticism by experts. For example, these definitions reflect the European monumentalist vision of cultural heritage (UNESCO 2000),[10] while undervaluing the intangible values of indigenous communities (Smith 2006, p. 96). Meanwhile, some definitions, for instance 'combined works of nature and of man,' were targeted due to their broadness, and were later developed into the modern notion of 'cultural landscape.'[11] This shows the expansion of the scope and contents of cultural heritage (Yusuf 2008, p. 29), and this kind of change can be further observed in the definition of the key term 'outstanding universal value' (Forrest 2010, pp. 232–240). The Operational Guidelines, which are the set of rules governing the implementation of the Convention, suggest ten criteria for the assessment of 'outstanding universal value,' along with additional criteria of authenticity for cultural heritage and integrity for both heritage types (paras. 77–95).

At the national level, States Parties are required to ensure protection of heritage and take effective measures in order to do so (Articles 4–5). They are sovereign and exercise exclusive rights over their cultural and natural heritage located within their territory, and this sovereignty is fully respected under the Convention. However, there also exists an international obligation to recognize the "duty of the international community as a whole to cooperate" for the protection of 'World Heritage,' as implied

[10] Indeed, when UNESCO hosted a "Meeting of experts to co-ordinate, with a view to their international adoption, principles and scientific, technical and legal criteria applicable to the protection of cultural property, monuments and sites" in 1968, more than half of the thirteen experts came from European countries, and all of the NGOs, except for the League of Arab States, were European ones as well (Cameron and Rössler 2016, p. 25).

[11] For further details concerning cultural landscape, see von Droste et al. (1995) and Gfeller (2013).

in its name (Article 6(1)), and this clearly illustrates the nature of the Convention's obligations *erga omnes* ("towards all") (Buzzini and Condorelli 2008, pp. 178–179).

The 'World Heritage List' is founded on the duty of each State Party to "identify and delineate the different properties situated on its territory" under Article 3, and is established by the Intergovernmental Committee for the Protection of the Cultural and Natural Heritage of Outstanding Universal Value (hereinafter, 'World Heritage Committee' or 'Committee') (Articles 8–14).[12] Before States Parties submit a specific nomination for the List, they are required to submit an inventory of properties for the possible inclusion as World Heritage to the Committee. This inventory is called the 'Tentative List.' Then, the Committee makes a final decision on their nomination and officially updates the World Heritage List. This World Heritage List is one of the key features of the Convention, and indeed the properties inscribed on the List are of outstanding universal value as cultural and natural heritage, as defined in Articles 1 and 2 of the Convention (Article 11(2)). However, when the properties on the List are threatened by serious and specific dangers, the Committee then can decide to include said properties on the 'List of World Heritage in Danger' (hereinafter, 'Danger List') (Article 11(4)). Unlike inclusion of properties on the World Heritage List (Article 11(3)), establishing the Danger List does not require the consent of the concerned territorial state(s), and it should also be noted that the removal of a property from the World Heritage List occurs under a similar process whereby consent is not required (Buzzini and Condorelli 2008, pp. 195–6 and p. 199).

The System of International Assistance, which is strictly linked to the World Heritage Fund established under Article 15, is another important operational core of the Convention. Through this international support, the "protection, conservation, presentation or rehabilitation" of the heritage mentioned in Article 13(1) can be secured. Details on the conditions that need to be met concerning requests and grants for, and types of, available International Assistance, are set out in Articles 19 to 26, while those of its source, the World Heritage Fund, are regulated under Articles 15–16. The World Heritage Committee decides on the action to be taken with regard to requests of International Assistance, but cooperates with international and national governmental and non-governmental organizations, particularly the International Centre for the Study of the Preservation and Restoration of Cultural Property (the Rome Centre),[13] the ICOMOS, and the IUCN (Article 11(7)), that have objectives similar to those of the Convention. These three organizations have contributed greatly to the introduction of the Convention and continue to closely cooperate with the Committee, assisting in general work such as helping update the World Heritage List and evaluating applications for International Assistance, and also by attending Committee meetings in an advisory capacity (Article 8(3)). The

[12] The Committee is composed of 21 States Parties elected at the General Conference of UNESCO, who equitably represent different regions and cultures of the world (Articles 8(1) and 8(2)).

[13] Later it became the International Centre for the Study of the Preservation and Restoration of Cultural Property (ICCROM).

Secretariat of UNESCO also works closely with the aforementioned advisory organizations in preparing the Committee's agenda and for the implementation of any decisions of the Committee (Article 14).

4.2 NSAs in the 1972 Convention

As with standard international law principles, the most important stakeholders of the 1972 Convention are the States themselves, in particular the 21 States making up the executive body, who are elected as members of the World Heritage Committee at the General Assembly of the Convention. According to the institutional framework established by the Convention (Vrdoljak 2008a, p. 221), these States are responsible for some key activities including inscription of properties on the World Heritage List and making determinations on matters for International Assistance.

As summarized in Table 4.1, the Convention also stipulates the status and roles of other NSAs that support and participate in the implementation of the Convention. In particular, the expert Advisory Bodies of the Convention and UNESCO are granted their authorities and roles from the provisions of the Convention as well as its Operational Guidelines. Other NSAs such as NGOs and the general public, including public and private organizations, are also mentioned in the texts of the Convention and Operational Guidelines. Furthermore, in order to ensure the smooth implementation of the Convention, several provisions of the Convention and Operational Guidelines specifically emphasize participation of the local or international community.

4.2.1 NSAs in the Text of the 1972 Convention

UNESCO

Among the various NSAs involved in the implementation of the 1972 Convention, one of the most important ones is UNSECO, whose roles are well stipulated under the Convention's Articles. According to Article 14(1), the World Heritage Committee is assisted by a Secretariat appointed by the Director General of UNESCO. Interestingly enough, although the Secretariat of UNESCO is one of the core pillars of the institutional framework of the Convention,[14] its role as described in the following paragraph is quite vague: "utilizing to the fullest extent possible the services of Advisory Bodies in their respective areas of competence and capability, [the Director-General of UNESCO] shall prepare the Committee's documentation and the agenda of its meetings and shall have the responsibility for the implementation of its decisions" (Article 14(2)).

[14] General Assembly of States Parties to the World Heritage Convention, the World Heritage Committee, and the Secretariat.

Table 4.1 Stakeholders of the 1972 convention and their status and roles

	Stakeholders	Status and roles	Goal
States	States parties	National implementation of the convention	Protection of world cultural and natural heritage
		Submission of world heritage nomination and international assistance, payment to the world heritage fund	
	General assembly	Election of member states of the world heritage committee	
	World heritage committee	Updating world heritage and its danger list, allocation of world heritage funds for international assistance	
NSAs	UNESCO	Preparation for the committee agenda and implementation of its decisions	
	Experts (advisory bodies: ICOMOS, IUCN, ICCROM)	Support for the secretariat and the committee, attendance at the world heritage committee in an advisory capacity	
	International/local NGOs	Participation in the national/international implementation of the convention, attendance at the world heritage committee representing local people's interest and/or in an advisory capacity	
	Local community	Participation in the national/international implementation of the convention, attendance at the world heritage committee representing own interest	

Source Author (based on the 1972 Convention and its Operational Guidelines)

However, this vagueness has also fostered a flexibility in the tasks of UNESCO, and thereby has enabled the evolution of its position from that which was originally defined in the Convention (Vrdoljak 2008b, p. 250). For example, initially, the Secretariat consisted of a permanent or temporary staff of UNESCO, but in evolving by necessity, it became a more independent and permanent administrative structure in 1992 within UNESCO: the World Heritage Centre. Further details on the evolving roles of the Secretariat will be provided in the following section dealing with the changes of the status of NSAs in the Operational Guidelines.

Experts

With regard to the experts, there are three official Advisory Bodies of the Convention: the ICCROM, the ICOMOS, and the IUCN. They are independent bodies without selection, nomination or authorization by the States Parties. Their unique roles are specifically addressed in several Articles of the Convention. Article 13(7) requires the Committee to cooperate with the Advisory Bodies for the implementation of its programs and projects, and Article 14(2) calls on UNESCO to utilize 'to the fullest extent possible the services of' the ICCROM, the ICOMOS and the IUCN in their respective areas of competence and capability.

Their distinct status originates from Article 8(3), whereby their participation in the meetings of the Committee in an advisory capacity is ensured at the request of the States Parties. The purpose of the Advisory Bodies' participation is mainly to provide expert opinion on the World Heritage List and International Assistance, which are specified in the Operational Guidelines of the Convention. Specializing in these technical or scientific roles, the Advisory Bodies, in acting as neutral parties, help buffer the Secretariat and the Committee from outside political pressure (UNESCO 1997, para. 44).

NGOs and Local Communities

However, the Committee does not exclusively cooperate with only these three organizations. Article 13(7) mentions that other 'international and national governmental and non-governmental organizations having objectives similar to those of this Convention' can be invited for the implementation of its programs and projects, and public and private bodies and individuals can be added to the list of cooperating partners as well. In addition, representatives of other intergovernmental or non-governmental organizations with objectives similar to those of the Convention may also attend the meetings of the Committee in an advisory capacity (Article 8(3)). However, the role of supporting the Secretariat for the Committee is exclusively the purview of the three organizations that make up the Advisory Bodies.

The legal ground for the participation of other international NGOs or the local community in the implementation of the Convention is mentioned in various places throughout the Convention. The participation of these NSAs differs from that of the Advisory Bodies or other core organizations, who are involved in the Convention due to their specific expertise in the fields of cultural or natural heritage. These other NSAs, rather, represent two differing but sometimes consistent interests, those of international and local communities. International interest for the protection of heritage derives from the concept of obligations *erga omnes,* which is an inherent obligation of the Convention. The Preamble notes that the "deterioration or disappearance of any item of the cultural or natural heritage constitutes a harmful impoverishment of the heritage of *all the nations of the world,*" and the safeguarding those properties is important "*for all the peoples of the world*" (paras. 2 and 5; emphasis added). More emphasis on the existence of the international collective interest is made by the recognition of certain heritage of outstanding interest which "need[s] to be preserved as part of the *world heritage of mankind as a whole*" (para. 6; emphasis added). The obligations *erga omnes* are imposed on States Parties in a concrete proviso as well, recognizing that "such heritage constitutes a world heritage for whose protection it is *duty of the international community as a whole to co-operate*" (Article 6(1); emphasis added).

Therefore, obligations *erga omnes* function as a legal vehicle for the promotion of international community interests in both international and domestic forums, not only by interested States, but also by private parties and by members of a civil society (Francioni 2007, p. 222). Although there is nothing in the Convention itself that suggests any intention to confer any rights to third parties, evolving interpretation of the Convention and changes to the Operational Guidelines reflect the existence of obligations *erga omnes* and the corresponding rights of the international community to participate in the implementation of the Convention. This enables many international NGOs to attend the World Heritage Committee, to speak on behalf of international civil society and to assert the top priority of the Committee, which is the protection of the value of World Heritage. Notwithstanding the issue of legitimacy, the accountability or transparency of NGO involvement in global governance and the recognition of States Parties, duties to cooperate for the collective interest of the international community under the Convention provide ample ground for non-specified international civil organizations to become one of the important stakeholders of the Convention.

Local entities also actively participate in implementation of the Convention. The motivation of their participation derives from not only obligations *erga omnes* but sometimes also for their own local interests. The obligations *erga omnes* are the area wherein local entities share their interest with the aforementioned international NGOs. In this case, international NGOs frequently represent the local people's opinion at the meetings of the Committee. However, in a practical sense, local NGOs or communities are more closely linked with the national and local implementation of the Convention by the States Parties. Although there is no specific provision of the Convention that stipulates their roles concerning its domestic implementation by the States Parties, the importance of their participation has gained attention gradually, and thus is well reflected in the text of the Operational Guidelines.

Meanwhile, the local communities have their own interests as well. These can be related to international interests—such as environmental protection or the rights of indigenous peoples—or might conflict with them, in that they could be solely focused on local interests, for example local economic development. Several cases of local communities' participation in the Committee to advocate their interests will be discussed in the following section.

4.2.2 NSAs in the Operational Guidelines of the 1972 Convention

The Operational Guidelines have set up detailed criteria and procedures to facilitate the implementation of the 1972 Convention (para. 1). They are periodically revised to reflect the decisions of the World Heritage Committee, such as when the Committee recognizes new requirements, or to adapt to the changing expectations of the international community.[15] The Operational Guidelines provide stakeholders of the Convention with useful tools with which to interpret key provisions of the Convention and tackle, thereby, new challenges in safeguarding cultural and natural heritage. For example, the criteria for Outstanding Universal Value of World Heritage according to the Operational Guidelines have been amended many times to reflect the decisions made by the World Heritage Committee in the 1970s, 1980s and 1990s (Francioni 2007, p. 20).

The Operational Guidelines consist of nine parts encompassing procedures and strategies concerning the World Heritage List, monitoring of the state of conservation of World Heritage properties, World Heritage Fund, International Assistance and so on. The basic roles of the different stakeholders of the Convention, and who they are, are laid out in the introductory part of the Operational Guidelines. They are States Parties, the General Assembly of States Parties, the World Heritage Committee, the Secretariat of UNESCO, Advisory Bodies, and other organizations and partners including local communities. Among them, NSAs like the UNESCO, Advisory Bodies and other organizations have broad and vague status and roles as stipulated in several Articles of the Convention, whereas local communities or civil organizations do not have any assigned official status or role under the Convention. In this sense, as discussed earlier in this chapter, the Operational Guidelines fill in the gaps regarding participation in the implementation of the Convention.

UNESCO

First of all, the Secretariat of the World Heritage Committee, which is the World Heritage Centre of UNESCO, finds a more defined and expanded role under the Operational Guidelines (para. 28). Their main tasks are organizing the meetings of the General Assembly and the Committee and the implementing of their decisions and resolutions. They also assist States Parties' implementation of the 1972 Convention. When seen in detail, many of these mandates go beyond the stated function of the Secretariat as stipulated under Article 14 of the Convention, which is merely to prepare the Committee agenda and follows-up on its decisions. For example, in the nomination process, the Secretariat plays an active role for the States Parties by assisting the process and providing information and guidance (paras. 125–127 and 140–141). A similar duty is performed for the Periodic Reporting of the States Parties as well (para. 200). In addition, UNESCO has the authority to grant the use of the emblem of the 1972 Convention, which is related to the credibility of both

[15] The historical development of the Operational Guidelines since their first adoption in 1977 is available at https://whc.unesco.org/en/guidelines/ (accessed 30 May 2021).

the Convention and the fundraising activities of UNESCO. These functions are not mentioned in the text of the Convention, and are derived entirely from that of the Operational Guidelines (paras. 275–278).

Compared with the 1954 Convention or the 1970 Convention, both of which enable UNESCO to initiate its own proposals, there is no explicit proactive role for UNESCO under the 1972 Convention or its Operational Guidelines. However, with regard to the Reactive Monitoring of World Heritage Sites,[16] UNESCO plays more than a coordinator's role. When UNESCO receives information from a source other than a State Party concerned, that a World Heritage property is under serious deterioration or that necessary corrective measures have not been taken in a timely manner, it must verify the source to check the accuracy of the information content with the State Party concerned and elicit its comments (para. 174). Then, it requests the relevant Advisory Bodies to forward comments based on the new information, and then the Secretariat compiles all of the collected information and presents it to the Committee (paras. 175 and 176). If the information presented to the Committee is deemed to be insufficient for the Committee to act upon, the Committee authorizes UNESCO to take necessary action such as dispatching a Reactive Monitoring mission, Advisory mission, or consultation with specialists (para. 176(e)). Although UNESCO follows the direction of the Committee, these actions are taken prior to the removal of a property from the World Heritage List, and therefore have the potential to place UNESCO outside of its neutral administrative role and into a potentially politically contentious arena (Vrdoljak 2008b, p. 253).

In addition, it is noteworthy that the director of the UNESCO World Heritage Centre has the authority to grant International Assistance up to US$ 5,000. In addition, in 2019, the Centre became responsible for assessment of all requests irrespective of the amount requested, in an effort to increase the efficiency of the assessment process (para. 247). Meanwhile, the Advisory Bodies do not have any power to approve requests from the States Parties for International Assistance, regardless of the amount requested.

Experts

Similar to those of UNESCO, the roles of the expert Advisory Bodies have become better defined in the Operational Guidelines. Advisory Bodies advise on the implementation of the World Heritage Convention in the field of their expertise by assisting the Secretariat of UNESCO and the World Heritage Committee. One of the most important roles of Advisory Bodies is the evaluation of new nominations for the World Heritage List and monitoring of the state of conservation of World Heritage properties (such as through Reactive Monitoring missions at the request of the Committee and

---

[16] Para. 169 reads: "Reactive Monitoring is the reporting by the Secretariat, other sectors of UNESCO and the Advisory Bodies to the Committee on the state of conservation of specific World Heritage properties that are under threat. To this end, the States Parties shall submit specific reports and impact studies each time exceptional circumstances occur or work is undertaken which may have an impact on the Outstanding Universal Value of the property or its state of conservation."

Advisory missions and at the invitation of States Parties) (para. 31). Their involvement in the nomination process is worth highlighting (para. 143), as their recommendations based on their scientific expertise is the baseline of the discussion at the Committee concerning its final decision on the inclusion of a site nominated for to the World Heritage List.

Two Advisory Bodies participate in the aforementioned nomination and evaluation processes: the ICOMOS for cultural heritage properties, the ICUN for natural heritage properties, and both for the purposes of cultural landscape or mixed properties (paras. 144–146). There are several factors that they need to consider when evaluating and presenting the nominations, and these factors set high standards reflective of a scientific, neutral, and systemic approach.[17] After finishing the review process for the nominations, the two Advisory Bodies make their recommendations, which fall into one of three categories: (a) properties that are recommended for inscription without reservation; (b) properties that are not recommended for inscription; (c) nominations that are recommended for referral or deferral (para. 151). Based on Article 8(3), these two Advisory Bodies attend the Committee meeting to present their recommendations on the nominations. Their scientific opinion has been historically respected and considered objective by the Committee Members; however, there is a growing trend of politicization regarding the Committee's decisions on the inscription of new World Heritage Sites.[18]

Advisory Bodies also support the States Parties' conduct of their duties under the Convention. In preparing the Periodic Reports for the UNESCO General Conference on their legislative and administrative measures adopted for the application by the Convention, the States Parties can request expert advice from the Advisory Bodies (paras. 199 and 200). They can also consult with those organizations when preparing their Tentative List of nominations for World Heritage Site consideration under Article 11.1 of the Convention (paras. 71–74, and 76). States Parties' application for International Assistance can be assisted by the Advisory Bodies as well,

---

[17] For example, para. 148 reads: "(a) adhere to the World Heritage Convention and the relevant Operational Guidelines and any additional policies set out by the Committee in its decisions; (b) be objective, rigorous and scientific including in considering all information provided to the Advisory Bodies regarding a nomination; (c) be conducted to a consistent standard of professionalism, equity and transparency throughout the evaluation process in consultation and dialogue with nominating States Parties; (d) comply to standard format, both for evaluations and presentations, to be agreed with the Secretariat and include names of all experts who participated in the evaluation process, except desk reviewers who provide confidential reviews, and, in an annex, a detailed breakdown of all costs and expenses related to the evaluation; (f) indicate clearly and separately whether the property has Outstanding Universal Value, meets the conditions of integrity and/or authenticity, a management plan/system and legislative protection; (g) evaluate each property systematically according to all relevant criteria, including its state of conservation, relatively, that is, by comparison with that of other properties of the same type, both inside and outside the State Party's territory; (h) include references to Committee decisions and requests concerning the nomination under consideration; and (j) provide a justification for their views through a list of references (literature) consulted, as appropriate."

[18] The issue of the politicization of the World Heritage Committee in not fully complying with the recommendations of the Advisory Bodies concerning nominations for the World Heritage List will be dealt with in a later part of this chapter.

who can be consulted in the process of the preparation of the requests (para. 242).[19] Requests with a budget above US$ 30,000 are assessed by the Advisory Bodies for final approval by the Committee and monitored by UNESCO in collaboration with the Advisory Bodies (paras. 247, 252, and 256).

NGOs and Local Communities

The third category of NSA respective of the Convention includes international NGOs, local NGOs, and communities. Unlike UNESCO or the Advisory Bodies, these entities do not have a statutory mandate to participate in the implementation of the Convention, but the Operational Guidelines have gradually recognized their roles by adding and revising several provisions. To begin with, the obligations *erga omnes* of the Convention for the protection of cultural and natural heritage of outstanding universal value are stressed when explaining key principles of the Convention in the introductory part of the Operational Guidelines (para. 4). These principles become realized by the contributions of key stakeholders of the Convention, such as the States Parties, General Assembly, Committee, UNESCO, and Advisory Bodies, and gradually have expanded to other entities, particularly local communities and NGOs, as well. In 1995, the Committee revised the Operational Guidelines to recognize the role of local people in the nomination process and management of properties (UNESCO 1995).[20] This first inclusion of the local community in the body of the Operational Guidelines occurred after several years of adding an interpretive part for cultural landscape, which emphasizes the local communities' collaboration and requires their full approval for a nomination (para. 12 of the Annex 3).[21]

Subsequently in 2005, the Operational Guidelines were revised to indicate that States Parties are encourage to ensure the participation of a wider variety of stakeholders,[22] meaning other NSAs such as NGOs, as well as private organizations. This was a theme during 2005, when similar overtures to better include these entities in more activities during the course of implementing the Convention took place. Examples would be participation in the preparation of the Tentative List,[23] and in the

[19] The work of the Advisory Bodies in the process of preparation, assessment, and monitoring of International Assistance is conducted in close cooperation with UNESCO.

[20] The added paragraph is as follows: "14. Participation of local people in the nomination process is essential to make them feel a shared responsibility with the State Party in the maintenance of the site."

[21] This text was prepared by an Expert Group on Cultural Landscapes (La Petite Pierre, 24–26 October 1992) and subsequently approved for inclusion in the Operational Guidelines by the World Heritage Committee at its 16th session (Santa Fe, 7–14 December 1992) (UNESCO 1992).

[22] Para. 12 reads: "States Parties to the Convention are encouraged to ensure the participation of a wide variety of stakeholders, including site managers, local and regional governments, local communities, non-governmental organizations (NGOs) and other interested parties and partners in the identification, nomination and protection of World Heritage properties."

[23] Para. 64 reads: "States Parties are encouraged to prepare their Tentative Lists with the participation of a wide variety of stakeholders, including site managers, local and regional governments, local communities, NGOs and other interested parties and partners."

nomination by the States Parties.[24] With regard to the protection and management of World Heritage Sites, the importance of full participation of the various stakeholders was specifically noted in 2011 (paras. 108 and 117). At that time, the necessity of the active and full participation of local communities and other stakeholders as relates to sustainable protection, management and presentation of the World Heritage properties was emphasized by the Convention (para. 119).[25] Special attention was given to community involvement during the application process for International Assistance. This was laid out in an explanatory note as a stated objective of Conservation and Management Assistance (Annex 8, p. 131). Moreover, the involvement of these stakeholders became one of the major criteria of the evaluation for International Assistance by the Advisory Bodies, in particular for preparatory assistance requests (Annex 9, p. 139).[26]

These changes concerning the increased and continuous involvement of local populations in World Heritage Sites are in line with the Strategic Objective of the Committee first adopted in 1992 (UNESCO 1992, Annex II). The Operational Guidelines continued to evolve as needed, and the current ones are referred to as "the 5 Cs."[27] This nomenclature was first used in the Budapest Declaration on the Implementation of the World Heritage Convention in 2002. The fifth 'C,' representing 'Community,' was added to Credibility, Conservation, Capacity-building, Communication in 2007, thanks to a proposal from New Zealand (UNESCO 2007b).

Furthermore, heightened attention to indigenous peoples was furthered in the 2015 version of the Operational Guidelines. It was at this time that indigenous peoples were recognized as one of the important partners in the protection of World Heritage. States Parties became encouraged to obtain the 'free, prior and informed consent' of indigenous peoples for World Heritage nominations in general (paras. 40 and 123 respectively). In 2019, the Committee adopted another revised version of the Operational Guidelines to reflect the importance of indigenous peoples' participation in the management of World Heritage Sites, capacity-building, research programs, and requests for International Assistance by concerned States Parties.[28]

[24] Para. 123 reads: "Participation in the nomination process of local communities, indigenous peoples, governmental, non-governmental and private organizations and other stakeholders is essential to enable them to have a shared responsibility with the State Party in the maintenance of the property. States Parties are encouraged to prepare nominations with the widest possible participation of stakeholders and to demonstrate, as appropriate, that the free, prior and informed consent of indigenous peoples has been obtained, through, inter alia making the nominations publicly available in appropriate languages and public consultations and hearings."

[25] This was added in 2011 following the recommendation of the Expert Meeting on the Relations between the World Heritage Convention, Conservation and Sustainable Development (Paraty, 29–31 March 2010) (UNESCO 2011b).

[26] Annex 9, p. 139 reads: "28. Is sufficient attention given to community involvement?"

[27] 1. Strengthen the **Credibility** of the World Heritage List; 2. Ensure the effective **Conservation** of World Heritage Properties; 3. Promote the development of effective **Capacity-building** in States Parties; 4. Increase public awareness, involvement and support for World Heritage through **Communication**; and 5. Enhance the role of **Communities** in the implementation of the World Heritage Convention. (Emphasis added by the author.)

[28] Paras. 12, 14.bis, 39, 64, 90, 111(a), 117, 119, 214bis, 215, and 239(j).

As for international NGOs with expertise in the field of cultural and natural heritage, their participation as prescribed has been expanded in more concrete terms than what was originally found in Articles 8(3) and 13(7) of the Convention. Those with appropriate competence to assist in the implementation of the program and projects of the Convention, such as Reactive Monitoring missions, became eligible for invitation to participate by the Committee in 2015 (UNESCO 2015b, Annex. para. 38). This shows that some international NGOs can have a dual identity as both experts of heritage and advocates for the local community.

Other areas in which the various NSAs participate in the implementation of the Convention are awareness-raising and promotion. Several paragraphs were added to the Operational Guidelines in 2005 to reaffirm the importance of participation of the local and national population with regard to the protection of heritage (paras. 211(c) and (d)). Under Article 27(2) of the Convention, States Parties are to develop educational activities related to World Heritage, and the participation of academic institutes as well as the relevant local and national educational authorities in such efforts is essential (para. 220). To achieve this goal, active fundraising activities by the States Parties for public and private foundations, associations, or partnerships (both public and private) developed in tandem with the Secretariat was encouraged (paras. 230–231). These provisions empowered NSAs as active participants in the promotion of the Convention; as such, NSAs could be detached from their locality but still contribute as donors to the common benefit of the international community.

The provisions in the Convention and its Operational Guidelines concerning the status and roles of NSAs, as analyzed thus far, are summarized in Table 4.2. As can be seen, the roles of UNESCO have become more concrete in the Operational Guidelines, including the proactive role for Reactive Monitoring. Additional roles have been added concerning International Assistance, in the same way as for the Advisory Bodies. The cooperation of the Advisory Bodies for the preparation of the agenda of the Committee has become substantive, ranging from the evaluation of nomination files to other technical advice for the States Parties. Without specific direct-reference Articles, the legal ground for the participation of NGOs and local communities has been gradually established along with additional relevant changes to the Operational Guidelines, particularly as concerns their rights and duties in the process of nomination preparation as well as management of properties.

4.3 NSAs in the Implementation of the 1972 Convention

Based on the provisions of the Convention and the Operational Guidelines mentioned above, NSAs have participated in the implementation of the Convention in various ways. In particular, the World Heritage Committee is by far the most important forum, where all stakeholders of the Convention, namely States Parties, UNESCO, Advisory Bodies, international NGOs, and local communities, gather and contribute to decisions on key issues of the Convention. The 21 Member States of the Committee

Table 4.2 Provisions of the 1972 convention and its operational guidelines concerning the status and roles of NSAs

NSAs	Status and roles	Convention (Art.)	Operational guidelines (Para.)
UNESCO	Preparation of the committee agenda and implementation of its decisions	14(1), 14(2)	28 (roles), 125–127, 140–141 (assistance for nomination), **174–176 (reactive monitoring)**, 200 (periodic report), 257–278 (emblem management), 242^{2}, 252^{3}, 256^{3} (international assistance assessment), 247^{6} (all international assistance assessment)
Experts (advisory bodies)	Cooperation with the committee for the implementation of its programs and projects	(13.7)	30–37 (roles), 71–74, 76 (tentative list), **143–151 (nomination evaluation)**, 199–200 (periodic report), 242^{3}, 247^{3}, 252^{3}, 256^{3} (international assistance assessment)
	Cooperation with UNESCO for preparation of the committee agenda	**(14(2))**	
	Attendance at the world heritage committee in an advisory capacity	8(3)	
Int'l/local NGOs	Attendance at the world heritage committee in an advisory capacity	8(3)	38^{2} (programs and project cooperation), 12^{2} (nomination), 40^{2} (protection), 64^{2} (tentative list), 108^{2} (management), 117^{2} (management), 123^{2} (nomination), 38^{5} (reactive monitoring)
	Cooperation with the committee for the implementation of its programs and projects	(13(7))	
Local community	**Obligations *erga omnes*to protect heritage and cooperate for its protection**	(Preamble, paras. 2, 5, 7), (6(1))	–

(continued)

adopt decisions concerning a shared agenda on the implementation of the Convention, and States Parties become subject to questioning.[29] UNESCO prepares relevant

[29] However, States Parties cannot speak to World Heritage properties in their own territories, except at the explicit invitation of the Chairperson within the allowed time for their speech and in response to specific questions posed. Representatives of a State Party, whether or not a member of the Committee, may be invited by the Chairperson to present their views after the Advisory Bodies have presented their evaluation of the site proposed by the State for inscription. The presentation

Table 4.2 (continued)

NSAs	Status and roles	Convention (Art.)	Operational guidelines (Para.)
	Participation in the nomination and management process	–	14[1] (nomination), 12[2] (protection), 64[2] (tentative list), 108[2] (management), 117[2] (management), 123[2] (nomination), 211[2] (protection), 220[2] (educational activities), 119[4] (participation for sustainable use), 40[4] (protection), **123[4] (nomination consent)**, 12[6], 14.bis[6], 39[5] (inclusive partnership), **64[6]**, **90[6]**, **111(a)[6] (management)**, **117[6] (management)**, 119[6], 214bis[6] (capacity-building), 215[6] (research), **239(j)[6] (international assistance participation)**

Note 1 Status and roles in bold are those considered important from the author's perspective in the evaluation of the status and roles of the NSAs in these provisions
Note 2 Articles or paragraphs in () connote the status and roles of each stakeholder
Note 3 Paragraphs with numbers mean the year when the paragraphs were added or revised. 1 means the 1995, 2 means 2005, 3 means 2008, 4 means 2011, 5 means 2015, and 6 means 2019
Note 4 Underlining indicates provisions with special attention to indigenous people
Source Author (based on the 1972 Convention and its Operational Guidelines)

documents and assists the Committee during the session. Advisory Bodies join the Committee to present their evaluations of sites proposed for inscription on the World Heritage List and relay the state of conservation of sites that are already inscribed on the List. Other NSAs such as international NGOs and representatives of local communities also attend the meeting and express their opinions concerning general matters of the Convention as well as on specific properties of interest. For a clearer idea of the roles and status of the NSAs in the implementation of the 1972 Convention, observation hereafter will focus on those roles conducted by NSAs at the World Heritage Committee. For UNESCO, which conducts activities year-round to implement decisions of the Committee, a noteworthy aspect of its reactive monitoring, mentioned in the previous section, will be selectively dealt with for observation.

shall be limited to a clarification or an update on the proposed site. See Rules 22.6 and 22.7 of the Rules of Procedure for the Intergovernmental Committee for the Protection of the World Cultural and Natural Heritage (2015).

4.3.1 UNESCO

At every session of the World Heritage Committee, UNESCO prepares a report for the World Heritage Centre on its activities and the implementation of the Committee's decisions, from its technical support for the State Parties on nominations, capacity-building and conservation to awareness-raising activities for the public upon the decision of the Committee. Above all, the proactive Reactive Monitoring role played by UNESCO enables it to depart from its conventional role as a neutral coordinator, often leading to a positive and productive result ensuring better conservation of World Heritage Sites.

From 1979 until 2019, a total of 3,796 state of conservation (SOC) reports on the 574 World Heritage Sites located in 147 States Parties were submitted.[30] Not all SOC reports invite Reactive Monitoring. For example, among 157 World Heritage Sites whose SOC reports were submitted to the Committee in 2018, only 21 were related to Reactive Monitoring.[31] As a coordinator for Reactive Monitoring, UNESCO receives and collects information on the SOC of specific properties, facilitates communication between the States Parties and the Advisory Bodies, and organizes and participates in the missions (Sheppard and Wijesuriya 2019, p. 33). Although there has been some concern about the duplication of roles between the Advisory Bodies and UNESCO, it has been widely understood that UNESCO's involvement in Reactive Monitoring complements the roles played by the Advisory Bodies, especially when politically sensitive issues are involved (Sheppard and Wijesuriya 2019, p. 36).

There are many examples demonstrating the proactive role conducted by UNESCO in Reactive Monitoring. In 2008, the UNESCO World Heritage Centre received media reports on mass construction projects in George Town in Historic Cities of the Straits of Malacca, Malaysia, and sent a letter to the State Party to request further information on the development project and the government's explanation.[32] The report from Malaysia contained the result of a heritage impact assessment (HIA) of the projects conducted by two experts, and clarified that the projects were not in conformity with the regulations that had been submitted to UNESCO in early 2007. Having been made aware of the need for consultation with UNESCO and the Committee, the State Party successfully modified the projects through close dialogue with the developers (Sheppard and Wijesuriya 2019, pp. 141–142).

Another example is the urgent Reactive Monitoring mission organized by UNESCO for the ancient city of Sigiriya, Sri Lanka.[33] In 2001, the national heritage authority of Sri Lanka provided information to UNESCO on the construction plans for a military airport within two kilometers of the Site, being concerned of possible

[30] The full list of the State of Conservation reports is available at http://whc.unesco.org/en/soc/ (accessed 30 May 2021).

[31] For the list of Reactive Monitoring missions carried out for the report of the Committee in 2019, see UNESCO (2019c), pp. 24–25.

[32] Melaka and George Town, Historic Cities of the Straits of Malacca was inscribed in the World Heritage List in 2008.

[33] The Ancient City of Sigiriya was inscribed in the World Heritage List in 1982.

negative impacts there. In response, UNESCO organized an urgent mission to the property, with the participation of the deputy director of the World Heritage Centre as well as an expert on airport planning engineering,[34] and had a meeting with concerned national officials. As a result of their substantive consultation, the site of the new airport was moved some 40 km from Sigiriya, thereby ensuring protection of the Site (Sheppard and Wijesuriya 2019, pp. 142–143).

4.3.2 *Experts*

Among the many roles that the Advisory Bodies undertake as per the Operational Guidelines, two of their most important are those of evaluating properties nominated for inscription on the World Heritage List and monitoring the state of conservation of World Heritage properties. These tasks are also clearly the most visible to the States Parties as well as to the general public. Since its establishment in 1978, the World Heritage List has been updated annually, and currently consists of 1,154 World Heritage properties located in 167 States Parties of the Convention.[35] Also, once a property is registered on the List, it becomes subject to Committee monitoring and, therefore too, Reactive Monitoring missions where applicable. These missions provide information on the state of conservation of specific World Heritage Sites under threat (para. 169).

First, to duly support the final decisions by the Committee concerning new nominations for the World Heritage List, the Advisory Bodies review all nomination dossiers submitted by the States Parties, and then make recommendations to the Committee concerning the eligibility of the property for inclusion to the List. There are four possible outcomes when evaluating a nomination for a potential recommendation by the Advisory Bodies: Inscription, Referral, Deferral, and Not to Inscribe.[36] In the past, the Committee tended to closely follow the Advisory Bodies' recommendation for nominations; however, the recent trend of Committee decisions has deviated from the science- and scholarship-based opinions of the Advisory Bodies (Bertacchini et al. 2016, p. 96). Several experts have pointed out increasing politicization over the previous 10 to 15 years, whereby the political alliances between Member States of the Committee and nominating States Parties have trumped the technical expertise of Advisory Bodies (Jokilehto 2011, pp. 67–69; Meskell 2012,

[34] ICOMOS was invited as well but could not join due to the short notice of the mission.

[35] As of 31 July 2021. The full list is available at http://whc.unesco.org/en/list/ (accessed 31 July 2021).

[36] Definitions of each option are provided in paras. 154–160 of the Operational Guidelines. Decisions Not to Inscribe imply that the proposed property does not have any Outstanding Universal Value and that the State Party may not apply for the inscription again. Meanwhile, Referral and Deferral allow for resubmission of the nomination to future sessions of the Committee. Nominations become referred when minor additional information is required and deferred when more in-depth study or a substantial revision is necessary.

Table 4.3 Nominations (#) according to advisory body recommendations and committee decisions (2003–2013)

		Committee decision				
		Inscription	Referral	Deferral	Not to Inscribe	Total
Advisory body recommendation	Inscription	170	3	2	0	174
	Referral	**27**	5	1	0	33
	Deferral	**33**	**23**	27	1	84
	Not to Inscribe	**1**	**3**	**9**	9	22
Total		231	34	39	10	314

Source Meskell et al. (2015, p. 428). Bold numbers represent Committee decisions upgraded based on Advisory Body recommendations

Table 4.4 Nominations (%) according to advisory body recommendations and committee decisions (2003–2007)

		Committee decision			
		Inscription (%)	Referral (%)	Deferral (%)	Not to inscribe (%)
Advisory body recommendation	Inscription	97.06	0.98	1.96	0
	Referral	**55.56**	33.33	11.11	0
	Deferral	**29.73**	**21.62**	45.95	2.7
	Not to Inscribe	**0**	**0**	**50**	50

Source Meskell et al. (2015, p. 428). Bold percentages represent Committee decisions upgraded based on Advisory Body recommendations

pp. 146–150). An external auditor of UNESO confirmed a risk to the List's credibility due to its recent reliance on geopolitical rather than scientific advice. In fact, 131 nominations out of 314 from 1977 to 2005 had received a favorable ruling by the countries on the Committee during their mandate (UNESCO 2011c, pp. 6–7).

The statistics well support this trend of pushing all recommendations of the Advisory Bodies in the direction of Inscription, e.g. from Referral to Inscription, and from Deferral to Referral or even Inscription, as seen in Table 4.3 (Meskell et al. 2015, pp. 427–428). Moreover, this trend has been accelerated recently, as Tables 4.4 and 4.5 illustrate. This is due to the nominating States Parties' ambition to have as many World Heritage properties in their territory and as soon as possible. Historically the preparation and entire nomination process is lengthy, sometimes taking over ten years. The process is also costly, requiring substantive financial and human resources and time.[37] Tellingly, whereas the Advisory Bodies intend Referral and

[37] For example, it took 14 years for the Bolgar Historical and Architectural Complex in the Russian Federation Republic of Tatarstan to be included on the World Heritage List, from its application in 1999 to final inscription in 2013, first because of the ICOMOS's concern over the development issue and later, due to changing historic substance in the nomination dossier (Meskell et al. 2015, pp. 433–435).

Table 4.5 Nominations (%) according to advisory body recommendations and committee decisions (2008–2013)

		Committee decision			
		Inscription (%)	Referral (%)	Deferral (%)	Not to inscribe (%)
Advisory body recommendation	Inscription	97.26	2.74	0	0
	Referral	**91.67**	8.33	0	0
	Deferral	**46.81**	**31.91**	21.28	0
	Not to Inscribe	**12.5**	**37.5**	**25**	25

Source Meskell et al. (2015, p. 428). Bold percentages represent Committee decisions upgraded based on Advisory Body recommendations

Deferral recommendations as tools with which States Parties can work towards and in line with Committee decisions in hopes of a better prepared future nomination and, ideally, inscription, States Parties consider them to be "poisoned gifts," taking them as criticism of towards individuals and groups who have already made countless efforts throughout the years (Meskell 2012, p. 147). In fact, many observers have opined that the Advisory Bodies began to present more favorable recommendations to the Committee in order to avoid tensions with the nominating State Parties (Meskell et al. 2015, p. 428).

Kishore Rao, former Director of the UNESCO World Heritage Centre, determined that there are systemic problems concerning the communication between the Advisory Bodies and States Parties in the nomination process (Rao 2010, p. 164). In practice, he introduced the 'Upstream Process' in 2010, which enables the Advisory Bodies and the Secretariat to provide advice directly to the States Parties for their nomination preparation in order to reduce significant problems encountered during evaluation, and his process subsequently was integrated into the Operational Guidelines in 2015 (paras. 71 and 122).

Meanwhile, the Advisory Bodies have other opinions, insisting that the credibility of the Convention is at risk and recommending, therefore, a greater role for them and other technical partners (IUCN 2012). Opinions of the States Parties, meanwhile are split on this thought. Several developing countries have called for reducing the role of the Advisory Bodies and the use of independent evaluators, while several European countries have expressed concern about the political pressures and dwindling expertise within delegations (Meskell et al. 2015, pp. 429–430).

The second task that the Advisory Bodies expend great efforts on is their monitoring of World Heritage properties. Throughout the year, the Advisory Bodies and the UNESCO World Heritage Centre review a considerable amount of information on the state of conservation of World Heritage Sites, either at the request of the World Heritage Committee, when provided by the States Parties themselves, or by third parties such as NGOs or individuals. The concerned States Parties are asked to submit detailed information on the issues raised in order to address possible impacts on the Outstanding Universal Value of a property (Veillon and UNESCO

World Heritage Centre 2014, p. 7). Through this Reactive Monitoring process, the Advisory Bodies in collaboration with the Secretariat suggest solutions to the States Parties to follow for better safeguarding of properties. Those solutions sometimes include adding properties to the Danger List under Article 11(4) of the Convention, the states of conservation of which are annually reviewed by the Committee.

Although including a property on the Danger List can be used to gain further assistance under the Convention, many States Parties tend to receive such a recommendation in a negative way, and even the lighter recommendation of 'possible inclusion' of the Site in question often is appealed by the States Parties concerned. For example, in 2011, the ICOMOS brought a recommendation for the Historic Areas of Istanbul in Turkey to be considered for possible inscription onto the Danger List the following year due to the existence in the area of uncontrolled development projects that had been ongoing for several years (UNESCO 2011d, pp. 159–165). However, the Turkish delegation actively lobbied to amend the decision, and finally succeeded in deleting, via the Australian delegation, the words 'possible inscription to the List in Danger' (UNESCO 2011e, 2011f, p. 137). Although the Committee adopted a decision requesting that the World Heritage Centre promote a better understanding of the implications and benefits of properties being inscribed onto the Danger List in order to overcome its negative perceptions (UNESCO 2017a, para. 39), only one recommendation for inclusion to the Danger List out of the five considered that year was agreed to by the Committee.[38]

4.3.3 NGOs and Local Communities

Other NSAs such as international and local NGOs and local communities also have participated in the Committee to represent their interests. They attend the Committee to express their opinions on various agendas ranging from policy- to property-related issues. With regard to policy issues, international NGOs usually intervene to emphasize their concerns, such as environmental protection or indigenous people's rights. These international NGOs also work closely with local NGOs or local communities on specific issues related to the nomination of properties to the World Heritage List or monitoring, as often these local NGOs have little to no experience in working at the international level. This relationship of working together with the international NGOs is quite beneficial for the local communities when considering the high cost of travel to the committee meetings, not to mention the expertise that the international NGOs can provide.

[38] Cerrado Protected areas: Chapada dos Veadeiros and Emas National Parks (Brazil), Islands and Protected Areas of the Gulf of California (Mexico), Historic Centre of Vienna (Austria), Kathmandu Valley (Nepal), and Fort and Shalamar Gardens in Lahore (Pakistan) were proposed for inscription on the List of World Heritage in Danger, but only Historic Centre of Vienna was included on the List in the end.

Over last two decades, the number of participants from this category of NSA has increased, along with the total number of participants on the Committee, notwithstanding slight variations due to where the Committee venues may be geographically located (see Table 4.6). In the past, rare were opportunities for NSAs to speak during a session of the Committee, but starting in 2010 and moving forward, there has been a slight uptake. In particular, the 41st session in 2017 enabled the highest number of interventions from international and local NGOs. This session allowed for this drastic uptick because of the leadership of the Chair, Jacek Purchla, who had hoped that the session would be remembered as a new chapter in this important relationship between heritage and society (UNESCO 2017b, p. 395). It was a success: the Committee adopted a decision encouraging States Parties and civil society organizations to work together in exploring newer possibilities of joint contribution and discourse at the national level and as well as at the international level (UNESCO 2017a, para. 40).

Table 4.6 Participation of NSAs (except advisory bodies and UNESCO) in the committee (1998–2017)

Year (venue)	NSA participants	NSA interventions	Year (venue)	NSA participants	NSA interventions
1998 (Japan)	34 (227)	0	2008 (Canada)	203 (606)	4
1999 (Morocco)	28 (227)	2	2009 (Spain)	161 (824)	1
2000 (Australia)	72 (342)	0	2010 (Brazil)	N/A	0
2001 (Finland)	20 (313)	3	2011 (France)	214 (1,182)	4
2002 (Hungary)	17 (305)	0	2012 (Russia)	115 (1,046)	6
2003 (France)	23 (437)	N/A	2013 (Cambodia)	205 (985)	2
2004 (China)	44 (435)	0	2014 (Qatar)	144 (974)	7
2005 (South Africa)	54 (426)	5	2015 (Germany)	381 (1,591)	9
2006 (Lithuania)	N/A	1	2016 (Turkey, UNESCO)	N/A	7
2007 (New Zealand)	N/A	6	2017 (Poland)	309 (1,525)	28

Note Numbers in () are the total numbers of participants including Committee Member States, Observer States Parties, Advisory Bodies, Secretariat of UNESCO, etc.
Source Author (extracted from the participant lists and summary records of each World Heritage Committee from its 22nd to the 41st Session, available at http://whc.unesco.org/en/committee/; accessed 30 May 2021)

The Operational Guidelines ensures the participation of the local community in the nomination process for properties to be inscribed onto the World Heritage List. However, there do exist outlier cases wherein a property was nominated for the List without consultation from the local community: for example, in 2011, the International Work Group for Indigenous Affairs (IWGIA) presented a statement on behalf of over 70 indigenous organizations and NGOs in relation to the nominations of three sites: Western Ghats (India), Trinational Sangha (Congo, Cameroon, and Central African Republic), and Kenya Lake System in the Great Rift Valley (Kenya). Concerns were raised given that these nominations had been prepared without adequate involvement and consultation of the indigenous peoples and without obtaining their free, prior and informed consent.

In response to these concerns expressed by local communities, there were calls to defer the nominations (UNESCO 2011f, p. 150). With regard to the first two sites, the recommendation of the Advisory Bodies were in the same vein as the relevant NGO's appeal, and subsequently amendments requesting that the States Parties involve the local communities were included (UNESCO 2011g, para. 2(e) and (f); 2011h, para. 2(b)). However, the concerns that the NGOs had with Kenya Lake System fell on deaf ears or were not even heard, as the Committee adopted the draft decision prepared by the Advisory Body without seeking input from the NGOs (UNESCO 2011i). This difference could have stemmed from the difference of the Advisory Body's attitude, as it already had recommended for inscription of the Kenya Lake System by the Committee (UNESCO 2011j, p. 31). This kind of problem was addressed only in 2015, when the Advisory Bodies became better aware of this dichotomy due to the various correspondence that had been received from NGOs and local communities. The Committee strongly urged the States Parties to ensure the full and effective participation of the local people in the management and decision-making of relevant properties (UNESCO 2015c, para. 5).

More recently, however, advocating for the rights of the local community and their participation in the nomination process has become one of the main reasons why nominations have been referred back to the States Parties. In 2015, the IUCN evaluated the nomination dossier of Kaeng Krachan Forest Complex submitted by Thailand, and recommended Referral owing to certain concerns about the Karen communities residing within the Kaeng Krachan National Park. The Committee acknowledged the concern, and adopted the decision asking Thailand to implement a participatory process in order to resolve issues of rights, to answer any concerns about the livelihood of the effected local communities, and to pursue the widest possible support of all stakeholders related to the nomination (UNESCO 2015d, para. 2(a)). It should be noted, though, that the additional recommendation by the IUCN for Thailand to operate under the principle of "free, prior and informed consent" in their bid for inscription onto the List was not adopted, as it had not gained the broad support of the Committee Member States hoped for by the IUCN (UNESCO 2015e, pp. 141–142).

Whereas international NGOs' and local communities' involvement in the nomination process is relatively recent and slowly developing, their involvement in issues of World Heritage property conservation is quite profound. Certainly, their lobbying prowess and ability to gain support has gained the attention of the Committee. For example, in 2011, international and local NGOs collaborated to push Tropical Rainforest Heritage of Sumatra in Indonesia to be placed on the Danger List, as it was under threat of road construction through the park's core zones (UNESCO 2011k, pp. 36–41; 2011l). By sending letters detailing the road construction and their proposals to the World Heritage Centre and the Advisory Body, as well as detailing how they, the local NGOs, had been able to partner with Flora and Fauna International in order to mitigate the threats to the park, they were able to successfully persuade the Committee to request more responsibility from the Indonesian government for conservation of the Site (UNESCO 2011f, pp. 83–87).

Another positive example of international NGOs and local communities working together for implementation of the Convention is the Great Barrier Reef Site in Australia. In 2014, the Committee adopted a decision requesting Australia to mitigate the effects on it of costal development such as ports and LNG (Liquefied Natural Gas) facilities, and signalled the Reef's possible inscription onto the Danger List the following year. Both the Australian government and NGOs organized an international campaign in order to persuade the Committee Members both before and during the Committee's session. An intense discussion occurred, displaying tension between the local community and the government (Davey and Gillespie 2014; UNESCO 2014c, pp. 76–81). When this issue was revisited in 2015, the Committee could see progress in the government measures, and continued paying attention to the appeal of international NGOs and local people.[39] Therefore, the Committee did not add the Great Barrier Reef to the Danger List and requested continuous monitoring of the Australian government's actions towards the property (UNESCO 2015e, pp. 86–92; 2015f).

However, when the wishes of the local community are in direct opposition to the Convention's goals, which is protection of heritage, their protestations may fall on deaf ears. Dresden Elbe Valley in Germany is a representative example. A year after its inscription on the World Heritage List in 2004, Dresden City conducted a referendum concerning the construction of a new bridge located in the core area of its cultural landscape, and 67.92% of the local people voted in favour of building the bridge (Gaillard and Rodwell 2015, pp. 21–22). In early 2006, the ICOMOS issued a statement opposing the bridge project and called for 'less harmful alternatives,' and the Committee inscribed the Site on the Danger List, asking Germany and the Dresden City authorities to urgently halt construction (UNESCO 2006). However, before the Committee was held in 2007, the State of Saxony Higher Administrative Court upheld the outcome of the 2005 referendum as the decision of the citizens, and

[39] It is also worth noting that there has been a tradition of the Australian government's compliance with the 1972 Convention after the *Tasmanian Dam* case in the early 1980s. The decision of the High Court reaffirmed Australia's international obligations under the Convention and ordered a stop to the construction of a large hydro-electric dam proposed for South-West Tasmania. The decision influenced the national environmental law of Australia, specifically in the form of the Environment Protection and Biodiversity Conservation Act 1999 (Cth) (EPBC Act). See *Commonwealth v. Tasmania* ("Tasmanian Dam case") [1983] HCA 21; (1983) 158 CLR 1 (1 July 1983), the details of which are available at http://envlaw.com.au/tasmanian-dam-case/ (accessed 30 May 2021).

this ruling was further affirmed by the German Federal Court. Although the local people of Dresden wanted to maintain World Heritage status as well as build the new bridge (UNESCO 2009a, p. 91), the Committee deemed that the construction of the bridge would bring irreversible harm to the Outstanding Universal Value of the property, and decided to delist it in 2009 (UNESCO 2009b).

Other than those issues relating to specific World Heritage Sites, international and local NGOs conduct their interventions during the Committee and have the authority to speak on general policy issues of the Convention as well. Usually, the issues are in line with the objectives of their organization or are within the field or scope of their specialty or expertise. In particular, indigenous peoples' rights have been emphasized at recent meetings of the Committee by several NGOs. When the Committee reviewed the reports of the 40th anniversary of the Convention, the NGO representing indigenous village leaders of Surinam expressed a concern that the nomination process to the World Heritage List and its management was not compatible with the United Nations Declaration on the Rights of Indigenous Peoples, and called for reform in the manner of requiring a form of consent from the indigenous people prior to the inscription of relevant properties. The NGO also called for direct participation by indigenous peoples in the management of relevant World Heritage Sites (UNESCO 2013b, p. 20). This request was well received and was subsequently added to the 2015 Operational Guidelines in paragraphs 40 and 123.[40]

General participation of civil society has been advocated for as well. NGOs often form alliances and endeavor to make one loud voice rather than multiple quieter voices. In 2015, a representative on behalf of World Heritage-relevant civil society organizations who had attended the pre-Committee event for civil society hosted by an NGO called the World Heritage Watch, expressed her hope for the Committee to give civil society a role in the process of the Convention in a spirit of open dialogue and cooperation, and urged consideration of various ways to strengthen their participation in the implementation of the Convention (UNESCO 2015e, p. 26). While continuing the event prior to the Committee, those NGOs collectively gathered ideas on the key policies of the Convention, and presented them to the Committee. In particular, after the Committee adopted the Sustainable Policy Paper in 2015, NGO alliances delivered their ideas on the SDG Target 11.4, related to heritage and its inappropriate indicators focusing on the amount of expenditure on heritage exclusively, and called for the Committee's attention to this issue (UNESCO 2016b, p. 23).

---

[40] Para. 40 of the Operational Guidelines reads: "Partners in the protection and conservation of World Heritage can be those individuals and other stakeholders, especially local communities, **indigenous peoples**, governmental, non-governmental and private organizations and owners who have an interest and involvement in the conservation and management of a World Heritage property." (Bold added by the author for the addition in 2015.) In addition, para. 123 reads: "Participation in the nomination process of local communities, **indigenous peoples**, governmental, non-governmental and private organizations and other stakeholders is essential to enable them to have a shared responsibility with the State Party in the maintenance of the property. States Parties are encouraged to prepare nominations with the widest possible participation of stakeholders and to demonstrate, **as appropriate, that the free, prior and informed consent of indigenous peoples has been obtained, through, inter alia making the nominations publicly available in appropriate languages and public consultations and hearings**." (Bold added by the author to indicate the additions in 2015.)

4.4 Main Findings

The protection of cultural and natural heritage of important value to humanity as a whole has become a universal concern. With almost all Member States of the UN as Contracting Parties,[41] the list of heritage of outstanding universal value has now reached over 1,000 property sites. This number shows that the 1972 Convention has proven to be a successful and effective legal instrument for the protection of cultural and natural heritage. This success certainly derives from the high visibility of the listing system as well as the international fund supporting the protection projects. In particular, the property on the World Heritage List brings not merely economic benefits to the States Parties where the heritage is located, but also becomes a recipient of attention from the international community regarding the site's protection as a symbol of the 'common heritage' of humankind.

There are various NSAs participating in the protection of World Heritage under the Convention. In particular, UNESCO and the Advisory Bodies have their distinct roles stipulated in the articles of the Convention as important partners of the World Heritage Committee; and as one of the main institutional pillars of the Convention, UNESCO prepares the agenda of the Committee and follows-up the Committee's decisions. UNESCO has a more active role in the process of Reactive Monitoring of the World Heritage properties, all the while coordinating information collected from States Parties and third parties and participating in other various missions with the Advisory Bodies.

The Advisory Bodies are the main pillars of the Convention's scientific and technical expertise. From the earliest discussions and the Convention's introduction, the IUCN, the ICOMOS, and the ICCROM have contributed to developing the idea of the protection of common heritage into tangible and actionable forms at the international level. Their participation in the Committee is ensured under the Convention, and their advisory service to the Secretariat, moreover, is codified. Additionally, the Advisory Bodies play a pivotal role in assisting the Committee in updating the World Heritage List and also as an objective evaluator for potential nominations to the World Heritage List. Furthermore, in order to satisfy one of the criteria for Outstanding Universal Value of World Heritage as defined in the Operational Guidelines, the Advisory Bodies are responsible for determining a property's value based on their scientific expertise and therefore have much influence on the successful inscription of a potential property.

Participation by the third category of NSAs, international NGOs and the local community, is not directly stipulated in the Convention, but rather is inferred from the obligations *erga omnes* of the Convention, which are the duties of the international community as a whole to cooperate for the protection of the world's shared heritage. This obligation enables the international community to be involved in the implementation of the Convention and to call for the Committee's action to pursue the Convention's goals without compromise. Similarly, local communities related to World Heritage Sites also have obligations *erga omnes* once their local property is

[41] One State Party of the 1972 Convention not a Member of the UN is Palestine.

deemed to be global heritage upon an inscription onto the World Heritage List. The recent development of the Operational Guidelines acknowledges the importance of the local population in the protection of heritage, and provisions requesting States Parties to involve local communities have been increasing. And as global attention to the indigenous peoples' rights continues to grow, the Convention accommodates the importance of indigenous peoples' participation in the process of its implementation as well. However, it is difficult to say that their 'right' to participation is guaranteed legally or systemically.

In practice, the status and roles of NSAs under the 1972 Convention have been changing in various ways. Recently, the scientific authority of the Advisory Bodies has waned, while the Committee changes more and more into a political forum where States Parties compete with each other in order to gain World Heritage status for as many of their properties (and as soon) as possible. Recommendations from the Advisory Bodies regarding potential nominations hold less sway than they once did. When it comes to reviewing the state of conservation of World Heritage Sites, States Parties now tend to avoid the decisive warnings of the Advisory Bodies and to try to find other political avenues in order to avoid being placed on the Danger List. But on the bright side, several measures including the Upstream Process have recently started to facilitate communication between States Parties and Advisory Bodies in an effort to revitalize the role of Advisory Bodies and rectify the politicization of the Committee.

In the meantime, NGOs and local communities have gained more visibility in the implementation of the 1972 Convention. Recent cases show that the Committee is now more aware of the importance of local people's participation in the process of nomination preparation as well as their future roles in the management of the property. In the monitoring process, local communities have become more active along with their close cooperation with international NGOs. Local groups can develop campaigns against their government's policies that differ from the direction of the Convention, and can attend the Committee meetings to present their argument. There have been many recent cases wherein local and international NGOs successfully influenced the Committee discussion, resulting in the concerned States Parties complying with their wishes. However, their voices are ignored where the local communities' goals run counter to those of the Convention, as shown in the case of Dresden Elbe Valley.

While many NSAs have expanded their roles in the implementation of the 1972 Convention and have the ability to suggest the directions of key policies of the Convention, the core mechanisms of the Convention seem to remain state-centric (Chechi 2018, p. 20). Basically, the Convention is based on a strong conception of state sovereignty over its immovable heritage sites within its territory. The rigid requirement of the territorial state's consent for the inscription of a property onto the List under Article 11(3) certainly can undermine the purpose of the Convention, which is the effective safeguarding of important heritage (Francioni 2003, pp. 13–38). This rule of consent can potentially hinder any protection that the Convention may provide, and this may be an issue not only in extreme cases of armed conflict or revolution where there is no identifiable government entity, but also in cases where ethnic minorities or indigenous peoples are treated with indifference or hostility by the government (Francioni and Lenzerini 2008, p. 405). The facts that the consent of the territorial State is not necessary for the inscription of the property onto the Danger List or even for a site's potential deletion from the World Heritage List only recently started to become a concern for the Committee, resulting in an increased awareness of and a willingness to listen to the voices of the local communities.

The accommodation of civil society and their opinions is growing. Actions to reestablish the authority of the Advisory Bodies are underway. Ultimately, however, the final decisions on the key issues as they relate to the implementation of the Convention are still in the hands of the 21 Member States of the World Heritage Committee. If there is a way to ensure the status and roles of NSAs, whether as Advisory Bodies or local communities, as key players in the Convention, it is probably via the establishment of more concrete mechanisms. This can be accomplished in a multitude of ways; for example, a rule might be made to invite those NSAs with specific and relevant agendas to the Committee, or to involve them in the final decision-making process. None have been tried or implemented yet. It seems that the time is ripe for the Convention to legally accommodate the changing status and roles of NSAs in this climate.

References

Bertacchini E, Liuzza C, Meskell L, Saccone D (2016) The politicization of UNESCO world heritage decision making. Public Choice 167(1):95–129

Buzzini GP, Condorelli L (2008) Article 11: list of world heritage in danger and deletion of a property from the world heritage list. In: Francioni F (ed) The 1972 world heritage convention: a commentary. Oxford University Press, Oxford

Cameron C, Rössler M (2016) Many voices, one vision: the early years of the world heritage convention. Routledge, London

Chechi (2018) Non-state actors and the implementation of the world heritage convention in Asia: achievements, problems, and prospects. Asian J Int Law 8(2):1–29

Davey M, Gillespie J (2014) The Great Barrier Reef world heritage marine protected area: valuing local perspectives in environmental protection. Aust Geogr 45(2):131–145

Forrest C (2010) International law and the protection of cultural heritage. Routledge, London

Francioni F (2003) Thirty years on: is the world heritage convention ready for the 21st century?" In: Conforti B (ed) The Italian yearbook of international law. Brill, Leiden

Francioni (2007) A dynamic evolution of the concept and scope: from cultural property to cultural heritage. In: Yusuf AA (ed) Standard setting in UNESCO vol. 1: normative action in education, science and culture. Martinus Nijhoff, Leiden

Francioni F, Lenzerini F (2008) The future of the world heritage convention: problems and prospects. In: Francioni F (ed) The 1972 world heritage convention: a commentary. Oxford University Press, Oxford

Gaillard B, Rodwell D (2015) A failure of process? Comprehending the issues fostering heritage conflict in Dresden Elbe valley and liverpool - maritime mercantile city world heritage sites. Hist Environ Policy Pract 6(1):16–40

Gfeller AE (2013) Negotiating the meaning of global heritage: 'cultural landscapes' in the UNESCO world heritage convention, 1972–92. J Glob Hist 8(3):483–503

IUCN (2012) A future for world heritage: challenges and responses to assure the credibility of the world heritage convention. Online Publication: IUCN. https://www.iucn.org/theme/world-heritage/resources/iucn-policies-world-heritage/future-challenges. Accessed 30 May 2021
Jokilehto J (2011) World heritage: observations on decisions related to cultural heritage. J Cult Herit Manag Sustain Dev 1(1):61–74
Lenzerini F (2008) Articles 15–16: world heritage fund. In: Francioni F (ed) The 1972 world heritage convention: a commentary. Oxford University Press, Oxford
Meskell L (2012) The rush to inscribe: reflections on the 35th session of the World Heritage Committee, UNESCO Paris, 2011. J Field Archaeol 37(2):145–151
Meskell L, Liuzza C, Bertacchini E, Saccone D (2015) Multilateralism and UNESCO world heritage: decision-making, states parties and political processes. Int J Herit Stud 21(5):423–440
Rao K (2010) A new paradigm for the identification, nomination and inscription of properties on the world heritage list. Int J Herit Stud 16(3):161–172
Redgwell C (2007) The impact of legal instruments adopted by UNESCO on general international law. In: Yusuf AA (ed) Standard-setting in UNESCO, vol 2. Conventions, recommendations, declarations and charters adopted by UNESCO. Martinus Nijhoff Publishers, Leiden, pp 1948–2006
Sheppard D, Wijesuriya G (2019) Evaluation of the world heritage reactive monitoring process: strengthening the effectiveness of the world heritage reactive monitoring process. UNESCO, Online Publication
Smith L (2006) Uses of heritage. Routledge, New York
Stott PH (2011) The world heritage convention and the national park service, 1962–1972. George Wright Forum 28(3):279–290
UN (1972) UN Doc. A/CONF.48/14/REV.1. Report of the United Nations conference on the human environment. Stockholm, 5–16 June 1972
UNESCO (1992) WHC-92/CONF.002/12. The 16th session of the World Heritage Committee. Santa Fe, 7–14 December 1992
UNESCO (1966) 14C/Resolution 3.3411. The 14th session of the general conference of UNESCO. Paris, 25 October-20 November 1966
UNESCO (1995) WHC-95/CONF.203/XVIII.1.A.1. The 19th session of the Bureau of the World Heritage Committee. Paris, 3–8 July 1995.
UNESCO (1997) WHC-97/CONF.208/5. The 21st session of the World Heritage Committee. Naples, 1–6 December 1997
UNESCO (2000) WHC-2000/CONF.202/INF.13. The 24th session of the Bureau of the World Heritage Committee. Paris, 26 June-1 July 2000
UNESCO (2006) Decision 30 COM 7B.77. The 30th session of the World Heritage Committee. Vilnius, 9–16 July 2006
UNESCO (2007a) World heritage—challenges for the millennium. UNESCO, Paris
UNESCO (2007b) Decision 31 COM 13B. The 31st session of the World Heritage Committee. Christchurch, 23 June–2 July 2007
UNESCO (2009a) WHC-09/33.COM/7A. The 33rd session of the World Heritage Committee. Sevilla, 22–30 June 2009
UNESCO (2009b) Decision 33 COM 7A.26. The 33rd session of the World Heritage Committee. Sevilla, 22–30 June 2009
UNESCO (2011b) WHC-11/35.COM/13. The 35th session of the World Heritage Committee. Paris, 19–29 June 2011
UNESCO (2011c) WHC/11/35.COM/9A. The 35th session of the World Heritage Committee. Paris, 19–29 June 2011
UNESCO (2011d) WHC/11/35.COM/7B.Add. The 35th session of the World Heritage Committee. Paris, 19–29 June 2011
UNESCO (2011e) Decision 35 COM 7B.111. The 35th session of the World Heritage Committee. Paris, 19–29 June 2011

UNESCO (2011f) WHC-11/35.COM.INF.20. The 35th session of the World Heritage Committee. Paris, 19–29 June 2011
UNESCO (2011g) Decision 35 COM 8B.9. The 35th session of the World Heritage Committee. Paris, 19–29 June 2011
UNESCO (2011h) Decision 35 COM 8B.4. The 35th session of the World Heritage Commit-tee. Paris, 19-29 June 2011
UNESCO (2011i) Decision 35 COM 8B.6. The 35th session of the World Heritage Committee. Paris, 19–29 June 2011
UNESCO (2011j) WHC-11/35.COM/INF.8B2. The 35th session of the World Heritage Committee. Paris, 19–29 June 2011
UNESCO (2011k) WHC-11/35.COM/7B.Add. The 35th session of the World Heritage Committee. Paris, 19–29 June 2011
UNESCO (2013b) WHC-13/37.COM/INF.20. The 37th session of the World Heritage Committee. Phnom Penh, 17–27 June 2013
UNESCO (2014c) WHC-14/38.COM.INF.16. The 38th session of the World Heritage Committee. Doha, 15–25 June 2014
UNESCO (2015b) Decision 39 COM 11. The 39th session of the World Heritage Committee. Bonn, 28 June–8 July 2015
UNESCO (2015c) Decision 39 COM 7B.5. The 39th session of the World Heritage Committee. Bonn, 28 June–8 July 2015
UNESCO (2015d) Decision 39 COM 8B.5. The 39th session of the World Heritage Committee. Bonn, 28 June–8 July 2015
UNESCO (2015e) WHC-15/39.COM.INF.19. The 39th session of the World Heritage Committee. Bonn, 28 June–8 July 2015
UNESCO (2015f) Decision 39 COM 7B.7. The 39th session of the World Heritage Committee. Bonn, 28 June–8 July 2015
UNESCO (2016b) WHC/16/40.COM.INF.19. The 40th session of the World Heritage Committee. Turkey, 10–20 July and Paris, 24–26 October 2016
UNESCO (2017a) Decision 41 COM 7. The 41st session of the World Heritage Committee. Krakow, 2–12 July 2017
UNESCO (2017b) WHC/17/41.COM.INF.18. The 41st session of the World Heritage Committee. Krakow, 2–12 July 2017
UNESCO (2019c) WHC/19/43.COM/5A. The 43rd session of the World Heritage Committee. Paris, 30 June-10 July 2019
Veillon, Richard and UNESCO World Heritage Centre (2014) State of conservation of world heritage properties: a statistical analysis (1979–2013). UNESCO, Paris
von Droste B, Plachter H, Rössler M (eds) (1995) Cultural landscapes of universal value: components of a global strategy. Gustav Fischer in cooperation with UNESCO, Paris
Vrdoljak AF (2008a) Article 13: world heritage committee and international assistance. In: Francioni F (ed) The 1972 world heritage convention: a commentary. Oxford University Press, Oxford
Vrdoljak AF (2008b) Article 14: The secretariat and support of the world heritage committee. In: Francioni F (ed) The 1972 world heritage convention: a commentary. Oxford University Press, Oxford
Yusuf AA (2008) Article 1-definition of cultural heritage. In: Francioni F (ed) The 1972 world heritage convention: a commentary. Oxford University Press, Oxford

Chapter 5
The Protection of Underwater Cultural Heritage

Based on two provisions for the protection of cultural heritage in international waters in the United Nations Convention on the Law of the Sea (hereinafter, 'UNCLOS') adopted in 1982, the UNESCO Convention on the Protection of the Underwater Cultural Heritage (2001; hereinafter, '2001 Convention') has further developed the idea according to several principles such as in situ preservation and prohibition of commercial exploitation of underwater cultural heritage.

The 2001 Convention requires participation of various NSAs, from UNESCO, experts, NGOs, and the general public for its implementation. The text of the Convention contains relevant provisions on the status and roles of NSAs. The Operational Guidelines for the implementation of the 2001 Convention (hereinafter, 'Operational Guidelines'), adopted in 2013, have made those provisions more concrete by adding several additional roles of NSAs. Compared with the other international cultural heritage laws within the purview of this book, the history of the implementation of the 2001 Convention is rather short, and the number of States Parties is small. However, several cases will be introduced to demonstrate the status and roles of NSAs that are practically related to the Convention.

5.1 Introduction of the Legal Protection for Underwater Cultural Heritage

5.1.1 History of the Adoption of the 2001 Convention

The importance of underwater cultural heritage, archaeological sites and other remains that are situated wholly or partially underwater, lies in that they are 'sealed time capsules' that can reveal as much about the past as about the event of their sinking or submergence. However, there are threats of incidental damage entailed in using the water for purposes ranging from simply fishing to exploitation of seabed resources or

J. Kim, *Non-State Actors in the Protection of Cultural Heritage*, Creativity, Heritage and the City 3, https://doi.org/10.1007/978-981-16-6659-9_5

offshore construction projects (Engelhardt 2006, p. 6). Among these threats, the activities of salvagers or 'treasure hunters' who see underwater objects of cultural heritage, especially sunken vessels, as profit-making enterprises, are especially dangerous.

The legal regime that developed from the ancient time to regulate the recovery of underwater property is the law of salvage, which aims to encourage recovery at sea by giving awards to the salvor as paid by the owner. With respect to the property of unknown owners, the law of finds may apply, by which the recovered property is awarded to the finder. No account has been taken of the historic or cultural value of recovered property or artifacts brought to the market (Forrest 2010, p. 288). Only with the increasing territorial claims of States over the oceans has the issue of cultural heritage even been touched on.

In the light of the notion of the 'common heritage of mankind' concerning underwater resources and treasures,[1] international negotiation on the status of the deep seabed commenced from 1968, and it evolved to an attempt to produce a single convention governing all aspects of the oceans. After a series of difficult negotiations (Koh and Jayakumar 1985, pp. 29–134), UNCLOS was finally adopted in 1982. In this substantive 'Constitution for the Ocean' (Koh 1982), there are only two provisions related to cultural heritage in international waters: Articles 149 and 303. Article 149 reads as follows:

> All objects of an archaeological and historical nature found in the Area[2] shall be preserved or disposed of for the benefit of mankind as a whole, particular regard being paid to the preferential rights of the state of country of origin, or the state of cultural origin, or the state of historical and archaeological origin.

This Article however addresses these two key notions in only vague and ambiguous ways, as it does not mention the manner in which objects are to be 'preserved or disposed of,' or exactly who is to do the preserving or disposing (Strati 1995, p. 300). Does preservation mean in situ preservation or removal from the site to museums or elsewhere? Does the term of 'benefit of mankind' imply that the responsibility for raising of funds for preservation or disposal of concerned objects should simply be divided, or is it a proclamation of intangible aspect of learning from those cultural properties (Newton 1986, p. 181)? Finally, the interpretation of 'preferential rights' also can be various, and moreover, it would be difficult to determine who has the most preferential rights among perhaps many interested parties.

The other Article in the UNCLOS referring to underwater cultural heritage is 303, which reads:

> 1. States have the duty to protect objects of an archaeological and historical nature found at sea and shall co-operate for this purpose.
> 2. In order to control traffic in such objects, the coastal State may, in applying Article 33, presume that their removal from the sea-bed in the zone referred to in that article

[1] See a historic speech made by Maltese Ambassador Arvid Pardo at the General Assembly of the United Nations (UN 1967).

[2] The Area is defined as the seabed and ocean floor and subsoil thereof beyond the limits of national jurisdiction (Article 1(1) of the UNCLOS). The Area is governed by rules devised for the benefit of mankind as a whole (Articles 136 and 137 of the UNCLOS).

without its approval would result in an infringement within its territory or territorial sea of the laws and regulations referred to in that article.

3. Nothing in this article affects the rights of identifiable owners, the law of salvage or other rules of admiralty, or laws and practices with respect to cultural exchanges.
4. This article is without prejudice to other international agreements and rules of international law regarding the protection of objects of an archaeological and historical nature.

Paragraph 1 of Article 303 imposes a general duty of protection for underwater cultural objects, as similarly stated for the Area in Article 149. However, paragraph 2 of Article 303 refers to the contiguous zone specifically, by mentioning the costal State's application of Article 33 that enables the power of a costal state to apply its laws of customs, immigration, fiscal and sanitary laws.[3] As the other paragraphs under Article 303 do not refer to specific maritime zones, para. 2 can be understood as a special clause for the contiguous zone, but this is unclear.[4] Paragraph 3 of Article 303 intends to maintain the previous *status quo*, leaving the issue of rights of wonders to national legislation and customary application of the salvage law or other commercial maritime laws (Forrest 2010, p. 328). Lastly, para. 4 of Article 303 leaves room for more concrete or specific agreements on underwater cultural heritage. Likewise, although the Convention tried to establish an international legal order applicable to oceans (Paik 2016, p. 366), the provisions of these two articles of the UNCLOS related to underwater cultural heritage remained vague.

Further discussion on underwater heritage followed. In particular, the Committee on Culture and Education of the Council of Europe examined the question of the preservation of underwater cultural heritage and prepared a report including a recommendation to develop a European Convention on the issue (Council of Europe 1978). A draft was prepared by an ad hoc committee of experts, but it could not be adopted due to an unrelated political dispute (O'Keefe and Prott 2011, p. 131). Meanwhile, the 1989 International Salvage Convention included an article allowing a State to enter a reservation for the application of the convention to historic wrecks.[5] However, the default position of the Convention was that its provisions could apply to underwater cultural heritage as well, and therefore, it was facing in a rather opposite direction as to the protection of underwater cultural heritage.

In 1988, the newly established Cultural Heritage Law Committee of the International Law Association (ILA) started to draft an international convention dedicated

[3] Article 33 reads: "1. In a zone contiguous to its territorial sea, described as the contiguous zone, the coastal State may exercise the control necessary to: (a) prevent infringement of its customs, fiscal, immigration or sanitary laws and regulations within its territory or territorial sea; (b) punish infringement of the above laws and regulations committed within its territory or territorial sea. 2. The contiguous zone may not extend beyond 24 nautical miles from the baselines from which the breadth of the territorial sea is measured."

[4] This interpretation, which assumes that paras. 1, 3 and 4 of Article 303 apply to all maritime zones while para. 2 applies to the contiguous zone can be quite controversial (Forrest 2010, pp. 323–328).

[5] Article 30(1)(d) reads: "when the property involved is maritime cultural property of pre-historic, archaeological or historic interest and is situated on the sea-bed."

to underwater cultural heritage, and forwarded the final version to UNESCO in 1994 for its consideration, with an Annex prepared by the International Council on Monuments and Sites (ICOMOS) concerning the rules for excavation of underwater cultural heritage.[6] After the feasibility study, a draft Convention was presented by the Secretariat of UNESCO and the UN Division of Ocean Affairs and the Law of the Sea (DOALOS) in 1998. After a series of contentious negotiations (O'Keefe 2002a, pp. 25–32; Garabello 2003, p. 89; Lund 2006, pp. 14–19), the 2001 Convention was finally adopted by a vote at the 31st General Conference of UNESCO.[7] Since its entry into force on 2 January 2009, the Convention has been ratified by 67 States.[8]

5.1.2 Key Contents of the 2001 Convention

The 2001 Convention consists of 35 Articles and an Annex titled Rules Concerning Activities Directed at Underwater Cultural Heritage.[9] Article 1(1) defines underwater cultural heritage as "all traces of human existence having a cultural, historical or archaeological character which have been partially or totally underwater, periodically or continuously, for at least 100 years." Article 2 provides several important principles of the Convention, such as in situ preservation, no commercial exploitation of underwater cultural heritage, and no regulation of jurisdiction.

First of all, the Convention stipulates the principle of in situ preservation (Article 2(5)). In particular, Rule 1 of the 2001 Convention clearly presents it as the first option to be considered for the protection of underwater cultural heritage. The rationale was that the maritime environment generally provides good conditions for preservation, though extremely fragile, placing the heritage in the time and context of sinking without contact from outside. However, this does not mean that the Convention bans any kinds of recovery of the heritage from the seabed. Recovery can be authorized for the purpose of more proper protection of the heritage or contributing to the body of knowledge on the concerned heritage (Rule 1). For example, underwater cultural heritage always is potentially exposed to the risk of illicit excavation and trafficking, as has happened in the cases of several underwater archaeological shipwrecks (Scanlan 1999), and recovery may be the best option to warrant protection in such situations.

Another important principle of the 2001 Convention is its prohibition of commercial exploitation of underwater cultural heritage (Article 2(7) and Rule 2). Similarly,

[6] ICOMOS, *Charter for the Management and Protection of the Underwater Cultural Heritage*, prepared by an ICOMOS Sub-Committee on the Underwater Cultural Heritage, and ratified by the 11th ICOMOS General Assembly in 1996.

[7] 87 Member States voted in favor, four States (The Russian Federation, Norway, Turkey and Venezuela) voted against, and 15 States abstained (including Brazil, Columbia, France, Germany, Greece, Israel, the Netherlands, Paraguay, Sweden, Switzerland, United Kingdom, Uruguay, etc.). The United States was not a member of UNESCO at that time and had no right to vote.

[8] As of 31 May 2021.

[9] According to Article 33 of the 2001 Convention, the Rules form an integral part of the Convention.

Article 4 stipulates the non-applicability of the law of salver or the law of finds to activities related to underwater cultural heritage. However, the Convention grants an exception to those authorized by competent bodies or otherwise in full conformity with the Convention. As mentioned above, if recovery of the heritage from the underwater site is the best option to maximize its protection, salvage law could be relevant as well. Even though salvage law is generally considered incompatible with the fundamental aims of the 2001 Convention, the Convention does try to be flexible to some extent, leaving the interpretation of this clause to States Parties so as to allow for continuous application of modified salvage law.[10]

Among the most difficult topics in the negotiation process for the 2001 Convention were those related to jurisdiction. Although the primary aim of the Convention was to establish a proper protective mechanism for underwater cultural heritage found beyond States' territorial jurisdictions, many States, especially maritime powers, strongly argued their concerns that the Convention would create new rights for costal States within the Exclusive Economic Zone (EEZ) and continental shelf, which might upset the balance of interests under UNCLOS.[11] In the negotiation process of the Convention, the attempt to give a State the right to declare a cultural heritage zone was highly criticized as amounting to "creeping jurisdiction (O'Keefe 2002b, p. 100)."

However, the Convention explicitly declares that it shall not prejudice the rights, jurisdiction or duties of States under international law, in particular UNCLOS (Article 3).[12] Instead, the Convention further develops the ideas of the duties to cooperate (as stated in its Preamble and Article 2(2)) and information-share (Article 19). This cooperation also extends to training and transfer of technology on the protection of cultural heritage among them (Article 21).

Specifically, as introduced above, the UNCLOS limits coastal States' jurisdiction over underwater cultural heritage to the contiguous zone (24 nautical miles) (Article 303(2) of the UNCLOS), and a similar provision is set out in the 2001 Convention (Article 8). However, the 2001 Convention goes further than to address those heritage located within EEZ or on the continental shelf, but not touching upon any jurisdictional issues but takes "constructive ambiguity (O'Keefe and Prott 2011, p. 132)." The Convention allows coastal States to request reporting to them of any activities directed at underwater cultural heritage in their EEZ or on the continental shelf (Article 9), and can authorize or prohibit any such activity to prevent interference with its rights under the UNCLOS (Article 10). In this process, a system of coordination among all States having a verifiable link to the heritage concerned

---

[10] Forrest (2010, pp. 345–346) considers this aspect of the Convention, however, as 'an unfortunate result' undermining the effect of the general principle of the Convention proclaiming no commercialization of underwater cultural heritage.

[11] This concern still exists. According to an internal evaluation survey of UNESCO for its Member States, 24% of countries identified inconsistency or incompatibility with UNCLOS as the reason for not ratifying the 2001 Convention (Rivière et al. 2019, pp. 9–10).

[12] However, although the provisions of UNCLOS are of a 'constitutional' nature, there exist general rules of treaty interpretation such as *lex specialis* or *lex posterior* (Lee 2006, pp. 20–26). In addition, Article 303.4 of UNCLOS stipulates that the article is 'without prejudice to other international agreement' as well.

can be established (Articles 9(5) and 10(3)–(6)), which is in fact another mechanism created by the 2001 Convention to deal with the delicate issue of jurisdiction. When it comes to the underwater cultural heritage found in the Area, the applicable rules are similar to those for the continental shelf and EEZ, except that there is no a coastal State playing the role of coordinator but rather a coordinating State elected by all interested States (Articles 11 and 12).

A costal State's exclusive jurisdiction over the remains of another State's vessels and aircraft is another subject of complex debate related to sovereign immunity but the Convention reached a compromise that asks the coastal State to inform the flag State of the discovery of any vessels or aircraft in the former's territorial sea (Article 7(3)). This is a recognition of the exclusive jurisdiction of the coastal States over their territorial waters. However, in an EEZ, on the continental shelf or in the Area, no activity directed to the State vessels or aircraft shall be conducted without the agreement of the flag State (Articles 10(7) and 12(7)).

The operational part of the Convention is found in Articles 14 to 18. States Parties are required to take measures to prevent illicitly exported underwater cultural heritage (Article 14), to prohibit use of their territory in support of any activities not in conformity with the Convention (Article 15), and to ensure that their nationals and vessels do not engage in any activities violating the provisions of the Convention (Article 16). The 2001 Convention also requires States Parties to impose sanctions for violation of measures implemented by the Convention (Article 17). Although the original draft of the Convention included State cooperation for extradition (UNESCO 1998; Forrest 2010, p. 354), but the discussion reached a conclusion to ensure those sanctions to be adequate in severity to be effective enough. In addition to this, a State Party is required to seize underwater cultural heritage that was not properly recovered under the Convention, take all measures to adequately conserve it, and cooperate with other States and UNESCO while ensuring public benefit (Article 18). Other than these obligations, and additionally to the duty of cooperation to share information and training (Articles 19 and 21) briefly mentioned above, States Parties have a duty to raise public awareness on the importance of protecting underwater cultural heritage (Article 20) and to establish or designate competent authorities for proper national implementation of the Convention (Article 22).

Articles 23 to 25 are related to the governance of the Convention and the roles of several key stakeholders of the Convention. These aspects will be analyzed in the following section.

5.2 NSAs in the 2001 Convention

As in many other international conventions, including those in the field of cultural heritage (the subjects of this book), States Parties are the main stakeholder of the 2001 Convention. Moreover, the characteristics of the sea, where the territorial or sovereignty issues of States are perhaps the most sensitive, give more authority to, and impose a greater duty on, States in the course of their protection of underwater cultural heritage. As already noted above, States Parties to the 2001 Convention are required to ensure and strengthen the preservation of underwater cultural heritage in situ, with different duties according to the areas of the sea, by regulating, authorizing, or reporting on activities of concern. Other domestic responsibilities such as imposing sanctions for violations, providing for seizure of heritage, raising public awareness, and appointing competent authorities are also imposed under the provisions of the Convention. The duty of international cooperation among States Parties through information sharing and technology transfer is another important pillar of the Convention.

NSAs such as UNESCO, NGOs, experts, and other individuals including the general public also are mentioned in the texts of the 2001 Convention and its Operational Guidelines. The number of provisions addressed to NSAs are fewer than those related to the States Parties. However, the texts stipulating the status and roles of NSAs imply the explicit participation of the NSAs in the implementation of the Convention. For example, UNESCO is stipulated as a Secretariat for the Convention, and a Scientific and Technical Advisory Body (STAB) is mentioned as a subsidiary body for the Meeting of States Parties.

There is no mention of NGOs in the text of the Convention, but its Operational Guidelines explicitly include them, together with other private entities, as partners in the implementation of the Convention. The rights, obligations, and roles of individuals are specified in the Rules Concerning Activities Directed at Underwater Cultural Heritage, annexed to the Convention. These various stakeholders of the 2001 Convention and their different roles are summarized in Table 5.1; more specific analysis focused on each category of NSA will follow below.

5.2.1 NSAs in the Text of the 2001 Convention

UNESCO

As it does with respect to other conventions for the protection of cultural heritage, UNESCO has a clear role as a depository of the 2001 Convention (Article 26(3)), being in charge of ratification, acceptance, approval or accession to the Convention (Article 26(1)), as well as its amendments (Article 31(1)) and denunciation (Article 32(1)). In addition, as a Secretariat of the Convention, it has been charged with a number of other, routine roles. Article 24 of the Convention requires UNESCO to organize Meetings of States Parties further to Article 23(1), and to provide assistance for States Parties to implement the decisions made at those Meetings.

The role of UNESCO also is to assist States Parties in the course of seizure of illegally recovered underwater cultural heritage within their territory. States Parties have a responsibility of taking all reasonable measures to stabilize the seized heritage and to notify, along with UNESCO, all other States that might have a verifiable cultural or historical link with the concerned heritage (Article 18). These two duties are inter-related, in that countries may need technical support in the process of their

Table 5.1 Stakeholders of the 2001 convention and their status and roles

Stakeholders		Status and roles	Goal
States	States parties	National implementation of the convention, including preventive measures	Protection of under-water cultural heritage
		International cooperation (information sharing, etc.)	
		Ensuring participation of various stakeholders (NGOs, experts, etc.)	
	Meetings of states parties	Elaboration and approval of the operational guidelines	
		Election of members to the advisory body (STAB) and adoption/amendment of its statutes	
		Examination of reports submitted by the states parties and advisory body (STAB)	
		Taking necessary measures for fundraising and others to further the objectives of the convention	
NSAs	UNESCO	Organization of meetings of states parties	
		Assistance to states parties for the implementation of the decisions made by their meetings	
		Appointment of a "Co-ordinating State" for the protection of underwater cultural heritage in the Area	
		Mediation to settle the disputes of States Parties	
		Authorization of the use of the Convention logo	
	Experts (STAB)	Assistance for the Meetings of States Parties in questions of a scientific or technical nature regarding the implementation of the Rules of the Convention	
		Evaluation of the requests for financial assistance of States Parties and their reports	
		Recommendation for accreditation of NGOs and review of their activities	

(continued)

Table 5.1 (continued)

Stakeholders		Status and roles	Goal
		Cooperation with States Parties for national implementation of the Convention	
	NGOs	Cooperation with States Parties for their implementation of the Convention	
	Individuals	Duty to report any discovery or activity directed at underwater cultural heritage to the States	
		Rights to enjoy educational and recreational benefits of access to the underwater cultural heritage	

Source Author (based on the 2001 Convention and its Operational Guidelines)

conservation of seized heritage. Therefore, the Convention expects UNESCO to provide its expertise to the State Party taking seizure, together with other interested States (Forrest 2010, p. 353).

Similar provisions for information sharing with a view to facilitating UNESCO's support for States Parties and cooperation among States Parties can be found in the activities of States Parties in the EEZ and the Area.[13] A State Party is requested to notify UNESCO of activities directed at underwater cultural heritage conducted by its national or vessel in the EEZ or on the continental shelf, so that UNESCO can make the information available to all other relevant States Parties (Articles 9(3) and 9(4)). Also, the Co-ordinating State, which is the State Party leading the consultation with all other Parties that have declared an interest over the protection of discovered underwater cultural heritage, is tasked with informing the UNESCO of the results from its preliminary research on the concerned heritage (Article 10(5)(c)). Then, UNESCO can inquire of any necessity for its technical support to the Co-ordinating State, while disseminating such information to other States Parties to encourage cooperation among all concerned.

In the Area as well, the Convention requires the States Parties to notify UNESCO and International Seabed Authority of any discoveries or activities of their nationals or vessels directed at underwater cultural heritage (Article 11(2)). Again, UNESCO then makes this information available to all relevant States Parties and receives declarations of interest from any having a verifiable link to the heritage concerned (Articles 11(3) and 11(4)). One thing different from the role of UNESCO in EEZ and on the continental shelf, UNESCO has the authority to invite all interested States Parties as well as the States Parties that conducted the activities, and even appoint a State Party to play the role of the Co-ordinating State in the Area (Article 12(2)). In other words, UNESCO functions as a facilitator of cooperation among States Parties by

[13] The 2001 Convention does not impose any duty to share information with UNESCO concerning activities of States Parties conducted in their territorial sea.

providing a platform for their consultation, in cases where there exists no coastal State that can work as a Co-ordinating State in the Area. Through this active intervention, UNESCO ensures that all information on the preliminary research of the Co-ordinating State is available to other States Parties (Article 12(5)).

A further role of UNESCO as a facilitator is set out in the process of dispute settlement. Article 25(1) requests States Parties to negotiate in good faith or seek for other peaceful means of settlement when any dispute between them is raised concerning the interpretation or application of the Convention. When such negotiations do not work within a reasonable period of time, UNESCO can intervene for mediation (Article 25(2)). However, UNESCO can function as a mediator only by agreement between the States Parties concerned; in fact, the States Parties can proceed with choosing the provisions relating to the dispute settlement under Part XV of the UNCLOS (Article 25(3)) directly, without inviting UNESCO for mediation. This reflects the constitutional status of UNCLOS as a governing legal instrument over any conflicts among States related to the sea.

Experts

As concerns the Scientific and Technical Advisory Body (hereinafter, 'STAB'), its establishment and functions are stipulated in Articles 23(4) and 23(5). Experts are nominated by the States Parties, and the final composition is decided by the Meetings of States Parties, considering both equitable geographical distribution and gender balance. STAB mainly assists the Meetings of States Parties with its expertise regarding questions on the implementation of the Rules Concerning Activities Directed at Underwater Cultural Heritage (hereinafter, 'Rules'). The Rules, drafted by the ICOMOS Sub-Committee on the Underwater Cultural Heritage, include regulations for the relevant project design, guidelines for the competence and qualifications required of persons for those projects, and best practices of underwater cultural heritage conservation and site management (UNESCO 2018c, p. 20). As the Rules function as ethical and professional standards for underwater archeology, it is reasonable and therefore natural for eminent international experts to monitor and advise their implementation by States Parties. The specific roles of STAB in performing this function under Article 23(5) are further developed by its Statues and the Operational Guidelines of the Convention, which will be analyzed in the following section.

NGOs

Unlike the Operational Guidelines, which have a dedicated chapter on NGOs, the 2001 Convention has no such provision in its text. It can only be assumed that they were included, implicitly, in the Convention's Preamble as one of the entities charged with protection of underwater cultural heritage, such as professional organizations, groups of archaeologists or divers, or other interested people.

Individuals

Individuals also lack any explicit provision related to them in the text of the 2001 Convention. However, there are several phrases in which the rights and obligations of individuals can be grasped. To begin with, like the other cultural heritage conventions, such as the 1954 Hague Convention[14] and the 1972 World Heritage Convention,[15] the 2001 Convention has a paragraph indicating the obligations *erga omnes* to protect underwater cultural heritage, acknowledging its important value as common heritage (para. 1). This becomes the grounds for barring any natural persons' unauthorized or illegitimate activities that may have negative impacts on the heritage (paras. 6 and 7).[16] In particular, Article 2(7) establishes the principle of banning commercial exploitation of underwater cultural heritage, and further, Rule 2 of the Convention restricts commercial activities entailing trading of heritage. Moreover, States Parties, according to Article 17, impose sanctions on individuals for violations of their national law for the protection of underwater cultural heritage. Illicitly trafficked underwater cultural heritage can be seized as well (Article 18). These provisions implicitly impose key obligations on individuals under the Convention.

A more specific duty of individuals is set out in the text of the 2001 Convention. When individuals discover or intend to engage in activities related to underwater cultural heritage in the EEZ or on the continental shelf, they are obliged to report such activity or discovery to their State or to both their State and another relevant State (Article 9(1)). The same duty is imposed for their activities in the Area as well, but this time only to their State, which is tasked with notifying UNESCO of its dissemination of such information to all other relevant States Parties of the Convention (Articles 11(1)–(3)).

While the rights of individuals to their activities related to underwater cultural heritage are confined to achieving the aim of the Convention or obligations *erga omnes* for the protection of underwater cultural heritage, their benefits to enjoy such heritage are protected by provisions of the Convention. In paragraph 5 of the Preamble, the public's right to enjoy the educational and recreational benefit of access to in situ underwater cultural heritage is noted, and the term 'public benefit' is referred to again in Article 18(4), which requires a State Party holding seized underwater cultural heritage to ensure its disposition. The necessity of public access is noted again in Article 2(10). This provision goes into further detail in the Rules.

The Rules envisage the necessity of promotion of public access (Rule 7), in particular concerning the archives of the projects related to underwater cultural heritage. The Rules provide guidelines for the archives to be available for professional and

[14] Para. 3 of the Preamble reads: "...Considering that the preservation of the cultural heritage is of great importance for all peoples of the world and that it is important that this heritage should receive international protection ...".

[15] Para. 6 of the Preamble reads: "...Considering that parts of the cultural or natural heritage are of outstanding interest and therefore need to be preserved as part of the world heritage of mankind as a whole ...".

[16] However, Article 5 of the Convention tries to provide minimum protection for activities that incidentally affect underwater cultural heritage, defined as "activities which, despite not may physically disturb or otherwise damage underwater cultural heritage" according to Article 1(7). Examples of such activities are commercial fishing, harbor or costal development, cable laying, and so on. The Convention leaves to the discretion of State Parties the determination of the 'best practicable means' to mitigate any adverse effects.

public access (Rule 33) and to be disseminated for public education and popular presentation as soon as the project is finalized (Rules 35 and 36). These rights of individuals to access have become a legal ground for their participation in the national implementation of the Convention by States Parties, the paragraphs pertaining to which can be found in the Operational Guidelines.

5.2.2 NSAs in the Operational Guidelines of the 2001 Convention

The Operational Guidelines for the implementation of the 2001 Convention were first drafted in 2009 upon the Convention's coming into force, and were adopted at the fourth session of the Meeting of States Parties in 2013. The current text is the revised version for 2015. As for the other Operational Guidelines or Directives for the cultural heritage conventions dealt with in this book, the one for the 2001 Convention also aims to facilitate the implementation of the Convention by means of practical guidance (para. 22). The Operational Guidelines of the 2001 Convention address States Parties, experts (STAB), UNESCO, other International Organizations, concerned NGOs, and other interested parties and partners in the protection of underwater cultural heritage as its key users (para. 24), and suggest to them, in more concrete language, ways in which the provisions of the Convention can be realized.

UNESCO

For UNESCO, the Operational Guidelines firstly provide a basic explanation of its roles as stipulated in the provisions of the Convention. For example, its roles in organizing the Meetings of States Parties under Article 23(1), receiving information from States Parties' activities directed at underwater cultural heritage under Articles 9(3) and 11(2), and accepting declarations of States Parties' interest in the heritage located in the Area under Article 11(4) (paras. 17, 26, and 27), are set out again in the Operational Guidelines without much added value. These roles are similar to UNESCO's function as a depository of information from States Parties with a view to facilitate international cooperation under Article 19 (paras. 55 and 56).

However, there are several roles added to UNESCO apart from the provisions of the Convention with the adoption of its Operational Guidelines. While introducing a mechanism for the accreditation of NGOs, UNESCO's work as a Secretariat has been expanded to check the completeness of the requests of NGOs for the consideration of the STAB and to maintain all relevant information up-to-date (paras. 84–86 and 88).[17] In 2015, a revised version of the Operational Guidelines was adopted, the new additions of which all relate to the work of UNESCO. The first addition is concerned with the use of the resources of the Underwater Cultural Heritage Fund, which was not mentioned in the Convention. The Fund needs to be well planned in advance for adequate allocation to projects directed at the protection of underwater cultural

[17] The role of UNESCO extends to the review process of accreditation as well (paras. 89 and 90).

heritage. UNESCO, as the managing body of the Fund, is commissioned to play the role of an executive bureau to prepare a draft budget to be submitted to the Meetings of States Parties for approval (para. 67). This role is connected with UNESCO's technical support for funded projects, and the Operational Guidelines enables it to make immediate use of funds received (para. 68). Although evaluation of requests for financial assistance for such projects and their reports is within the purview of the STAB (para. 78), UNESCO has found justification for its more active engagement in project execution in the field.

Another addition in the revised 2015 version of the Operational Guidelines is the new chapter dedicated to the logo of the 2001 Convention. To increase the visibility and encourage the promotion of the Convention, a special logo was created.[18] It can be used both independently and together with the UNESCO logo, but the latter is strongly encouraged (para. 96). Therefore, in that latter case, UNESCO has the authority to govern the use of the logo,[19] as utilized by States Parties, subsidiary organs of the Convention including the STAB, NGOs, the private sector or civil society (paras. 101, 106, and 110–114). Although all uses of the logo are reported to the Meeting of States Parties, UNESCO enjoys its freedom to use and grant the logo without prior authorization of the Meeting (paras. 115 and 104), and receives legal protection in that regard as well (paras. 116, 117 and 118).

As for the other active roles of UNESCO as stipulated in the Convention, such as appointing a Co-ordinating State for the protection of underwater cultural heritage in the Area (Article 12(2)), and moderating negotiations between States Parties to settle disputes (Article 25(2)), there are no further details or explanations that are relevant to this book.

Experts

The Operational Guidelines further develop specific and additional roles of experts (STAB) as well. Like the new role requested for UNESCO concerning coordination of financial assistance for projects by States Parties, the role of evaluation of such requests and their report goes to STAB for its advice to the Meeting of States Parties (paras. 72, 74 and 78). For the accreditation of NGOs as well, the role of STAB is focused on the evaluation of the applications of NGOs as well as their renewal requests (paras. 85 and 89). Although the final decisions on these matters are made by the Meeting of States Parties, STAB has the authority to suspend their collaboration with an NGO before the decision of the Meeting (para. 93).

According to paragraph 19 of the Operational Guidelines, the functions of STAB are regulated by its Statutes. Its general role to assist the Meeting of States Parties in

[18] The logo depicts waves representing the sea and the underwater cultural heritage site of the shipwreck San Juan, a whaling ship built in Passaia, Spain in 1565 and sunk in Red Bay, Canada two years later. This site was chosen to represent the multi-culturality and the cultural connections of the heritage, which important values of the Convention. The round shape of the logo is a symbol of global protection for underwater cultural heritage.

[19] For the stand-alone logo, the Meeting of States Parties delegates the authority to grant its use to UNESCO, but for the joint logo (para. 106), UNESCO has the power of authorization for its use (para. 110).

terms of scientific or technical advice in the implementation of the Rules becomes concrete in the Statutes, such as in making technical and scientific recommendations, identifying and monitoring practical issues in underwater cultural heritage, identifying the means of developing best practices, proposing workshops of seminars, and facilitating actions for further achievement of the 2030 Agenda (Article 1(b)). Upon the decision of the Meetings or their Bureaus, STAB can also conduct missions to the requesting States Parties or deliver presentations during the Meetings to provide their expert advice to States Parties (Article 1(c)). Apart from direct assistance to the Meetings of the States Parties, STAB is also invited to provide consultation for elaboration of draft Operational Guidelines related to the Rules and give guidance on questions directly related to the Rules for State cooperation mechanisms as well (Article 1(a)(ii) and (iii)).

The Statutes require STAB to consult and collaborate with various partners, in particular with NGOs, UNESCO UNITWIN Networks, UNESCO Chairs, and Category II Centers in the course of its activities (Article 1(e)). In addition to this cooperation, the Statutes enables STAB to receive assistance from international experts by its own selection, and also from UNESCO for its missions to States Parties and elaboration of relevant reports (Articles 1(f)–(g) and 5(c)–(d)). The States Parties are responsible for funding the activities of STAB (Article 8(a)). This financial and non-financial support from various partners, experts, UNESCO and States Parties is considered to ensure STAB's appropriate functioning.

Provisions requiring participation of other experts are mentioned in several parts of the Operational Guidelines. States Parties are encouraged to bring their underwater cultural heritage experts to the Convention on a regular basis to discuss the latter's proper implementation (para. 11). Relevant Rules in the Convention specifying mandatory participation of a qualified expert for management of the activities of project teams consisting of specialists in the field are repeated, with an additional mandate for the State Parties to appropriately consult experts for preliminary investigations (paras. 32–34 and 36).

NGOs

NGOs are never mentioned in the text of the 2001 Convention, but are referred to in the Operational Guidelines as important key partners of cooperation for States Parties in the implementation of the Convention together with expert groups and private entities such as local communities and the public at large (paras. 11, 79 and 81). To ensure the participation of NGOs in the process of protection of underwater cultural heritage, the Operational Guidelines introduce a mechanism of NGO accreditation. In particular, to enable the STAB to work with NGOs (Article 1(e) of the Statutes), criteria and a procedure for their accreditation as well as for renewal of such partnerships are laid out in detail (paras. 82–93). This kind of NGO accreditation to facilitate the implementation of the Convention can be found in the 2003 Convention, where NGOs play an important role in safeguarding and transmitting intangible cultural heritage in local, regional and international communities. It is assumed that the importance of NGO expertise in various fields related to the protection of underwater cultural heritage, such as marine archaeology and diving industry, increases the necessity of their further involvement in practice, and therefore led to the actual formulation of these provisions in the Operational Guidelines. However, the Operational Guidelines do not go further concerning NGOs' specific roles and do not enumerate any examples of their involvement.

Individuals

Provisions addressed to individuals are set out in the context of the protection of their rights. As a local community directly linked to underwater cultural heritage sites, a State should engage with individuals in any relevant activities (para. 49). The participation of the local community is emphasized in other provisions of the Operational Guidelines as well, where, for example, they mention the importance of the participation of various actors. The rights of the public at large are further ensured in the process of authorizing activities related to underwater cultural heritage, in that any plan that is not appropriately addressed to the general public as well as the scientific community cannot obtain authorization (para. 50). The events of communities or specific public associations focusing on the protection of underwater cultural heritage, moreover, are eligible for support from the respective States Parties (para. 54(c)).

Now, as concerns the obligations of individuals for the protection of underwater cultural heritage, specifically the duty to report concerning their relevant activities, and possible sanctions for offences made against the aims of the 2001 Convention, they are not mentioned in any further detail within the Operational Guidelines.

The provisions of the 2001 Convention and its Operational Guidelines concerning the specific status and roles of NSAs, as analyzed thus far, are summarized in Table 5.2. The Table shows that the status and roles of NSAs are further specified and added to the Operational Guidelines. With regard to UNESCO, whose several technical roles were added in 2015, no further active role can be witnessed apart from those stipulated in the Convention for the coordination and mediation of States Parties. However, for the experts (STAB) and NGOs, several new roles are added in the Operational Guidelines without particular reference from the Convention. In particular, the role of the experts has been strengthened along with its authority in relation to NGOs. The Statute of the STAB also enhances the status of the Body as a recipient of support from UNESCO and States Parties. Last but not least, it is noteworthy that the educational right of general individuals is well recognized both in the text of the 2001 Convention and its Operational Guidelines, not to mention their duty of respect for the protection of underwater cultural heritage.

Table 5.2 Provisions of the 2001 convention and its operational guidelines concerning status and roles of NSAs

NSAs	Status and roles	Convention (Art.)	Operational guidelines and statute of STAB (Para.)
UNESCO	Organization of the meetings of states parties and assistance for states parties for the implementation of the decisions made by their meetings	23(1), 24	17, 21
	Assistance for the experts (STAB)	–	21
	Information-sharing with states parties	9(3), 9(4), 10(5)(c), 11(2)–(4), 12(5), 18(3)	26–27, 55–56
	Appointment of "Co-ordinating State" for the protection of underwater cultural heritage in the Area	**12(2)**	–
	Mediation to settle the disputes of States Parties	**25(2)**	–
	Support of the work of advisory bodies related to NGOs	–	84–86, 88
	Drafting of budget and support of execution of the underwater cultural heritage fund		67–68*
	Authorization of the use of the logo of the convention		101*, 104*, 106*, 110–115*
Experts (STAB)	Assistance for the meetings of states parties regarding questions of a scientific or technical nature on the implementation of the rules of the convention	23(4), 23(5)	19, Statute 1(b), (c)
	Drafting of operational guidelines related to the rules	–	Statute 1(a)(ii)–(iii)

(continued)

Table 5.2 (continued)

NSAs	Status and roles	Convention (Art.)	Operational guidelines and statute of STAB (Para.)
	Evaluation of the requests for financial assistance of States Parties and their reports		**72, 74, 78**
	Recommendation for accreditation of NGOs and review of their activities		**85, 89**
	Suspension of collaboration with NGOs		**93**
	Cooperation with partners (NGOs, UNITWIN Networks, UNESCO Chairs, etc.)		Statute 1(e)
	Receiving technical support from international experts, UNESCO and funds from States Parties		**Statute 1(f)-(g), 5(c)-(d), 8(a)**
	Cooperation with states parties for national implementation of the convention (as experts)		32–33 and 36(experts)
NGOs	Cooperation with states parties for implementation of the convention	–	11, 79, 81
	Cooperation with the experts (STAB)		82–93, Statute 1(e)
Individuals	Cooperation with states parties for national implementation of the convention (as local communities, etc.)	–	11, 79, 81
	Duty to respect for the protection of underwater cultural heritage (no commercial activities, etc.)	(2.7, 6, 7, 17, 18)	(1)
	Duty to report any discovery or activity directed at underwater cultural heritage to the States	9(1), 11(1)–(3)	–

(continued)

Table 5.2 (continued)

NSAs	Status and roles	Convention (Art.)	Operational guidelines and statute of STAB (Para.)
	Right to enjoy the educational and recreational benefits of access to the underwater cultural heritage	**Para. 5 of the Preamble, 2(10), (18.4), Rule 7, 33, 35, 36**	**50, 65**

Note 1 Status and roles in bold are those considered important from the author's perspective in the evaluation of the status and roles of the NSAs in these provisions
Note 2 Articles or paragraphs in () connote the status and roles of each stakeholder
Note 3 Paragraphs of the Guidelines with * are those added in 2015 after the first draft of the Operational Guidelines adopted in 2013
Source Author (based on the 2001 Conventions and its Operational Guidelines)

5.3 NSAs in the Implementation of the 2001 Convention

Due mainly to the short history of the implementation of the 2001 Convention as well as the small number of Contracting Parties,[20] there are not many cases of NSA participation to observe relative to other cultural heritage conventions relevant to this book. Moreover, unlike the 2003 Intangible Cultural Heritage Convention, which has a similarly short history of adoption but a long history as a UNESCO program before its development to an international convention, the 2001 Convention does not have any precedents in realizing the core ideas of the Convention with various stakeholders.

In addition, the implementation of the Convention by States Parties also remains rather fragmentary (Petrig and Stemmler 2020, pp. 398–399).[21] In many countries, in particular the United States, cases related to underwater cultural heritage still rely on salvage law (Nafziger 2018, p. 382), which has never developed with heritage in mind, and indeed, much of the pertinent litigation is nearly endless.[22] Considering these limitations, a closer look at the rights, obligations and roles of each category of NSA will be provided here in reference to relevant working documents of UNESCO, both at the international and national levels. Several cases from States that are not Parties of the 2001 Convention will be looked at as well for further reference.

[20] Since its entry into force on 2 January 2009, the Convention has been ratified by 67 States as of 31 May 2021. This is the lowest number of States Parties among the five UNESCO Conventions for the protection of cultural heritage analyzed in this book.

[21] STAB recommended to the States Parties to 'draw attention to the problems of the participation of nationals of States Parties or vessels under the of States Parties in the pillage or exploitation of historic shipwrecks in non-State Parties' (UNESCO 2018d, p. 6).

[22] For example, the *Cobb Coin* line of cases is now nearly 40 years old. See, most recently, *Salvors, Inc. v. Unidentified Wrecked & Abandoned Vessel*, 861 F.3d 1278 (11th Cir. 2017).

5.3.1 UNESCO

Other than organizing statutory meetings every two years for the Meeting of States Parties and every year for the meetings of the STAB, UNESCO actively encourages the ratification by its Member States of the 2001 Convention by providing practical tools, such as a Model for a National Act on the Protection of Cultural Heritage, and the Model Sheet for Inventories of Underwater Cultural Heritage. A strategy for further ratification and implementation of the Convention was also developed by UNESCO and adopted in 2017 (UNESCO 2017c). In addition, to support due implementation of the Convention, many regional and national policy meetings as well as technical workshops and meetings have been held by UNESCO.[23] UNESCO also provides a comprehensive manual, training course books, and promotional publications and videos to contribute to enhanced understanding and raised awareness of the Convention.[24]

One of the important duties of UNESCO as the Secretariat of the 2001 Convention is sharing information among States Parties concerning the discovery or activities of underwater cultural heritage made in the EEZ, on the continental shelf, and in the Area, with a view to facilitating international cooperation. In 2017, Italy discovered an underwater cultural heritage site located on the Tunisian continental shelf, where there exist the remains of Roman wrecks dating to between the first century B.C. and the fourth century AD, along with modern shipwrecks from the two World Wars on Skerki Banks (UNESCO 2018e, pp. 7–9). The site was at risk from uncontrolled fishing and the passage of container ships (Gaskell and Forrest 2019, p. 340), and so Italy, according to Article 9 of the 2001 Convention, notified its discovery to UNESCO and all other States Parties in early 2018. While Tunisia was designated as the Co-ordinating State for the protection of the site (because the Skerki Banks are located on its continental shelf), UNESCO supported it to convene a meeting of interested Parties at UNESCO Headquarters in Paris.[25] The participants were delegations from six countries who had expressed an interest based on their verifiable cultural, historical or archaeological links to the case.[26] Although the full cooperation mechanism is still not fully in place, the cooperation mechanism of the 2001 Convention, which is expected to be further facilitated by the UNESCO Secretariat, will enable the concerned States Parties to have close discussion over key site protection issues such as financial and technical resources and sanctions on illicit activities

[23] For example, between May 2017 and June 2019, twelve policy meetings and seven technical meetings were organized by UNESCO or in cooperation with its partners (UNESCO 2019d, pp. 3–6). UNESCO uses and gives grant for the use of the 2001 Convention logo for these events.

[24] Resources produced by UNESCO are available at http://www.unesco.org/new/en/culture/themes/underwater-cultural-heritage/publications-resources/ (accessed 30 May 2021).

[25] The meeting was held on the 6th of February, 2019 (UNESCO 2019e).

[26] France, Italy, Spain and Tunisia expressed their interest in participating in the protection of the site, and attended the meeting held at UNESCO Headquarters in Paris. Algeria, Egypt and Morocco sent their declarations of interest after the first meeting. The first meeting of the international consultation on the Skerki Banks was held in June 2019 in Tunis, Tunisia, in cooperation with UNESCO (ANSAmed 2019).

of nationals and vessels at the site, not to mention increased visibility of their cooperation (Rivière et al. 2019, pp. 32–33). Other than this case related to cooperation with States Parties, there has been no case of UNESCO appointing a Co-ordinating State or working as a mediator to settle a dispute between States Parties.

To support the work of experts as it relates to NGOs, UNESCO has not only prepared NGO applications for accreditation and renewal, but has also organized the meetings of accredited NGOs of the Convention since 2018, in conjunction with the meetings of the STAB and other international meetings, in order to provide a forum for NGOs seeking for improved collaboration and better implementation of the 2001 Convention thereby (UNESCO 2019d, pp. 7–8).

In terms of the management of the Underwater Cultural Heritage Fund, there has been no voluntary contribution made to the account since its creation in 2009, and therefore, no budget planning has yet been executed by UNESCO.

5.3.2 Experts

The expert advisory body of the 2001 Convention, STAB, is composed of fourteen experts elected by the Meeting of States Parties.[27] Since its first election in December 2009, STAB has met once a year to discuss its technical assistance for States Parties, in particular through missions, as well as other evaluation issues such as selection of best practices and accreditation for NGOs. It also develops practical tools to aid implementation of the Convention, one of which is the Code of Ethics for Diving on Submerged Archaeological Sites, adopted by the Meeting of States Parties in 2011.

The representative role of STAB as an Advisory Body of the 2001 Convention is conducting missions to the States Parties in cases of lack of expertise related to underwater cultural heritage. So far, STAB Members have led five missions to Haiti (2014), Madagascar (2015), Panama (2015), Bulgaria (2017) and Guatemala (2019), respectively. These missions were requested by the States Parties and were intended to meet their specific needs. For example, Barry Clifford, an underwater explorer from the U.S., claimed that a shipwreck on Gran Mouton Reef, Haiti, might be that of the Santa Maria, Christopher Columbus' flagship during his first expedition to America, and expressed his wish to excavate it (Mullen and Assefa 2014). Haiti, as a Party to the 2001 Convention, requested a mission from STAB to mediate the argument. Members of STAB received assistance from the UNESCO Secretariat as well as the receiving State. The mission discovered that the wreck was not that of the Santa Maria but that, regardless, it was exposed to ongoing pillaging in the bay, which situation required attention from the local government as well as neighboring countries (UNESCO 2014d).

In a mission to Panama in 2015, STAB examined the wreck of a seventeenth century Spanish galleon, the San Jose, that had sunk in waters off the Las Perlas

[27] It can, according to its Statute (Article 2), have up to twenty-four Members, depending on the number of States Parties.

archipelago. Since 2003, Investigaciones Marinas del Istmo (IMDI), a commercial company, had been salvaging the shipwreck, but the government of Panama was concerned about their obedience to the rules and standards stipulated in the 2001 UNESCO Convention. Through its mission, STAB uncovered many problems regarding the activities of IMDI, including their involvement in commercial trading of recovered objects as well as their lack of technical and scientific competence, and recommended that the government of Panama to revise and supplement its administrative and legal provisions related to underwater cultural heritage so as to move them more in line with those of the 2001 Convention, and also suggested systemic research and public promotion (UNESCO 2015g).

With regard to the functions of the STAB as pertaining to various evaluations, such as requests of financial assistance from States Parties and accreditation of NGOs and their renewals, there has been no request of financial assistance from a State Party, and therefore, STAB has never proceeded with any such evaluation. Evaluations by STAB for NGO accreditation, however, have been numerous: already it has recommended accreditation of fifteen NGOs to the Meetings of States Parties. Notably, there is as yet no NGO whose cooperation with STAB has been suspended.

Another duty added to the STAB without any provisions from the Convention or its Operational Guidelines but rather, with the decision of the Meeting of the States Parties, is to review examples of Best Practices of underwater cultural heritage (UNESCO 2015h). STAB's idea of developing the Register of Best Practices stems from Article 2(10) of the Convention,[28] which was written with a view to promoting the diffusion of information on underwater cultural heritage for public awareness. Upon the application of the States Parties, STAB evaluates them based on its own recommended criteria and the endorsement of the Meeting of the States Parties. Twelve cases have been registered so far.[29] Considering that the creation of the List of Best Practice to promote the public access to the underwater cultural heritage was suggested by STAB and maintained with a crucial role of STAB for evaluation of applications from States Parties, this shows another aspect of the experts' additional important role in the implementation of the 2001 Convention.

5.3.3 NGOs

In practice, the roles of NGOs in the implementation of the 2001 Convention are various according to each NGO's characteristics. In general, at international meetings such as the Meetings of States Parties or the STAB, NGOs are observers, and it is difficult to say whether they are very active therein in terms of their participation in the discussion of the agenda or influence on the final decisions of the meetings.

---

[28] It reads that "Responsible non-intrusive access to observe or document in situ underwater cultural heritage shall be encouraged to create public awareness, appreciation, and protection of the heritage except where such access is incompatible with its protection and management."

[29] As of 30 May 2021.

NGOs from time to time take a floor at meetings of the STAB in order to share their experiences and new information on relevant issues, but they rarely do so at the Meetings of States Parties. Above all, as mentioned above, their status as accredited NGOs of the Convention depends on the evaluation of the STAB and the decision made by the States Parties.

However, all fifteen accredited NGOs differently contribute to the effective implementation of the Convention in various ways.[30] For example, ICOMOS International Committee on Underwater Cultural Heritage (ICOMOS-ICUCH), the author of the draft Rules within the 2001 Convention, has been involved in the missions of the STAB, specifically as a member of the teams to Panama and Madagascar in 2015. They also have provided technical editorial services and authorship to the UNESCO publications, and have conducted core components of the training programs organized by UNESCO. ICOMO-ICUCH has sent a project proposal to a State as well (Underwood 2016, p. 1). In 2018, it expressed several concerns about the recovery of cultural materials from the wreck of the San Jose located in the territorial waters of Colombia,[31] such as the reimbursing of the contractor of the recovery work with cultural objects and the lack of any detailed research project design (ICOMOS-ICUCH 2018). Many members of ICOMOS-ICUCH have been active in delivering their advice regarding national policy on the protection of underwater cultural heritage (Underwood 2016, pp. 2–12).

Likewise, the Australasian Institute for Maritime Archaeology (AIMA), as a community NGO, has continually advocated for the ratification of the Australian government's Underwater Cultural Heritage Bill of 2018.[32] Together with another accredited NGO, Nautical Archaeology Society (NAS), AIMA has taught training courses on maritime archaeology since 2017, including the 2001 Convention as an integral part of its courses, which course are currently run in many countries including New Zealand, South Africa, Canada, Micronesia, Australia and the UK (AIMA 2019, p. 2). In addition to these courses, many promotional activities such as newsletters and annual conferences have been conducted to raise the awareness of the public, including the local community and young researchers. These kinds of activities have been expanded to a regional level, the Asia–Pacific, through its scholarship program sponsoring projects on underwater cultural heritage (AIMA, pp. 2–3).

These examples of the activities of NGOs are not exhaustive. As the STAB recognized in calling them the best means of making the Body's recommendations heard and the ethical principles and guidelines of the Convention known (UNESCO 2012d, p. 3), NGOs have practical insights and expertise in the field of underwater archaeology, with many experiences of fostering the development of underwater archaeology at the national, regional and international levels. However, as the UNESCO Internal Oversight Service (IOS) pointed out in its report, accredited NGOs have

[30] The list of accredited NGOs and their reports on the activities related to the Convention is available at http://www.unesco.org/new/en/culture/themes/underwater-cultural-heritage/partners/accredited-ngos/ (accessed 30 May 2021).

[31] As of 31 May 2021, Colombia had not ratified the 2001 Convention.

[32] Austria had not ratified the 2001 Convention as of 31 May 2021.

been under-utilized so far and, therefore, a more collaborative way of working with them is needed (Rivière et al. 2019, p. 38).

As individual experts, members of NGOs, like many members of ICOMOS-ICUCH mentioned above, actively participate in the activities of government. They support advocacy for the introduction of national legal provisions for the protection of underwater cultural heritage and/or the ratification of the 2001 Convention in the non-States Parties of the Convention. They also are engaged in promotional activities such as public lectures, exhibitions, and campaigns to raise public awareness.

5.3.4 Individuals

One of the most fundamental duties of individuals under the 2001 Convention is to respect underwater cultural heritage. Among others, the sport diving community has played a crucial role in discovering new underwater sites and raising public appreciation for underwater heritage. It is said that the number of active scuba divers worldwide is about six million (DEMA 2019), which group is growing, particularly in the younger generation (PADI 2019); therefore, it is important that they be strongly encouraged to support responsible public access for sustainable protection of underwater cultural heritage. In practice, divers are educated to follow the Code of Ethics for Diving on Submerged Archaeological Sites, mentioned above as a technical contribution of the STAB. In fact, the World Underwater Federation (CMAS), one of the accredited NGOs of the Convention, has utilized UNESCO manuals at their professional training sessions for scientific divers (CMAS 2019, p. 2).

Many commercial salvage activities have been regulated recently, even before the introduction of the 2001 Convention. The *Titanic*, the most famous shipwreck, which sank in 1912 and was later discovered by RMS Titanic Inc. (RMST), a U.S. salvage corporation, in 1985, was protected as underwater cultural heritage in order to prevent destructive research and commercial exploitation. Although the United States District Court acknowledged RMST as the salvor in possession as well as the "true, sole and exclusive owner of any items salvaged from the wreck" in 1996,[33] it later served an injunction ordering the salvor not to penetrate the Titanic or to sell any of the artifacts from it.[34]

However, not all activities of individuals are under regulation for the protection of cultural heritage under the Convention. For example, while commercial fishing

[33] *R.M.S. Titanic, Inc. v. The Wrecked and Abandoned Vessel*, 924 F.Supp. 714 (E.D. Va. 1996). For further information on the litigation concerning the *Titanic*, see Forrest (2000), pp. 1–11.

[34] *R.M.S. Titanic, Inc. v. The Wrecked and Abandoned Vessel*, Civ. No. 2:93cv902 (July 28, 2000 E.D. Va.) and *R.M.S. Titanic, Inc. v. Wrecked and Abandoned Vessel*, 742 F. Supp. 2d 784, 790 n. 6 (E.D. Va. 2010).

activities can be banned if they have any chance of destroying underwater cultural heritage, the traditional right of fishing of individuals is protected.[35]

Individuals' right to enjoy the educational and recreational benefits of access to underwater cultural heritage has been increasingly recognized in practice. Even in the case of the *Titanic* mentioned above, the court favored RMST on the understanding that all artifacts recovered from the wreck would be exhibited to the public and not sold or disposed of (Blake 2015, p. 90). Indeed, some of the recovered objects were displayed in the National Maritime Museum in London at the start of a world tour to cover RMST's salvage costs (Williams 1994). After the finalization of the Agreement Concerning the Shipwrecked Vessel RMS Titanic (Titanic Agreement) in 2000, the case came under the application *ratione materiae* and *ratione temporis* of the 2001 Convention on 15 April 2012 (Aznar and Varmer 2013, p. 101). Article 4(3) of the Titanic Agreement clearly states that "[n]o Party shall authorize, award or grant exclusive salvage right to RMS Titanic and the artifacts in its vicinity that would preclude non-intrusive public access consistent with this Agreement." Rule 4 of the Annex to the Agreement also indicates that "[p]ersons undertaking [activities directed to the *Titanic*] shall ensure proper recording and dissemination to the public of historical, cultural and archaeological information." A similar emphasis on ensuring public access through documentation and dissemination can be seen in Rules 21, 22, 31 and 32 as well.[36]

Recently, many States Parties have endeavored to expand public access to the sites of underwater cultural heritage in situ by the establishment of official dive trails for access, making replicas of underwater heritage, or establishing virtual museums.[37] Through these efforts, the rights of individuals to access to underwater cultural heritage could be protected further. For example, the National Oceanic and Atmosphere Administration (NOAA) of the United States amended its policy to expand public access to historic shipwrecks. In the 1990s, NOAA rejected public requests for permission to dive in the *Monitor* National Marine Sanctuary (Varmer et al. 2010, p. 138). However, having sensed and considered the rise in public's interest in the management of and access to *Monitor*, NOAA began to issue "special use" permits for non-intrusive diving in the sanctuary (NOAA 2008).

[35] *Dispute regarding Navigational and Related Rights (Costa Rica v. Nicaragua)*, Judgment, I.C.J. Reports 2009. The International Court of Justice (ICJ) concluded that fishing by the inhabitants of the Costa Rican bank is to be respected by Nicaragua as a customary right.

[36] Rule 21: "[p]rojects shall be thoroughly documented in accordance with professional archaeological standards current at the time the project is to be undertaken";

Rule 22: "[d]ocumentation shall include, at a minimum, the systematic and complete recording of the provenance of artifacts moved or removed in the course of the project, field notes, plans, sections, photographs and recording in other media";

Rule 31: "[p]rojects shall provide for public education and popular presentation of the results"; and Rule 32: "[a] final synthesis shall be provided to relevant national authorities and made available to the public as soon as possible, having regard to the complexity of the Project."

[37] Examples are available at www.unesco.org/new/en/culture/themes/underwater-cultural-heritage/access/ (accessed 30 May 2021).

5.4 Main Findings

The journey to introduce an international convention dedicated to the protection of underwater cultural heritage was not easy. Two Articles in the 1982 UNCLOS, which stipulated a duty of protection of underwater cultural objects for the benefit of mankind, provided a good opportunity to develop more concrete ideas to establish the principles of in situ preservation and non-commercial exploitation of underwater cultural heritage. Albeit difficult due to concerns about the "creeping jurisdiction," the 2001 Convention successfully introduced a mechanism of cooperation in the EEZ, on the continental shelf, and in the Area to share information and seek for further collaboration for training or transfer of technology related to the protection of underwater cultural heritage. The Convention also included a set of detailed Rules—concrete guidelines—for activities directed at underwater cultural heritage.

The Convention and its Operational Guidelines suggest the status and roles of NSAs, the actual participation of which in the implementation of the Convention has been analyzed in this chapter through a number of examples. UNESCO, as the Secretariat of the Convention, plays the main role in organizing Meetings of States Parties and providing assistance for them. In doing so, UNESCO has developed many practical tools and organized capacity-building meetings for further ratification of the Convention and development of relevant national policy. Other, technical support, for example to STAB or the management of the Underwater Cultural Heritage Fund and Convention's logo, are concrete additional work done by UNESCO according to the Operational Guidelines.

Due to the unique cooperation mechanism among States Parties in the EEZ, on the continental shelf and the Area, UNESCO works as a depository of information on the States' discovery or research of underwater cultural heritage in those areas. The recent case of Skerki Bank demonstrated the successful functioning of UNESCO for facilitation of collaboration among concerned States. However, more active roles for UNESCO, which are stipulated in the Convention and enable it to appoint a "Co-ordinating State" for the protection of underwater cultural heritage in the Area or to mediate disputes between States Parties, have not been conducted yet. This seems mainly due simply to the short history of the Convention.

The 2001 Convention officially established a STAB to support the Meetings of States Parties concerning questions relating to the implementation of the Rules. STAB has continuously conducted missions to States Parties that have requested investigations of underwater objects or diagnoses of the state of implementation of the Rules. As the Operational Guidelines require, relevant States Parties, UNESCO and international experts have supported those missions well. However, if sufficient funding had been available, more missions would have been possible. This would have enabled STAB to expand its influence over the implementation of the Convention, and certainly, more States Parties would have benefited from the STAB's expertise.

The Operational Guidelines have created more concrete roles for STAB, in particular for evaluation. STAB's evaluations of the accreditation of NGOs have been well conducted, resulting in fifteen accredited NGOs so far, whereas delivery of financial assistance to States Parties has never been done, due to a lack of funding. Other evaluation work was assigned to STAB by the Meeting of the States Parties, which calls on STAB to review the applications of States Parties for the List of Best Practice of underwater cultural heritage. So far, STAB's recommendations of applications have been duly respected at the Meetings of the States Parties.

NGOs, though lacking any reference in the text of the Convention, are the most promoted in the Operational Guidelines. As one of the key partners of States Parties in the implementation of the Convention as well as of the STAB in performing its function, NGOs have played various roles. They have actively provided their technical input to States' policies on underwater cultural heritage, and have sometimes participated in the missions of the STAB. Although there is no legal provision for cooperation between NGOs and UNESCO, NGOs have contributed to the latter's publications and training programs. Also, many NGOs have not confined themselves to cooperation with UNESCO, but have explored capacity-building and awareness-raising projects for the general public. Several national, regional, and international training courses were mentioned above as examples. However, in spite of their various activities, it is said that NGOs have been underutilized in the course of the Convention's implementation.

The status of private individuals is not explicit in the text of the 2001 Convention; rather, there are only some provisions implying their general duty to respect and protect underwater cultural heritage, along with statements on their right to enjoy the educational and recreational benefits of access to same. Individuals' obligation to report any discovery or activity directed at underwater cultural heritage to the pertinent States can be taken to be implicit in several provisions requesting action on the parts of States Parties. However, the Operational Guidelines do emphasize their participation in the national implementation of the Convention. The right of individuals to access to underwater cultural heritage has been ensured through non-authorization of any activities lacking affordable programs catering to the general public.

In practice, the diving community, the closest group to the underwater cultural heritage in the physical sense, has generally respected the value of underwater cultural heritage in following the Code of Ethics in their training and activities. The right of commercial activities or trade of individuals has been regulated in the name of the protection of underwater cultural heritage, as witnessed in the *Titanic* case. The case also showed that the individuals' right to enjoy access to the sites of underwater cultural heritage was ensured, and certainly, there are many cases showing States Parties' efforts to expand the public access.

Indeed, after an extensive document review and survey and an interview with UNESCO Member States, the UNESCO Secretariat, STAB, NGOs, and experts, the UNESCO IOS report published in 2019 made several recommendations for UNESCO and the Advisory Bodies (Rivière et al. 2019, p. iii). Among them, UNESCO was advised to introduce a monitoring mechanism for both national and global levels, and this was envisaged to further expand the role of UNESCO as the Secretariat of the Convention. The recommendations on partnership, meanwhile, were several, for example, for UNESCO with NGOs and other UNESCO networks to launch capacity-building programs, and for the STAB to promote, with local communities, a long-term capacity-building approach. Also, States Parties were encouraged to engage in more cooperation with NGOs (UNESCO 2019f, p. 9). All of this notwithstanding, greater engagement of NSAs is pivotal to ensure effective implementation of the Convention. New mechanisms and practices that enable further participation of NSAs will help to further the Convention's goal: the protection of underwater cultural heritage by the entire international community.

References

AIMA (2019) 2019 Report. http://www.unesco.org/new/fileadmin/MULTIMEDIA/HQ/CLT/images/AIMA_report_2019.pdf. Accessed 30 May 2021

ANSAmed (2019) Meeting on protection of Skerki Banks underwater heritage: first two-day conference with countries in UNESCO convention. http://www.ansamed.info/ansamed/en/news/sections/culture/2019/06/11/meeting-on-protection-of-skerki-banks-underwater-heritage_cd098747-3157-48fd-812f-f0c6143c415c.html. Accessed 30 May 2021

Aznar MJ, Varmer O (2013) The Titanic as underwater cultural heritage: challenges to its legal international protection. Ocean Dev Int Law 44(1):96–112

Blake J (2015) International cultural heritage law. Oxford University Press, Oxford

CMAS (2019) Report to UNESCO 2017–2019. http://www.unesco.org/new/fileadmin/MULTIMEDIA/HQ/CLT/images/CMAS_Report_2017-2019.pdf. Accessed 30 May 2021

Council of Europe (1978) Recommendation 848. Doc. 4200-E. Parliament Assembly. Strasbourg, 4 October 1978

DEMA (2019) Fast facts: recreational Scuba diving and Snorkeling. Online Publication: DEMA. https://www.dema.org/store/download.aspx?id=7811B097-8882-4707-A160-F999B49614B6. Accessed 30 May 2021

Engelhardt R (2006) The Asian pacific underwater heritage and the UNESCO convention 2001. In: Prott LV (ed) Fishing the interrupted voyage: papers of the UNESCO Asia-pacific workshop on the 2001 convention on the protection of the underwater cultural heritage. Institute of Art and Law, Leicester

Forrest C (2010) International law and the protection of cultural heritage. Routledge, London

Garabello R (2003) The negotiating history of the convention on the protection of the underwater cultural heritage. In: Garabello R, Scovazzi T (eds) The negotiating history of the convention on the protection of the underwater cultural heritage: before and after 2001 UCH convention. Martinus Nijhoff, Leiden

Gaskell N, Forrest C (2019) The law of wreck. Information Law from Routledge, New York

ICOMOS-ICUCH (2018) Report of activities in support of the 2001 UNESCO convention on the protection of the underwater cultural heritage. http://www.unesco.org/new/fileadmin/MULTIMEDIA/HQ/CLT/images/ICUCH_2018_Report.pdf. Accessed 30 May 2021

Koh TTB (1982) A constitution for the oceans. In: Remarks by the president of the third United Nations conference on the law of the sea at the final session of the conference (Montego Bay, 6–11 December 1982). https://www.un.org/depts/los/convention_agreements/texts/koh_english.pdf. Accessed 30 May 2021

Koh TTB, Jayakumar S (1985) The negotiating process of the third United Nations conference on the law of the sea. In: Nordquist M (ed) United nations convention on the law of the sea 1982: a commentary, vol 1. Martinus Nijhoff, Dordrecht

Lee K-G (2006) An inquiry into the compatibility of the UNESCO convention 2001 with UNCLOS 1982. In: Prott LV (ed) Fishing the interrupted voyage: papers of the UNESCO Asia-Pacific

workshop on the 2001 convention on the protection of the underwater cultural heritage. Institute of Art and Law, Leicester
Lund C (2006) The making of the 2001 UNESCO convention. In: Prott LV (ed) Fishing the interrupted voyage: papers of the UNESCO Asia-pacific workshop on the 2001 convention on the protection of the underwater cultural heritage. Institute of Art and Law, Leicester
Mullen J, Assefa H (2014) 500-year-old mystery: wreck off Haiti may be Columbus' flagship Santa Maria. CNN. https://edition.cnn.com/2014/05/13/world/americas/christopher-columbus-santa-maria/index.html. Accessed 30 May 2021
Nafziger JAR (2018) The UNESCO convention on the protection of the underwater cultural heritage: its growing influence. J Marit Law Commer 49(3):371–400
National Oceanic and Atmosphere Administration (NOAA) (2008) Monitor national marine sanctuary state of the sanctuary report 2008. http://monitor.noaa.gov/publications/general/sos2.pdf. Accessed 30 May 2021
Newton CF (1986) Finders Keepers—the Titanic and the 1982 law of the sea convention. Hast Int Comparat Law Rev 159(10):159–197
O'Keefe PJ (2002a) Shipwrecked heritage: a commentary on the UNESCO convention for the protection of underwater cultural heritage. Institute of Art and Law, Leicester
O'Keefe PJ (2002b) The Buenos aires draft convention on the protection of the underwater cultural heritage prepared by the international law association: its relevance seven years on. In: Camarda G, Scovazzi T (eds) The protection of the underwater cultural heritage: legal aspects. Giuffrè editore, Milan
O'Keefe PJ, Prott LV (eds) (2011) Cultural heritage conventions and other instruments: a compendium with commentaries. Institute of Art and Law, Builth Wells
PADI (2019) 2019 worldwide corporate statistics. Online Publication: PADI. https://www.padi.com/sites/default/files/documents/2019-02/2019%20PADI%20Worldwide%20Statistics.pdf. Accessed 30 May 2021
Paik J-H (2016) Standard of review in the law of the sea: reflections from the bench. In: Espósito C, Kraska J, Scheiber HN, Kwon M-S (eds) Ocean law and policy: 20 years under UNCLOS. Brill/Nijhoff, Leiden/Boston
Petrig A, Stemmler M (2020) Article 16 UNESCO convention and the protection of underwater cultural heritage. Int Comparat Law Quart 69(2):397–429
Rivière ES, Dlamini T, Varmer O, Kourkoumelis D (2019) Evaluation of UNESCO's standard-setting work of the culture sector: Part VI – 2001 convention on the protection of underwater cultural heritage. UNESCO, Online Publication
Scanlan D (1999) Pirates Sink Low, Steal Cannons from St. Augustine Shipwreck. Florida Times-Union. https://www.questia.com/newspaper/1G1-55517369/pirates-sink-low-steal-cannons-from-st-augustine. Accessed 30 May 2021
Strati A (1995) The protection of the underwater cultural heritage: an emerging objective of the contemporary law of the sea. Martinus Nijhoff, Leiden
UN (1967) Official records of the 1515th meeting of first committee. In: The 22nd session of the general assembly of the United Nations. New York, 1 November, 1967
Underwood CJ (2016) Statement indicating ICUCH's continuing support for the UNESCO convention for the protection of the underwater cultural heritage during the period 2013–2016. Online Publication: UNESCO. http://www.unesco.org/new/fileadmin/MULTIMEDIA/HQ/CLT/pdf/UCH_ICUCH_2016_STATEMENT.pdf. Accessed 30 May 2021
UNESCO (1998) CLT-96/CONF.202/5. Draft convention on the protection of the underwater cultural heritage. Paris, April 1998
UNESCO (2012d) UCH/12/3.STAB/220/9. The third meeting of the scientific and technical advisory body of the convention on the protection of the underwater cultural heritage. Paris, 19 April 2012
UNESCO (2014d) Report and evaluation of the mission of the scientific and technical advisory body to Haiti. 5–15 September 2014. http://www.unesco.org/new/fileadmin/MULTIMEDIA/HQ/CLT/images/Haiti-STAB-en.pdf. Accessed 30 May 2021

UNESCO (2015g) Report of the mission to Panama (6–14 July and 21–29 October 2015) to evaluate the Project related to the wreck of the San José. http://www.unesco.org/new/fileadmin/MULTIMEDIA/HQ/CLT/pdf/STAB-Panama-Report-EN-public.pdf. Accessed 30 May 2021

UNESCO (2015h) RESOLUTION 4/MSP 5. The fifth meeting of states parties to the convention on the protection of the underwater cultural heritage. Paris, 28–29 April 2015

UNESCO (2017c) UCH/17/6.MSP/INF.7REV2. The sixth meeting of states parties to the convention on the protection of the underwater cultural heritage. Paris, 30–31 May 2017

UNESCO (2018c) Information kit: the UNESCO convention on the protection for the underwater cultural heritage. http://www.unesco.org/new/fileadmin/MULTIMEDIA/HQ/CLT/pdf/GB-2001CONVENTION-INFOKIT-2018.pdf. Accessed 30 May 2021

UNESCO (2018d) UCH/18/9.STAB/10. The ninth meeting of the scientific and technical advisory body of the convention on the protection of the underwater cultural heritage. Paris, 24 April 2018

UNESCO (2018e) UCH/18/9.STAB/11. The ninth meeting of the scientific and technical advisory body of the convention on the protection of the underwater cultural heritage. Paris, 24 April 2018

UNESCO (2019d). UCH/19/7.MSP/5. The seventh meeting of states parties to the convention on the protection of the underwater cultural heritage. Paris, 20–21 June 2019

UNESCO (2019e) Cooperation in international waters—protection of the Skerki Banks. UNESCO Press Release. https://en.unesco.org/news/cooperation-international-waters-protection-skerki-banks. Accessed 30 May 2021

UNESCO (2019f) UCH/19/7.MSP/3REV. The seventh meeting of states parties to the convention on the protection of the underwater cultural heritage. Paris, 20–21 June 2019

Varmer O, Gray J, Alberg D (2010) United States: responses to the 2001 UNESCO convention on the protection of the underwater cultural heritage. J Marit Archaeol 5(2):129–141

Williams R (1994) Titanic show goes on despite grave-robbing row: maritime museum says it is satisfied none of the artefacts have been taken from the wreck. Rhys Williams reports. Independent. https://www.independent.co.uk/news/uk/titanic-show-goes-on-despite-grave-robbing-row-maritime-museum-says-it-is-satisfied-none-of-the-1430981.html. Accessed 30 May 2021

Chapter 6
The Protection of Intangible Cultural Heritage

The adoption of the Convention for the Safeguarding of the Intangible Cultural Heritage in 2003 (hereinafter, '2003 Convention') was a historical event in terms of the marked changes it represented to the notion of cultural heritage and the measures introduced for its protection. Lacking tangibleness, intangible cultural heritage essentially requires its bearers and transmitters for its very existence. This special characteristic of intangible cultural heritage is the necessary starting point for any study on the status and roles of NSAs in the implementation of the 2003 Convention relative to the other international cultural heritage laws considered in this book.

Although the 2003 Convention has several texts referring to the status and roles of NSAs, the Operational Directives that support its practical implementation have expanded on those texts. Similarly to the governance system of the 1972 Convention Concerning the Protection of the World Cultural and Natural Heritage (hereinafter, '1972 Convention'), that of the 2003 Convention enables NSAs to be deeply involved in its implementation. Cases witnessed both at the intergovernmental committee of the Convention and in the course of national implementation show their active participation in practice. However, there exist some difference in terms of status and roles between the text and reality as well as among the various categories of NSAs.

In this chapter, after the introduction of the 2003 Convention concerning the history of its adoption and key contents, a statutory and empirical analysis of the status and roles of NSAs in it will be provided.

J. Kim, *Non-State Actors in the Protection of Cultural Heritage*, Creativity, Heritage and the City 3, https://doi.org/10.1007/978-981-16-6659-9_6

6.1 Introduction of the Legal Protection for Intangible Cultural Heritage

6.1.1 History of the Adoption of the 2003 Convention[1]

Legal protection for intangible cultural heritage started only in the 1970s. After several decades of disjointed practices by and between countries that adhered to different standards and norms of culture, a normative instrument for the protection of intangible cultural heritage finally was made possible in 2003 at UNESCO. This push to establish an international standard for the protection of intangible cultural heritage was primarily led by non-Western countries. Indeed, the 2003 Convention signaled a historic turning point in terms of the concept and definition of heritage and of actions for its safeguarding (Bouchenaki 2007, p. 106).

The first attempts toward the international protection of intangible cultural heritage took place during the 1970s and 1980s, and sought to root its protection by means of copyright law (Aikawa 2004, p. 138). UNESCO prepared a draft document of the international instrument in 1971, but, as it turned out, it was unrealistic to apply copyright principles to the protection of folklore (Sherkin 2001, pp. 42–44). UNESCO's subsequent joint effort with the World Intellectual Property Organization (WIPO) to establish a model provision in 1982 was again considered premature, due to a lack of understanding of the protection of folklore and its workable mechanism in the form of international convention (Ficsor 1997, pp. 3–4; WIPO 2003).

However, UNESCO was not discouraged from developing a framework for safeguarding folklore, and kept discussions going while leaving the copyright issue to WIPO. Establishment of expert committees and independent sections at the Secretariat led to the adoption of the Recommendation on the Protection of Traditional Cultural and Folklore in 1989 (hereinafter '1989 Recommendation'). The 1989 Recommendation was the first international normative instrument recognizing folklore, or intangible cultural heritage, as an object of protection, and became the source of various programs before the adoption of the 2003 Convention. In particular, the proposal of the Republic of Korea to establish a system of Living Human Treasure (UNESCO 1993), modeled after the World Heritage List of the 1972 Convention, inspired many countries to adopt similar systems. The concept of an international list was further explored in 1998, when a new program entitled Proclamation of Masterpieces of Oral and Intangible Heritage of Humanity (hereinafter, 'Masterpiece Program') was launched, its inspiration drawn from a case study of Jemaa el-Fna in Morocco (Schmitt 2008, pp. 99–101).

Listing intangible cultural heritage elements received much attention from the Member States of UNESCO, and gave rise to many lively debates on its concepts and notions. Moreover, the global assessment of the 1989 Recommendation at the Washington International Conference in 1999 concluded with a request for stronger

[1] Some parts of Sect. 6.1 have been extracted from the author's earlier publication (Kim and Nam 2016). Reflecting up-to-date information, some contents have been revised accordingly.

legal instruments to address the question of intangible cultural heritage protections more thoroughly (Bouchenaki 2007, p. 107). This recommendation was well received by UNESCO, and a feasibility study on developing a new standard-setting instrument was then undertaken (UNESCO 2001a). With concerns over the duplication of work with WIPO, a few States expressed reservations over the format of the new instrument, but it was ultimately decided that it would take the form of an international convention (UNESCO 2001b).

While the Guidelines for the Establishment of National Living Human Treasure Systems were disseminated by UNESCO in 2002, several inter-governmental meetings of experts were organized to further develop the draft convention. These events served to fill-in the gaps—bring together the ideas of various countries on a number of issues, including the listing system—and enabled the final draft of the Convention to be adopted without amendment at the 32nd session of the General Conference in October 2003.[2] This resulted in both a rapid and a high ratification rate for the 2003 Convention by the Member States compared with other conventions of UNESCO, even by several countries that had been hesitant or passive with regard to the introduction of this new instrument. So far, 180 of 193 Member States of UNESCO have joined the Convention.[3]

6.1.2 Key Contents of the 2003 Convention

The 2003 Convention consists of 40 Articles divided into nine Parts. The general provisions of Part I (Articles 1 to 3) deal with the purpose and definitions of the key terms of the Convention, followed by Part II (Articles 4 to 10), where the organs of the Convention are defined. Part III (Articles 11 to 15) deals with national measures for safeguarding of intangible cultural heritage, while Part IV (Articles 15 to 18) addresses those measures at the international level. Provisions regarding international cooperation are stipulated in Part V (Articles 19 to 24), and the modalities of the International Fund are established under Part VI (Articles 25 to 28). The reporting system of the Convention is explained in Part VII (Articles 29 to 30), with a transitional clause, Part VIII (Article 31), on the incorporation of the Masterpiece Program into the Representative List of the Intangible Cultural Heritage. Lastly, Part IX (Articles 32 to 40) closes out the final clauses of the Convention.

As Article 1 clearly states, the purposes of the Convention are:

(a) to safeguard the intangible cultural heritage;

(b) to ensure respect for the intangible cultural heritage of the communities, groups and individuals concerned;

(c) to raise awareness at the local, national and international levels of the importance of the intangible cultural heritage, and of ensuring mutual appreciation thereof;

---

[2] Adopted on 17 October 2003 by the General Conference of UNESCO at its 32nd session and entered into force on 20 April 2006.

[3] As of 27 July 2020.

(d) to provide for international cooperation and assistance.

Intangible cultural heritage—the primary subject of the Convention—is defined under Article 2. According to Article 2(1):

> The "intangible cultural heritage" means the practices, representations, expressions, knowledge, skills – as well as the instruments, objects, artefacts and cultural spaces associated therewith – that communities, groups and, in some cases, individuals recognize as part of their cultural heritage. This intangible cultural heritage, transmitted from generation to generation, is constantly recreated by communities and groups in response to their environment, their interaction with nature and their history, and provides them with a sense of identity and continuity, thus promoting respect for cultural diversity and human creativity. For the purposes of this Convention, consideration will be given solely to such intangible cultural heritage as is compatible with existing international human rights instruments, as well as with the requirements of mutual respect among communities, groups and individuals, and of sustainable development.

It should be noted that this definition assumes a community to be a group of people who recognize a particular cultural element as a symbol of their identity (Kurin 2007, p. 12). This means that intangible cultural heritage cannot be detached from its community who share the value of heritage; in other words, the community shares the duty to safeguard the elements of the self-identified intangible cultural heritage. Thus, safeguarding intangible cultural heritage can be achieved only by recognizing the central role of communities in creating and transmitting these cultural elements (Blake 2006, p. 35). It should be further noted that the community is not permitted limitless protection of self-identified cultural elements as intangible cultural heritage. Article 2 includes a proviso attached to the definition to exclude any cultural elements that contravene international human rights standards. This is in line with the human rights framework established regarding the safeguarding of intangible cultural heritage, as stated in the preamble of the Convention (para. 1).

At the national level, the Convention requires each State Party to draw up one or more inventories of intangible cultural heritage (Article 12(1)). National inventory works as a basic tool for the efficient safeguarding of heritage. Therefore, the governments of each respective State Party first need to take action to "identify and define the various elements of the intangible cultural heritage present in its territory, with the participation of communities, groups and relevant non-governmental organizations" (Article 11(2)). Appropriate legal, technical, administrative and financial measures for safeguarding of intangible cultural heritage—e.g., adopting relevant policies, designating or establishing competent bodies for safeguarding actions, and fostering research and training—can ensure the establishment of inventories and appropriate protection for listed elements (Article 13). Education is a key method of transmission of intangible cultural heritage to future generations, and various educational means should be promoted by States Parties (Article 4). Last but not least, it should be noted that the Convention strongly calls for the participation and involvement of individual bearers or practitioners, groups, and communities in all of these safeguarding efforts of governments (Article 15). Considering the characteristics of intangible cultural heritage whose value is defined by the communities, the role of these stakeholders cannot be overestimated.

At the international level, the Convention addresses the collective duties of the States Parties through its General Assembly and Intergovernmental Committee for the Safeguarding of the Intangible Cultural Heritage (hereinafter, 'Intangible Cultural Heritage Committee' or 'Committee'). In particular, Articles 16–18 introduce three different lists under the Convention. In a shift away from the World Heritage Lists of the 1972 Convention, which consisted of *normal* and *in-danger* lists, as well as the 1998 Masterpiece Program, the 2003 Convention made a deliberate and substantial effort to avoid the notion of *superiority*, something previously implied in prior instruments. This reflects an intention to refrain from paying too much attention to the international lists and nominating countries (Kurin 2007, p. 17), based on the new definition of intangible cultural heritage. Firstly, concerning the Representative List of the Intangible Cultural Heritage of Humanity, the Operational Directives of the Convention suggest five criteria for inscription,[4] none of which reference concepts, such as, "Outstanding Universal Value," of the World Heritage Sites. Rather, as stated in criterion R.2, they emphasize, through their inscriptions on the List, the contribution of elements to enhancing the visibility of the intangible cultural heritage, cultural diversity and human creativity. This approach is derived from the belief that each individual cultural tradition cannot be evaluated or does not need to be of "Outstanding Universal Value," as they are all part of the diversity of culture.

There are two other lists of the Convention: List of Intangible Cultural Heritage in Need of Urgent Safeguarding, and Register of Good Safeguarding Practices.[5] The Urgent Safeguarding List aims to draw attention to endangered intangible cultural heritage elements around the world (Article 17); this mechanism serves as one of several grounds for international assistance. The Register for Good Practices, which is a new list not previously contained in prior cultural heritage preservation instruments such as the 1972 Convention, also contributes to facilitating international cooperation between States Parties. By listing exemplary national programs or projects that seek to safeguard intangible cultural heritage, countries can share and exchange experiences so as to more effectively implement the Convention (Article 18).

In addition to the list systems at the international level, the Convention emphasizes the principles of international cooperation. By joining the Convention, States Parties recognize the safeguarding of intangible cultural heritage as a general interest to humanity, and are asked to participate in the relevant collective actions (Article 19). International Assistance for individual States Parties is available, whether it is to

---

[4] I.2.2 of the Operational Directive of the 2003 Convention reads: "R.1. The element constitutes intangible cultural heritage as defined in Article 2 of the Convention; R.2. Inscription of the element will contribute to ensuring visibility and awareness of the significance of the intangible cultural heritage and to encouraging dialogue, thus reflecting cultural diversity worldwide and testifying to human creativity; R.3. Safeguarding measures are elaborated that may protect and promote the element; R.4. The element has been nominated following the widest possible participation of the community, group or, if applicable, individuals concerned and with their free, prior and informed consent; and R.5. The element is included in an inventory of the intangible cultural heritage present in the territory(ies) of the submitting State(s) Party(ies), as defined in Articles 11 and 12 of the Convention."

[5] In 2016, 'Register of Programs, Projects and Activities that Best Reflect the Principles and Objectives of the Convention' was changed to 'Register of Good Safeguarding Practices.'

safeguard the State's elements on the Urgent Safeguarding List or to support its capacities to duly implement the Convention (Article 20).

6.2 NSAs in the 2003 Convention

The standard-setting work of the 2003 Convention can be divided into two levels, national and international, so as to identify stakeholders at each level and demonstrate their mandates, as illustrated in Table 6.1.[6] The General Assembly and Intangible Cultural Heritage Committee are the collective entities of the States Parties, and therefore the stakeholders at the international level can be divided into three categories: States Parties, UNESCO, and experts.

Experts according to the 2003 Convention usually are advisory organizations including individual experts or NGOs with expertise in various fields of intangible cultural heritage.[7] Other NSAs, in particular those creators and bearers of intangible cultural heritage, such as communities, groups, and sometimes individuals, are not found in Articles 15–18 (safeguarding measures at the international level). However, at the national level, the involvement of these NSAs is included in several Articles of the Convention, and in at least two different functions: participants in national measures and beneficiaries of those measures. These are referenced accordingly in the Operational Directives guiding the implementation of the Convention.

6.2.1 NSAs in the Text of 2003 Convention

UNESCO

The only NSA that has an explicit role in the text of the Convention is UNESCO, as the Secretariat that assists the Committee, prepares the documents of the General Assembly and the Committee and ensures the implementation of their decisions (Article 10). Compared with some of the other conventions, which include several provisions concerning UNESCO's own initiatives,[8] it seems that the text of the 2003

---

[6] Unlike the other conventions considered in this book, the 2003 Convention explicitly divides two levels of implementation. Therefore, the framework of analysis on the status and roles of the different actors follows that division.

[7] Article 9 of the Convention refers to accredited NGOs as advisory organizations for the Committee. However, in practice, a consultative body (evaluation body) for the Committee includes both representatives of accredited NGOs and individual experts.

[8] For example, Article 17 of the 1970 Convention on the Means of Prohibiting and Preventing the Illicit Import, Export and Transfer of Ownership of Cultural Property (hereinafter, '1970 Convention') reads: "2. The United Nations Educational, Scientific and Cultural Organization may, on its own initiative conduct research and publish studies on matters relevant to the illicit movement of cultural property; ...4. The United Nations Educational, Scientific and Cultural Organization may, on its own initiative, make proposals to States Parties to this Convention for its implementation."

Table 6.1 Stakeholders of the 2003 convention at two different levels and their status and roles

Levels	Stakeholders	Status and roles	Goal
Int'l	General assembly	Election of the committee	Protection of intangible cultural heritage
		Approval of the fund plan, operational directives	
	Inter-governmental committee	Decision on the lists of the convention	
		Examination of the reports submitted by states parties	
	States parties	International cooperation and assistance	
	UNESCO	**Preparation of the documents for the general assembly and the committee**	
		Assistance to the committee	
	Experts (NGOs, public or private bodies and persons with expertise)	**Advisory service to the committee**	
Nat'l	States parties	Establishment of national inventory of intangible cultural heritage	
		Adoption of a general policy, designate competent bodies, foster studies, and adopt legal, technical, administrative and financial measures	
		Conduct of educational, awareness-raising and capacity-building programs	
		Ensuring participation of communities, groups, and individuals in safeguarding activities	
	Local communities (NGOs, communities, individuals)	**Participation in national safeguarding activities (identify and define the various elements of intangible cultural heritage and their management)**	
		Beneficiary of educational and training programs	

Note Stakeholders in bold are NSAs
Source Author (based on the 2003 Convention)

Convention does not provide room for UNESCO to perform an active role. This limit is complemented by the Operational Directives with detailed provisions on the roles of UNESCO, to be introduced in the following section.

Local Communities

Though not explicitly defined, the impact of other NSAs—NGOs, communities, groups and individuals—is found throughout the Convention. Departing from traditional treatment as mere beneficiaries of international law, those NSAs are considered to be important stakeholders of the Convention. From as early as the Preamble, the Convention recognizes the role of communities (in particular, indigenous communities), groups and, in some cases, individuals, in the production, safeguarding, maintaining, and recreating of intangible cultural heritage (para. 7 of the Preamble). Although there are no clear definitions of the terms 'communities,' 'groups' or 'individuals,'[9] the relevant provisions of the Convention raise important questions concerning the 'ownership' of heritage and the 'process' of its official recognition (Blake 2015, p. 185). As stated in Article 2(1), these NSAs are the entities that identify intangible cultural heritage as an element of their cultural heritage, and transmit it to the next generation through its re-creation. Unlike tangible heritage recognized by its artistic or historic value, and appreciated as a product itself without clear linkage to specific groups, intangible cultural heritage is intrinsically attached to a certain community due to its unique 'intangible' form. This means that intangible cultural heritage cannot be created and included on the national list arbitrarily by governments. At the same time, this echoes certain intrinsic rights of minority groups to preserve cultural identity and continuity, as reflected in Article 27 of the ICCPR (International Covenant on Civil and Political Rights, 1966).[10]

Provisions concerning the involvement of NSAs in implementing the Convention at the national level are set out in the several Articles of the Convention. Under Article 11(b), States Parties are required to identify and define intangible cultural heritage

[9] In particular, the term 'communities' raised several issues during the drafting the 2003 Convention (Blake 2015, p. 29). Later, in the Conclusions and Recommendations of the Report of the Expert Meeting on Community Involvement in Safeguarding Intangible Cultural Heritage: Towards the Implementation of the Convention for the Safeguarding of the Intangible Cultural Heritage (Tokyo, Japan, 13–15 March 2006), organized by UNESCO and ACCU, these terms were defined as follows: "1. Communities are networks of people whose sense of identity or connectedness emerges from a shared historical relationship that is rooted in the practice and transmission of, or engagement with, their ICH; 2. Groups comprise people within or across communities who share characteristics such as skills, experience and special knowledge, and thus perform specific roles in the present and future practice, re-creation and/or transmission of their intangible cultural heritage as, for example, cultural custodians, practitioners or apprentices; 3. Individuals are those within or across communities who have distinct skills, knowledge, experience or other characteristics, and thus perform specific roles in the present and future practice, re-creation and/or transmission of their intangible cultural heritage as, for example, cultural custodians, practitioners and, where appropriate, apprentices." For convenience, such entities are called 'local communities' in this book.

[10] Article 27 of ICCPR reads: "In those States in which ethnic, religious or linguistic minorities exist, persons belonging to such minorities shall not be denied the right, in community with the other members of their group, to enjoy their own culture, to profess and practice their own religion, or to use their own language."

with the participation of communities, groups, and relevant NGOs. The essential role of those entities as key participants for safeguarding intangible cultural heritage is reaffirmed, and this principle works as the premise to all actions taken by the States Parties, per Articles 12–14. As is the case with many other international laws, the 2003 Convention also confers beneficiary status to NSAs regarding the States Parties' legal, technical, financial, and administrative protective measures, as well as educational and training programs under Articles 13 and 14. However, it is noteworthy that the status of heritage bearers as key participants in safeguarding activities of intangible cultural heritage is clearly preserved in a separate and independent provision of Article 15, which requests of States Parties to endeavor to "ensure the widest possible participation of communities, groups and where appropriate, individuals" and to "involve them actively in its management." This Article functions as a general provision recognizing the role of these NSAs bearing intangible cultural heritage and is further detailed in the Operational Directives of the Convention.

Experts

Beyond recognizing communities and groups as beneficiaries of the Convention, the Convention also references the role of other NSA entities. Inspired by Article 10(2) of the 1972 Convention,[11] Article 8(4) of the 2003 Convention enables public or private bodies as well as private persons to exert their expertise in the various fields of intangible cultural heritage at the international level. Here, "private persons" are different from those individuals associated with defining and safeguarding specific intangible cultural heritage; rather, they play the role of independent experts based on recognized competence, and not as representatives of the communities or organizations (Blake 2006, p. 56).

Official recognition for organizations related to intangible cultural heritage is stipulated in Article 9. The Convention allows NGOs to play their advisory roles by an accreditation process carried out at the Intangible Cultural Heritage Committee and General Assembly. This Article, like 8(4), arose from the 1972 Convention, which allowed for representatives of ICCROM, ICOMOS and IUCN to attend the World Heritage Committee in an advisory capacity (Article 8(3)). However, unlike the 1972 Convention that specifically named those three organizations, the 2003 Convention does not mention the names of any NGOs in its text as advisory organizations.[12] This is due to the fact that there were numerous NGOs in the field of intangible cultural heritage at the time of the drafting of the Convention, and the Committee intended to

[11] Which reads, "The Committee may at any time invite public or private organizations or individuals to participate in its meetings for consultation on particular problems."

[12] In this vein, the advisory organizations are more similar to the Scientific and Technical Advisory Body under the Meeting of States Parties of the 2001 Convention on the Protection of the Underwater Cultural Heritage, which consists of experts and assists the Meeting. See Article 23 of the 2001 Convention.

exploit the existing expertise of those NGOs rather than develop their own expertise or establish new NGOs (Blake 2006, p. 57).[13]

The involvement of these experts, including NGOs and individual experts, in their advisory capacity has taken place at the international level through the Intangible Cultural Heritage Committee, whereas community-based NSAs who bear the intangible cultural heritage elements affect States Parties' activities at the national level. Indeed, this differentiation between NSAs bearing heritage and NSAs with expertise have been supported by several countries during the meetings of the subsidiary body on modalities for the participation of communities or their representatives, practitioners, experts, centers of expertise and research institutes held in late 2007 and early 2008. Several countries argued that communities must be excluded from participation at the international level if they lack expertise to contribute effectively to international cooperation (UNESCO 2008, pp. 10–12). Further, the adopted text of Modalities for the Participation of Communities or their Representatives, Practitioners, Experts, Centers of Expertise and Research Institutes in the Implementation of the Convention also explains the different roles of bearers of intangible cultural heritage and those of experts (UNESCO 2008, Annex 2, paras. 3.1 and 3.2).

However, this dyadic approach toward NSAs has become functionally meaningless, as NSAs bearing heritage also have direct influence on the activities of the States Parties at the international level. Furthermore, experts have become more active participants in the domestic activities of States Parties, in addition to their role in national inventorying under Article 11(b). This interplay will be further illustrated in the following section with specific provisions in the Operational Directives of the Convention.

6.2.2 *NSAs in the Operational Directives of the 2003 Convention*

According to Article 7(e) of the Convention, the Intangible Cultural Heritage Committee is required to prepare Operational Directives for the implementation of the Convention for the Safeguarding of the Intangible Heritage and submit them to the General Assembly for approval. The General Assembly adopted the Operational Directives for the first time in 2008. States Parties considered that the Operational Directives should evolve over time and be amended periodically as experience is gained with the implementation of the Convention (UNESCO 2016c, para. 1). As

[13] However, recent NGO symposiums organized on the occasions of Intergovernmental Committees started to support capacity-building of accredited NGOs. Further details are available at the website of the NGO Forum: http://www.ichngoforum.org/ (accessed 30 May 2021).

such, the General Assembly has amended them six times since their implementation—2010, 2012, 2014, 2016, 2018, and 2020—and will continue to take into consideration any revisions and amendments in future meetings.[14]

As the Operational Directives provide specific measures to be taken to fulfill the mandate of the Convention, the rights, obligations and roles of each stakeholder can be inferred from their provisions. In other words, several hidden statuses and roles of NSAs can be pulled from the text of the Directives. Further, the amendments to the Operational Directives reflect the changing attitudes of the international community toward the status and roles of each type of NSA.

UNESCO

For example, the 2010 amendment of the Operational Directives expanded the role of UNESCO in departing from its previously supportive role to the States Parties as a Secretariat of the Convention (paras. 28, 31, 48, 52, 73, 74, 76, 77, 92, 93, 97, 98, 99, 165, and 166). Its added functions as a clearinghouse for collection, exchange and dissemination of information on intangible cultural heritage, a facilitator of the exchange of information among NSAs, a provider of training and workshops, and a promoter of awareness-raising activities should not be overlooked (para. 123). The role of coordinating or sometimes authorizing the use of the emblem of the 2003 Convention by States Parties and other stakeholders of the Convention was added to UNESCO as well in 2010 (paras. 138, 144, 147, and 150), giving it its own authority to use the emblem independently (paras. 129 and 140).

Local Communities

Most of all, the Operational Directives (and the relevant subsequent amendments) note the importance of NSAs who bear intangible cultural heritage, such as communities, groups, and individuals, at both the international and national levels. In particular, their "free, prior and informed consent" is one of the requirements for the inscription or change of intangible cultural heritage elements on the Lists under the Convention.[15] Although many States were initially opposed to the idea, this informed consent by local communities has been emphasized by scholars as one of the most

[14] The version adopted in June 2018 was used in the present analysis. Most recently, at the Eighth session of the General Assembly (Paris, 8–10 September 2020), the Directives were revised again.

[15] Para. 1 of the Operational Directives suggests criterion U.4 for the Urgent List nomination, noting that "the element has been nominated following the widest possible participation of the community, group or, if applicable, individuals concerned and with their free, prior and informed consent." For the Representative List, para. 2 of the Operational Directives suggests criterion R.4, saying that "the element has been nominated following the widest possible participation of the community, group or, if applicable, individuals concerned and with their free, prior and informed consent." Inscription on an extended or reduced basis also requires consent of the concerned communities, according to paras. 16 and 17 of the Operational Directives. As for the Good Practice Register, criterions P.5 (The program, project or activity is or has been implemented with the participation of the community, group or, if applicable, individuals concerned and with their free, prior and informed consent) and P.7 (The submitting State(s) Party(ies), implementing body(ies), and community, group or, if applicable, individuals concerned are willing to cooperate in the dissemination of best practices, if their program, project or activity is selected) are outlined in para. 7 of the Operational Directives.

important components in handling the protection of intangible cultural heritage from the earliest stages of discussion of the 2003 Convention (Simon 2001, pp. 111–142). Although many scholars deem this role of the local communities to be limited to the national level (Lixinski 2013, p. 53; Blake 2015, p. 186), the provisions of the Operational Directives can be interpreted as strong proof of the influence of the NSAs at the international level.

On the international front, participation of local communities serves as one of the important criteria for successful inscription of the intangible cultural heritage element on the Lists and for the Committee granting International Assistance.[16] Moreover, these NSAs as bearers of intangible cultural heritage may even make the nomination of heritage elements subject to extreme urgency protection, vis-à-vis the Urgent Safeguarding List, to the attention of the Bureau of the Committee (para. 32). Although urgent nomination by communities has never yet occurred, this provision enabling NSAs to request nomination implies the exceptionally expanded role of NSAs in an area where typically only the States Parties enjoy such privileges. In addition to the involvement in the process of inscription for the list or international assistance application, local communities are also invited to participate in the regional cooperation of States Parties stipulated in Article 19(2) (para. 88).

The amendments to the Operational Directive adopted in 2010 and 2016 envisaged an expanded role for local communities regarding the implementation of the Convention at the national level. Under the overarching principle stipulated in Article 15 of the Convention ensuring the participation of communities, groups, and individuals in safeguarding intangible cultural heritage, specific provisions calling for their participation in awareness-raising and sustainable-development activities conducted by States Parties have been added to the amendments.[17] In particular, States Parties are asked to seek the prior consent of the local communities before engaging in awareness-raising activities (para. 101(b)), and are further required to ensure the full respect of the States Parties concerning these communities' customary practices or traditional rights.[18] These provisions emphasize the role of local communities not only as primary beneficiaries of awareness-raising (paras. 101(d) and 104) or sustainable-development activities (paras. 171(b), 184, 185(b), 186(b), and 187(b)) but also as important partners in those activities.

Experts

NSAs with expertise, such as research centers, institutions, individual experts or NGOs, play active roles both at the international and national levels. Internationally,

[16] Para. 12(A.1) of the Operational Directives reads: "The community, group and/or individuals concerned participated in the preparation of the request and will be involved in the implementation of the proposed activities, and in their evaluation and follow-up as broadly as possible."

[17] *Ibid.*, paras. 101(b), 107(e), 108, and 109 for awareness raising and paras. 171(a), 175, 178(a), 179(a), 180(c), 181(c), (d), 182(a), 185(a), 186(a), 189(b), 190(a), 191(b), 191(c), 195(a), and 196(a) for sustainable-development activities.

[18] *Ibid.*, paras. 101(c), 179(b), 180(a), 189(a), (c), and 191(a) for the respect of customary practice and paras. 104, 173(b), and 178(c) for the recognition of their rights.

with respect to the process of examining nominations for the Lists under the Convention and requests for International Assistance, the role and influence of experts can be detected in more concrete aspects. The nomination process at the international level begins with the submission of applications by States Parties to the Committee. As a private expert or representative of an NGO with expertise in the field of intangible cultural heritage, these NSAs have acted as examiners or members of the Consultative or Evaluation Body in screening nominations for the Urgent and Representative Lists, proposals for the Good Practice Register, or requests for International Assistance.[19] By reviewing all relevant files, they submit their recommendations concerning the applications with several options for the Committee's final decision (para. 30).[20] In addition to this nomination evaluation role, experts, like NSAs bearing heritage elements that require urgent protection, are also eligible for bringing the nomination to the attention of the Bureau of the Committee (para. 32).

At the national level, experts are invited to provide data on the implementation of the Convention to the States Parties, not to mention their participation in national inventorying under Article 11(b) (para. 151). NGOs, in particular, are considered to be contributors of research on intangible cultural heritage and sustainable development (para. 175). Other NSAs with expertise, such as research centers, institutions and individuals, are invited to participate in developing plans, policies and programs on intangible cultural heritage and sustainable development (para. 171(d)). They have become involved in awareness-raising activities of the Convention as well (para. 109).

With the exception of para. 151 concerning the participation of NGOs in the Periodic Report of the States Parties to the Committee,[21] these expanded roles of experts were added to the Operational Directives by amendments in 2010 and 2016, when the General Assembly adopted new Chapters of the Directives on Raising Awareness about Intangible Cultural Heritage and Use of the Emblem of the Convention and Safeguarding Intangible Cultural Heritage and Sustainable Development at the National Level, respectively. These additions were a reflection of the international community's recognition of the experts' increasing impact on the implementation of the Convention.

---

[19] Independent expert examiners appointed by the Committee reviewed nominations for the Urgent List from 2009 to 2010. The Consultative Body, consisting of six experts and six accredited NGOs, was established in 2011 to examine nominations for the Urgent List and Good Practice Register as well as requests for International Assistance of more than 25,000 USD. The Body terminated its mandate in 2014, when the Evaluation Body, consisting of six experts and six accredited NGOs, was created and started its work (in 2015) to review all Lists, Registers, and requests for International Assistance. The minimum dollar value for applications for International Assistance was increased to 100,000 USD in 2016. See para. 27 of the Operational Directives.

[20] For the Urgent and Representative Lists, the recommendations are inscription, referral, or non-inscription, and for the Good Practice Register, they are selection, referral, or non-selection. The options for International Assistance requests are approval or non-approval.

[21] Actually, this provision was not in the original draft of the Operational Directives as submitted by the Intergovernmental Committee in 2008, but was added by the General Assembly during the discussion (Blake 2015, pp. 38–39).

Table 6.2 Provisions of the 2003 convention and its operational directives concerning the status and roles of NSAs at two different levels

Levels	NSAs		Status and roles	Convention (Article)	Operational directives (para.)
Int'l	UNESCO		Preparation of the committee and general assembly and implementation of their decisions	10	28, 31, 48, 52, 73, 74, 76, 77, 92, 93, 97, 98, 99, 138*, 144*, 147*, 150*, 165, 166
			Clearinghouse and organizer of awareness-raising activities	–	123*
			Coordination and authorization of the use of Emblem	–	129*, 140*
	Local communities (communities, groups, individuals bearing intangible cultural heritage)		**Right to consent to nomination**	–	**1(U.4), 2(R.4), 7(P.5, P.7), 12(A.1), 16, 17**
			Nomination for urgent request		**32**
			Participant in regional cooperation		88
	Experts	Public/ Private Bodies, Individual experts	Advice for the committee	8(4)	84, 89
			Evaluation of nominations		**27, 28, 30**
			Nomination for urgent request		**32**
			Participant in regional cooperation	–	88
		Accredited NGOs	Advice for the committee	9	91–99
			Evaluation of nominations		**27, 28, 30**
			Nomination for urgent request		**32**

(continued)

In summary, a comparison of the status and roles, at both the international and national levels, of the various groups of NSAs and their corresponding provisions in the 2003 Convention and its Operational Directives is provided in Table 6.2.[22] At the international level, it is observed that the role of UNESCO has been specified in the

[22] Some roles can be conducted by several different NSA groups, as noted repeatedly in the 2003 Convention and its Operational Directives.

Table 6.2 (continued)

Levels	NSAs	Status and roles	Convention (Article)	Operational directives (para.)
Nat'l	Local communities (communities, groups, individuals bearing intangible cultural heritage)	Participant and partner in safeguarding activities (in general)	(Preamble. para.7), (Article 11(b), 15)	79, 90
		Participation in inventorying	(11(b))	80(a), (b)
		Participation in nominating	–	80(d), (e)
		Right to consent to awareness-raising activities	–	**101(b)[*]**
		Participation in awareness-raising activities	(14)	80(c), 101(b)[*], 107(e)[*], 108[*], 109[*]
		Participation in periodic reporting of states parties	–	157, 160
		Receipt of respect as customary practitioner and traditional right(s) holder	**(2(1))**	**101(c)[*], 104[*], 173(b)[**], 178(c)[**], 179(b)[**], 180(a)[**], 189(a), (c)[**], 191(a)[**]**
		Receipt of benefit-sharing	–	**101(d)[*], 116[*], 171(b)[**], 184[**], 185(b)[**], 186(b)[**], 187(b)[**]**
		Participation in planning policy for sustainable development	–	171(a)[**], 191(c)[**]
		Participation in research on sustainable development	(14(a))	175[**], 178(a)[**], 179(a)[**], 180(c)[**], 181(c), (d)[**], 182(a)[**], 185(a)[**], 186(a)[**], 189(b)[**], 190(a)[**], 191(b)[**], 195(a)[**], 196(a)[**]

(continued)

Table 6.2 (continued)

Levels	NSAs		Status and roles	Convention (Article)	Operational directives (para.)
	Experts	Research centers, institutions, individual experts	Participation in inventorying	11(b)	79, 80(a), (b)
			Participation in nominating	–	80(d), (e)
			Participation in awareness-raising activities	(14)	80(c), 109*
			Participation in planning policy for sustainable development	–	171(d)**
		NGOs	Participation in inventorying	11(b)	90
			Participation in periodic reporting of states parties	–	151**, 157, 160
			Participation in research on sustainable development	(14(a))	Para. 175**

Note 1 Status and roles in bold are those considered important from the author's perspective in the evaluation of the status and roles of the NSAs in these provisions
Note 2 Articles in () connote the status and roles and activities of each stakeholder
Note 3 Paras with * indicate addition in 2010 and with **, in 2016, after the first adoption of the Operational Directives in 2008
Source Author (based on the 2003 Convention and its Operational Directives)

Operational Directives with many relevant provisions. Local communities as bearers of intangible cultural heritage found a firm right of giving consent to nominations and applying for nominations based on the provisions added to the Operational Directives, without any input from the text of the Convention itself.

At the domestic level, it is noteworthy that local communities again find a right to consent, as witnessed at the international level, concerning the activities conducted by the States for awareness-raising. Their right to benefit-sharing has been gradually recognized as well. Overall, their customary rights are well respected in the recently added concrete provisions of the Operational Directives.

6.3 NSAs in the Implementation of the 2003 Convention

The protections offered by the Convention and Operational Directives mentioned in the previous section can be realized only when the provisions therein are actually implemented. Therefore, observation of the operation of the Convention at both the international and domestic levels is critical to evaluating the legal effectiveness of those provisions. This observation also exhibits the status and roles of different NSAs with respect to various activities related to safeguarding intangible cultural heritage. Thus, the status and roles of each NSA at the different levels, especially their specific roles and activities (see again Table 6.2), require closer scrutiny.

6.3.1 NSAs in the International Implementation of the Convention

The activities of the NSAs in the international arena can be observed at the statutory meetings of the Convention: the Intangible Cultural Heritage Committee and the General Assembly. The Intangible Cultural Heritage Committee deals with the nomination of the intangible cultural heritage elements to the Lists—which directly affect local communities, groups, or sometimes individuals—and also review NGO accreditation requests under Article 9 of the Convention for recommendation to the General Assembly for final endorsement. Notwithstanding issues directly related to NSAs, other important matters concerning the Convention are usually dealt with at the Committee in advance, prior to the final adoption of relevant resolutions at the General Assembly. NSAs' activities at the international level are mainly relegated to the realm of Committee practices.

Experts

The role of experts in the evaluation of nomination files for the Lists of the 2003 Convention has been active so far, as the numbers of elements inscribed on the Lists shows. As for participation of NSAs on the Committee, it should be acknowledged that local bearers of intangible cultural heritage have limited opportunity to attend the sessions, except by invitation of their governments to represent their community regarding a newly nominated intangible cultural heritage item.[23] NGOs, however, have been involved with the Committee from the early stages, and have been regularly invited to attend these sessions. The increasing number of accredited NGOs since 2010 has paved the way for new NGO representatives to join the Committee.[24] The NGO Forum established in 2010 also explored their contributions through thematic symposiums. In fact, except several sessions of the Committee have been held off the European continent, where more than 50% of the accredited NGOs are located,

---

[23] On this occasion, these NSAs bearing heritage usually deliver their thank-you speeches together with representatives of their country after the successful nomination of their heritage item. However, opportunities for them to speak have been relatively few due to the limited time for speeches during the Committee, and they rather show themselves up with performances related to the nominated item conducted on the stage or played in the video clips. These NSAs are usually registered to the Committee under their respective States Parties.

[24] The first request for NGO accreditation was reviewed by the Committee in 2009, and the official accreditation became effective by the 3rd session of the General Assembly in 2010.

Table 6.3 Number of NSA participants and their interventions at the intangible cultural heritage committee (2006–2017)

Year/venue	NGOs	Examiners or consultative body	Other participants	NSA interventions
2006/Algiers	4	–	–	1
2007(Ext.)/China	4	–	–	1
2007/Japan	14	–	–	5
2008(Ext.)/Bulgaria	30	–	–	1
2008/Turkey	30	–	9	4
2009/France	42	19	80	3
2010/Kenya	85	11	53	3
2011/Indonesia	59	11	17	2
2012/France	95	–	89	2
2013/Azerbaijan	101	–	177	9(1)
2014/France	137	–	122	4(1)
2015/Namibia	75	–	47	9(2)
2016/Ethiopia	89	–	77	6(1)
2017/South Korea	168	–	102	6(7)

Note 1 Other participants include individual experts as observer
Note 2 Numbers in () indicate thank-you speeches made by the representatives of communities bearing inscribed intangible cultural heritage elements
Source Author (Extracted from the Related Item Documents of the Intangible Cultural Heritage Committees (from its 1st to 12th sessions)

the number of NGO participants to the Committee has been increasing (see Table 6.3).[25]

During the sessions, these NGOs have intervened on various issues on behalf of communities bearing intangible cultural heritage related to their expertise. For example, at the 8th session of the Committee in 2013, the representative of Traditions Pour Demain (France) took the floor on an item of the amendments to the Operational Directives on Safeguarding, Commercialization and Sustainable Development to express his concern about the unintentional damage to the living traditions by the measures of sustainable development that often risk social cohesion within the communities themselves (UNESCO 2014e, p. 152). The representative of the Centre for Peacebuilding and Poverty Reduction (Nigeria) also pointed out the potential damage incurred by excessive commercialization that could compromise the cultural character of intangible cultural heritage elements, and called for a balanced approach—a necessary component of sustainable development—for the beneficial

[25] The participation of these individual experts in the Committee was counted separately in 2009, 2010 and 2011, but later they were included in the delegation of the States Parties. As regards the representatives of NGOs that were members of the Consultative Body from 2011 to 2014, they were integrated into the category of NGOs except for the year 2011. After 2015, they were included in the delegations of the States Parties.

advantages and viability of intangible cultural heritage (para. 975, p. 152). Although it is not clear whether these interventions had any direct impetuses, these perspectives were duly reflected in the new paragraphs of the Operational Directives.[26]

In addition, NGOs have also called to pay attention to other key issues of the Convention's implementation. For example, at the 11th session of the Committee in 2016, a Representative of the NGO Forum expressed a collective concern regarding the recommendations of the Evaluation Body that had been almost systematically overturned during the Committee, recalling the essential role of the Body in respecting the values and spirit of the Convention (UNESCO 2017d, para. 1306). A similar statement was made again at the 12th session of the Committee the following year (UNESCO 2018f, para. 919). Although it is difficult to measure the impact of these statements, it is clear that the growing participation of the NGOs in the NGO Forum and the Committee has enabled them to gather and strengthen their common views on some of the general topics of the Committee, and thereby, has increased their chances to influence the decisions of the Committee on the implementation of the Convention.

Local Communities

One of the most important criteria that applications should meet is a community-related one (paras. 1(U.4), 2(R.4), 7(P.5, P.7), 16, and 17). When States Parties prepare required files for nomination, they must endeavor to guarantee the involvement of communities bearing intangible cultural heritage elements in the domestic process. Thus, the very fact that the States Parties must seek the consent or participation of local communities prior to submission to the Consultative or Evaluation Body (and ultimately the Committee, for its final decision) suggests the influence of those NSAs with respect to the implementation of the Convention at the international level.

In fact, there have been many nominations, requests or proposals that have failed to satisfy the community-related criteria, as demonstrated in Table 6.4. For example, during the years subsequent to the first evaluations of nominations to the Representative List, from 2009 on, approximately half of the unsatisfactory nominations were related to criterion R.4.[27] Similarly, approximately half of the unsatisfactory nominations for the Urgent List were related to criterion U.4.[28] Moreover, it has been recognized that the free, prior and informed consent of communities to the nomination is not something to be obtained retroactively (UNESCO 2012e, para. 23). Requests for International Assistance must also ensure the participation of relevant communities in the preparation of the application and demonstrate their future

[26] Chapter VI (Safeguarding intangible cultural heritage and sustainable development at the national level). Specifically, para. 194 for social cohesion and equity and para. 187 for the impact of tourism on the safeguarding of intangible cultural heritage.

[27] Criterion R.4: "The element has been nominated following the widest possible participation of the community, group or, if applicable, individuals concerned and with their free, prior and informed consent."

[28] Criterion U.4: "The element has been nominated following the widest possible participation of the community, group or, if applicable, individuals concerned and with their free, prior and informed consent."

Table 6.4 Number of nominations, requests, or proposals that did not satisfy criteria related to community (2009–2017)

Year/List	Urgent list		Representative list		International asistance		Good practice register	
	Unsatisfactory nominations	U.4 unsatisfied	Unsatisfactory nominations	R.4 unsatisfied	Unsatisfactory requests	A.1 unsatisfied	Unsatisfactory proposals	P5 and/or P7 unsatisfied
2009	1*(15)	0	35(111)	16	2(5)	0	2(5)	0
2010	1(4)	1*	8(54)	7	0(1)	0	–	–
2011	18(23)	9	31 + 1*(49)	12	4(4)	2	7(12)	3
2012	5(8)	3	17 + 1* (36)	5	8(10)	2	1(2)	0
2013	9(12)	7	8(31)	2	1(1)	1	1(2)	1
2014	5(8)	5	14(46)	7	2(2)	2	3(4)	3
2015	5(8)	2	16(35)	6	1*(2)	1*	–	–
2016	2(5)	0	19(37)	5	0(1)	0	4(7)	2
2017	3(6)	0	12(35)	1	1(3)	1	2(4)	2

Note Numbers with * indicate nominations evaluated with diverged opinion, and numbers in (), the total number of nominations, requests or proposals evaluated
Source Author (extracted from the Related Item Documents of the Intangible Cultural Heritage Committees from its 4th to 12th sessions)

involvement in the proposed activities, without which the Consultative Body does not recommend for approval of the request.[29] With respect to proposals to the Register of Good Practices, the Consultative Body specifically noted that a reason for rejection of several unsatisfactory proposals was due to the fact that the safeguarding methodologies were driven by experts, NGOs or government officials, and not by the communities themselves.[30]

However, whereas NSAs do have some degree of influence, ultimately, their influence is limited with respect to implementing the Convention internationally, because the final arbiter for successful nominations, requests, or proposals is the Committee consisting of the 24 States Parties of the Convention. Indeed, there have been several occasions where recommendations made by the Consultative or Evaluation Body (consisting of individual experts and NGO evaluators) to reject certain applications or proposals were overturned by the Committee after discussion, even though these applications did not meet several criteria, including community-related requirements. This can happen upon a strong appeal of the submitting State Party before or during the Committee.

For example, in the report on the examination of the Chinese file nominating Meshrep for inscription on the Urgent List in 2010, the opinion of two expert examiners diverged, mainly concerning criterion U.4 (the assessment of participation of the communities, groups, or individuals and their free, prior and informed consent for the nomination). One expert examiner, Rachel Harris, pointed out that "in practical terms, the government network of cultural organs which reach right into Xinjiang's villages is the only feasible mechanism for interventions of this nature, and the active participation of the peasantry in this region is still to a large extent dependent on the support and approval of these government organizations." She also raised a question on the consent letters signed by transmitters in the villages. Considering that many of the Uyghur peasants were illiterate and very unlikely to read Chinese, she suggested that personal statements written or dictated in their native Uyghur tongue would

---

[29] Criterion A.1: "The community, group and/or individuals concerned participated in the preparation of the request and will be involved in the implementation of the proposed activities, and in their evaluation and follow-up as broadly as possible." For example, when Pakistan requested International Assistance in the amount of US$ 90,590 for Safeguarding of the ibex dance and song of Pakistan (No. 00554) in 2013, the Committee decided not to approve the request because it did not meet criterion A.1 together with other criteria. Decision 8.COM 7.c.1 para. 2 reads: "(A.1) In the absence of an adequate identification of the community concerned or an explanation of the representativeness of the local organizations responsible for implementing the proposed project, the widest possible involvement of the community in the preparation of the request and in the design of the proposed activities is not demonstrated; the relation of practitioners to their own intangible cultural heritage and attention to their own modes of transmission are neglected in favor of formalized instruction by professionals from outside the community." (UNESCO 2013d, pp. 27–28).

[30] Criterion P.5: "The programme, project or activity is or has been implemented with the participation of the community, group or, if applicable, individuals concerned and with their free, prior and informed consent."

Criterion P.7: "The submitting State(s) Party(ies), implementing body(ies), and community, group or, if applicable, individuals concerned are willing to cooperate in the dissemination of best practices, if their programme, project or activity is selected.".

For the comments of the Consultative Body, see UNESCO (2012f), para. 493.

surely have been more appropriate and signaled a more active involvement from those key actors of the element (UNESCO 2010b, Annex 1, pp. 20–28). However, in spite of her concern and the insufficiency of documents related to community consent and involvement, the nomination succeeded with the support of many Member States of the Committee, who were ultimately persuaded by the appeal made by the Chinese government (UNESCO 2011m, pp. 16–22).

Recent trends demonstrate that States Parties have become more attentive to involving communities in the preparation of applications, as reflected by the decreasing number of unsatisfied U.4 and R.4 nominations, shown in Table 6.4. Comments by the Evaluation Body also have inclined to rather technical issues rather than questioning of fundamental characteristics of the local communities' consent, and indeed, various ways for the States Parties to accommodate consent from relevant communities have been considered.[31] However, this tendency of paying attention to technical issues of community consent in the evaluation process should not be interpreted as decreased influence of local communities on the recommendation of the Consultative or Evaluation Body. Still, community consent and participation serves as one of the most critical criteria that the submitting States Parties are required to consider, as applications without it would be envisaged to encounter considerable difficulty.

As noted in the Periodic Reports submitted by the States Parties examined in 2014,[32] NSAs—both heritage-bearers and experts—are also actively involved in joint international projects or activities, particularly those related to their intangible cultural heritage elements (UNESCO 2014f, para. 39). Shared intangible cultural heritage elements work as an important bond for bilateral and regional cooperation, and provide opportunities for all kinds of NSAs to develop and maintain international networks (UNESCO 2016d, para. 20).

UNESCO

The contribution of UNESCO to the international cooperation of NSAs should not be ignored. The Periodic Reports have regularly noted that UNESCO Field Offices are active facilitators of various instances of cooperation among communities, experts, institutions and governments, either by providing financial support or organizing capacity-building activities (UNESCO 2015i, para. 24).

In fact, the role of UNESCO has expanded dramatically since the adoption of the Convention. Whereas, for the purposes of this book, it is not necessary to describe in detail all of the functions of the Secretariat in implementing the actions of the Committee and General Assembly, it is worth noting that their extended work includes a close partnership with Category 2 Centers (hereinafter, 'Centers') under the auspices of UNESCO. These Centers are established and funded by Member

[31] For example, more diversified formats for the consent letters were recommended (UNESCO 2017e, paras. 49–50).

[32] Per para. 152 of the Operational Directives of the Convention, States Parties are required to submit their periodic reports to the Committee every six years on the basis of a rotation region by region.

States by means of formal agreements between UNESCO and the host country, and serve to achieve Strategic Program Objectives and priorities as well as the themes of UNESCO (UNESCO 2013c). Specifically, the Centers' key objectives are:

> (a) to promote the UNESCO Convention for the Safeguarding of the Intangible Cultural Heritage and contribute to its implementation; (b) to reinforce capacities in the Region for actively implementing the 2003 Convention on the regional and international level; (c) to increase the participation of communities, groups and individuals in safeguarding intangible cultural heritage in the Region; and (d) to foster regional and international cooperation for safeguarding intangible cultural heritage.[33]

Currently, there are seven Category 2 Centers in the field,[34] and they operate various capacity-building, policy support, or training workshops in partnership with the UNESCO Secretariat. However, considering that those Centers are not part of UNESCO but operate only under the auspices of UNESCO, it is difficult to conclude that these Category 2 Centers perform the same functions as UNESCO.

6.3.2 NSAs in the Domestic Implementation of the Convention

States Parties need to submit, on a six-year cycle, Periodic Reports on legislative, regulatory and other measures taken toward the implementation of the Convention, in accordance with Article 29.[35] So far, seven cycles of period reporting have been reviewed by the Intangible Cultural Heritage Committee, in which 130 States Parties participated.[36] Among other things, these Periodic Reports contain ample information regarding the implementation of the Convention at the domestic level, and help to exhibit the general trend of NSA involvement in national safeguarding activities of intangible cultural heritage. In addition to these materials, in 2013, the Evaluation Section of the UNESCO Internal Oversight Service (IOS) conducted an overall evaluation of four culture conventions[37] with regard to the relevance and effectiveness of

---

[33] https://ich.unesco.org/en/category2 (accessed 30 May 2021).

[34] The list is available at https://ich.unesco.org/en/category2 (accessed 30 May 2021).

[35] Para. 152 of the Operational Directives. In June 2018, the General Assembly approved amendments to the Operational Directives on Periodic Reporting in order to change the cycle of each State Party so as to follow a regional cycle instead. As a result, a transition period for reforming of the Periodic Reporting mechanism started ended on 15 December 2020 and the submission of reports from the first region is made.

[36] So far, 181 reports have been submitted, which are available at the dedicated homepage for Periodic Reporting: https://ich.unesco.org/en/submissions-and-deadlines-00861 (accessed 30 May 2021).

[37] The 1970 Convention on the Means of Prohibiting and Preventing the Illicit Import, Export and Transfer of Ownership of Cultural Property, the 1972 Convention Concerning the Protection of the World Cultural and Natural Heritage, the 2003 Convention for the Safeguarding of the Intangible Cultural Heritage, and the 2005 Convention on the Protection and Promotion of the Diversity of Cultural Expressions.

UNESCO's role in standard-setting, with a focus on its impact on ratification, legislation, policies, and strategies of the States Parties and their implementation at the national level (hereinafter, '2013 IOS Report') (Torggler and Blake 2013). As several activities to safeguard intangible cultural heritage at the national level are conducted by multiple NSAs together, the following observations on the roles and status of NSAs in the domestic implementation of the Convention will be made according to the specific safeguarding-activity categories.

Inventory

One of the most important duties of States Parties regarding the domestic implementation of the Convention is identifying and inventorying intangible cultural heritage elements, as it is an initial and essential step toward safeguarding intangible cultural heritage. Indeed, according to the Periodic Reports of various States Parties, many countries have put inventorying as a leading priority, and many also have introduced intangible cultural heritage inventories after ratifying the Convention. As such, the States Parties endeavor to involve communities as guided by the Operational Directives. However, the degree of participation of the communities is unclear, as the process of establishing inventories often varies depending on the respective countries. An in-depth study was conducted in 2014 examining Periodic Reports between 2011 and 2014 concerning the general trend of inventory-making practices of States Parties (UNESCO 2014f, paras. 40–85). The study noted that information meetings and consultations with communities were frequently held, and that the informed consent of the communities and their participation in field surveys, workshops or seminars were also secured (UNESCO 2014f, para. 77). However, the 2013 IOS Report found that the inventory-making practices of the States Parties were driven primarily by government leadership and academic institutions, relegating traditional bearers of intangible cultural heritage as mere informants rather than active participants (Torggler and Blake 2013, p. 41). This finding reflects a similar finding on the limited role of local communities in the international implementation of the Convention, specifically as regards the application for the nomination of intangible cultural heritage elements onto the international Lists, as previously discussed (Torggler and Blake 2013, p. 50).

On the other hand, the participation of experts (i.e., individual experts, institutions, and NGOs) in identifying intangible cultural heritage elements and safeguarding measures has been observed to be more active. It is assumed that such inventorying work leads to assistance to States Parties in the preparation of the nomination files. According to the Periodic Reports, experts and NGOs play varied roles in the process of inventorying, particularly as advisors to the local and central authorities, and as mediators between local communities and those authorities. An in-depth study on inventory-making conducted in 2014 drew attention to NGOs' special roles in identifying and inventorying living heritage in provincial and remote localities and in specialized areas of intangible cultural heritage such as traditional crafts, performing arts, and dance (UNESCO 2014f, para. 81). Based on their specialties, NGOs and institutions often offer academic consultancy to both governments and communities on the methodology or approach for inventorying, and mediate the inventorying process between two entities by participating in the official research teams that train communities for inventorying work (UNESCO 2017f, para. 14).

Awareness-Raising

The impact of the NSAs as bearers of intangible cultural heritage is greatest in their awareness-raising function. In this regard, NSAs play a pivotal role in giving consent to relevant programs of the government (para. 101(b)). Although government entities lead the charge on most such activities, local communities are active participants, often by means of establishing and maintaining cultural associations. According to the Periodic Reports in 2014, in African States such as Namibia, Mali, and Kenya, traditional authorities such as elders or chiefs have played a central role in transmitting, safeguarding and managing intangible cultural heritage items and conserving natural spaces and resources related to them (UNESCO 2014f, para. 11). The role of cultural associations becomes central in terms of non-formal education as well. Either independently or with the support of the government bodies or institutions, communities bearing intangible cultural heritage are closely involved in fairs, festivals, cultural programs, and/or youth centers, thus providing a non-formal setting for the preservation of intangible cultural heritage elements (UNESCO 2016d, para. 18).

Active participation of experts can be readily observed in awareness-raising activities as well. An in-depth 2015 transmission and education study examining Periodic Reports between 2013 and 2014 found that NGOs served as organizers of educational and training programs both within communities and for the general public (UNESCO 2015i, paras. 25–33). Those experts, NGOs, and educational institutions had been invited to participate in educational classes, and provided complementary non-formal education by taking advantage of external resources. Through these practices, these experts have played an important bridging role between the bearer communities of intangible cultural heritage and the local and central authorities that would safeguard it. This role as mediator is possible not only because experts have an excellent understanding of the Convention,[38] but also because they are connected to both the local communities and the government (Torggler and Blake 2013, p. 66). The Committee took notice of this special role of NGOs and institutions, and encouraged States Parties to further engage them to gain information for periodic reporting and demonstrate their roles in the reports (UNESCO 2015j, para. 10).

Monitoring

The process of preparing Periodic Reports, however, is an area wherein communities, unlike experts, play a relatively passive role. Typically, the central government requests local authorities or institutions to collect information from relevant associations or organizations representing the communities bearing intangible cultural heritage.[39] The local communities are not invited to participate in the actual drafting

[38] Particularly in the case of accredited NGOs.

[39] A typical example is Lithuania, where a questionnaire was sent to all communities concerned in order to reflect their answers in the final national report (UNESCO 2012g, para. 96).

of the report; rather, they are relegated to serve as an information provider in the process of inventorying. Furthermore, it is unclear to what extent the opinions of those NSAs are taken into account during the drafting of the reports. In fact, in 2015, the Committee directed States Parties to more actively involve the communities in monitoring and periodic reporting, which fact would indicate a prior lack of community involvement (UNESCO 2015j, para. 9).

Others

Another aspect of the involvement of local communities in the safeguarding process is their customary rights or benefit-sharing, which is something that has been pushed for recently. These rights and benefits, though not explicitly addressed in the text of the Convention, are based in the 2010 and 2016 Amendments to the Operational Directives concerning raising awareness and sustainable development.[40] In practice, several States Parties, including the Seychelles, reported that they had established policies providing intellectual property protection for the artistic creations and traditional knowledge that constitute intangible cultural heritage (UNESCO 2016d, para. 30). Additionally, some countries, Belarus, Cyprus, and Hungary for example, have endeavored to involve rural communities in development-policy-making by providing funding for local cultural festivals and fairs (para. 32, p. 12).

6.4 Main Findings

The long and complex journey to introduce a new international standard for safeguarding intangible cultural heritage is itself evidence of the difficulties in forming legal protection for incorporeal heritage. Unlike tangible cultural heritage, intangible cultural heritage does not have any visible and fixed form and is at risk of disappearance at any time. This type of heritage is most appreciable to its bearers, and cannot be transmitted without them. The importance of NSAs in safeguarding intangible cultural heritage is rooted here, with the drafters of the 2003 Convention paying particular attention to those local communities, groups, or individuals who create and bear intangible cultural heritage elements. Even States that were once reluctant to acknowledge these groups began to join the Convention, which has since become the standard for international protection of intangible cultural heritage.

Several Articles of the Convention recognize the status and roles of local communities and require States Parties to ensure their participation in the implementation of the Convention. The Convention also provides space for other NSAs, in particular individual experts and NGOs, to perform advisory functions based on their expertise. That said, provisions concerning the NSAs is relatively limited in the text of the Convention: local communities should serve as participants of national implementation and experts as advisors for international implementation of the Convention, without any further roles, or rights and obligations explicitly stated in the text.

[40] See Table 6.1.

However, with the adoption of the Operational Directives and their subsequent amendments—documents that guide the actual implementation of the Convention by the States Parties—those NSAs found themselves with more secured status and roles at both the domestic and international levels. Specifically, the consent of local communities worked as an essential criterion for the inscription of nominated intangible cultural heritage elements onto the international Lists and for the approval of International Assistance. The traditional rights and benefits of local communities were further entrenched by the amendments of the Operational Directives, providing an avenue by which these NSAs were ensured participation rights in the national implementation of the Convention by the States Parties.

Experts also found their roles expanded in the Operational Directives, particularly in the international forum, and most actively as evaluators of nomination dossiers. Other kinds of NSAs, such as the UNESCO Secretariat and donor NSAs, have based their roles in the preservation of intangible cultural heritage within the provisions of the Operational Directives as well. This increased prominence of NSAs was only made possible because of the flexibility of the Operational Directives in accommodating the changing environments required in safeguarding intangible cultural heritage, not to mention the foresight against the difficult process of revision in the Convention (O'Keefe and Prott 2011, p. 12).

In practice, when local communities are not appropriately consulted prior to applications for the inscription of national intangible cultural heritage elements on the international Lists or for the approval of International Assistance, States Parties have encountered unfavorable recommendations for their failure to satisfy this essential criterion. The strengthened participation and influence of experts has also been observed in the recent sessions of the Committee, and they often work as spokespersons for local communities who usually cannot attend the Committee. Both expert and local communities have been involved in regional or international cooperation as well, and the UNESCO Secretariat has facilitated this cooperation while enlarging its role of implementing the decisions of the Intangible Cultural Heritage Committee and General Assembly to support States Parties.

At the national level, experts actively participate in and contribute to various intangible cultural heritage safeguarding activities, performing their advisory role for both government and local communities and working as a mediator between them. They are the collaborators for Periodic Reports and partners of research for various topics on sustainable development and intangible cultural heritage as well. With respect to participation of local communities, there have been many positive reports of States Parties actively involving them in their national implementation of the Convention. Newly recognized NSAs' rights of participation related to the discourse of sustainable development also have started to be ensured by the States Parties.

It is important to be mindful of two things, however. The first is the critical evaluation mentioned in the 2013 IOS Report concerning the top-down approach of their policy, and the second is the different and varied degrees of involvement of the local communities that vary State to State. Policies on intangible cultural heritage should be drawn from the community level up, with guidance of experts, in order to ensure that bearers of intangible cultural heritage are afforded a full and fair opportunity to participate in the protection of intangible cultural heritage elements.

This demonstrates the limit of international law, in that it cannot be fully effective without the States Parties' will to duly carry out their duties under the Convention domestically. A lack of understanding concerning the importance of NSAs in safeguarding intangible cultural heritage, and a lack of experience in working with them through bottom-up approaches, are two of the reasons NSAs' roles may be limited in the domestic sphere.

Moreover, it appears that the international operation of the 2003 Convention is still led by the States Parties, particularly Members of the Committee, as evidenced by the incident in which the Committee, in spite of insufficient proof of prior consent by the concerned community, overturned an expert recommendation to reject a nomination for inscription to the List on account of pressure from the concerned State, as similarly witnessed in the World Heritage Committee of the 1972 Convention.[41] In addition, even where the rights of the NSAs are infringed by the States Parties, there is no instrument for them to pursue their appeal internationally, except as part of an independent campaign to influence the Committee's decision on the issue.

Overall, there have been many positive steps made toward increasing the role of NSAs and ensuring their rights under the Convention. It should be noted that progress is ongoing (Kurin 2007, p. 15). However, that progress still comes up short of fully establishing the NSAs' proper right to check State behavior both domestically and internationally, in departing from their traditional role as just participants in or beneficiaries of international law (Lixinski 2013, p. 55). Since the successful safeguarding of intangible cultural heritage cannot be achieved without the participation of NSAs, in particular those bearers who create the heritage and transmit it to future generations, more room must be made for such a role. Apparently, this will require considerable change of States' attitudes towards the implementation of the 2003 Convention.

References

Aikawa N (2004) A historical overview of the preparation of the UNESCO international convention for the safeguarding of the intangible cultural heritage. Museum Int 56:137–149

Blake J (2006) Commentary on the UNESCO 2003 convention on the safeguarding of the intangible cultural heritage. Leicester, Institute of Art and Law

Blake J (2015) International cultural heritage law. Oxford University Press, Oxford

Bouchenaki M (2007) A major advance towards a holistic approach to heritage conservation: the 2003 intangible heritage convention. Int J Intang Herit 2:106–109

Ficsor M (1997) Attempts to provide international protection for folklore by intellectual property rights. Online Publication: UNESCO. https://www.wipo.int/edocs/mdocs/arab/en/2003/ip_tip/doc/wipo_ip_tip_03_12.doc. Accessed 30 May 2021

[41] See Sects. 4.3.2 and 6.3.1 of this book.

Kim J, Nam S (2016) National response to international conventions: the case of the 2003 UNESCO intangible cultural heritage convention and the New Korean legislation. J Int Area Stud 23(2):39–59

Kurin R (2007) Safeguarding intangible cultural heritage: key factors in implementing the 2003 convention. Int J Intang Herit 2:10–19

Lixinski L (2013) Intangible cultural heritage law. Oxford University Press, Oxford

O'Keefe PJ, Prott LV (eds) (2011) Cultural heritage conventions and other instruments: a compendium with commentaries. Institute of Art and Law, Builth Wells

Schmitt TM (2008) The UNESCO concept of safeguarding intangible cultural heritage: its background and Marrakchi roots. Int J Herit Stud 14(2):95–111

Sherkin S (2001) A historical study on the preparation of the 1989 recommendation on the safeguarding of traditional culture and folklore. In: Seitel P (ed) Safeguarding traditional cultures: a global assessment. Smithsonian Center for Folklife and Cultural Heritage, Washington

Simon BS (2001) Global steps to local empowerment in the next millennium: an assessment of UNESCO's 1989 recommendation on the safeguarding of traditional culture and folklore. In: Seitel P (ed) Safeguarding traditional culture: a global assessment. Smithsonian Center for Folklife and Cultural Heritage, Washington

Torggler B, Blake J (2013) Evaluation of UNESCO's standard-setting work of the culture sector: part I–2003 convention for the safeguarding of the intangible cultural heritage. UNESCO, Online Publication

UNESCO (1993) 142 EX/18. The 142nd session of the executive board of UNESCO. Paris, 11 October–15 November 1993

UNESCO (2001a) 161 EX/15. The 161st session of the executive board of UNESCO. Paris, 28 May–13 June 2001

UNESCO (2001b) 31 C/INF.24. The 31st session of the general conference of UNESCO. Paris, 15 October–3 November 2001

UNESCO (2008) ITH/08/2.EXT.COM/CONF.201/INF.4. The second extraordinary session of the intergovernmental committee for the safeguarding of the intangible cultural heritage. Sofia, 18–22 February 2008

UNESCO (2010b). ITH/10/5.COM/CONF.202/5 Rev. The fifth session of the intergovernmental committee for the safeguarding of the intangible cultural heritage. Nairobi, 15–19 November 2010

UNESCO (2011m). ITH/11/6.COM/CONF.206/4 Rev. The sixth session of the intergovernmental committee for the safeguarding of the intangible cultural heritage. Bali, 22–29 November 2011

UNESCO (2012e) ITH/12/7.COM/8. The seventh session of the intergovernmental committee for the safeguarding of the intangible cultural heritage. Paris, 3–7 December 2012

UNESCO (2012f) ITH/12/7.COM/5 Rev. The seventh session of the intergovernmental committee for the safeguarding of the intangible cultural heritage. Paris, 3–7 December 2012

UNESCO (2012g) ITH/12/7.COM/6. The seventh session of the intergovernmental committee for the safeguarding of the intangible cultural heritage. Paris, 3–7 December 2012

UNESCO (2013c) 37/C Resolution 93. The 37th session of the general conference of UNESCO. Paris, 5–20 November 2013

UNESCO (2013d) ITH/13/8.COM/Decisions. The eighth session of the intergovernmental committee for the safeguarding of the in-tangible cultural heritage. Baku, 2–7 December 2013

UNESCO (2014e) ITH/14/9.COM/4 Rev. The ninth session of the intergovernmental committee for the safeguarding of the intangible cultural heritage. Paris, 24–28 November 2014

UNESCO (2014f) ITH/14/9.COM/5.a. The ninth session of the intergovernmental committee for the safeguarding of the intangible cultural heritage. Paris, 24–28 November 2014

UNESCO (2015i) ITH/15/10.COM/6.a. The tenth session of the intergovernmental committee for the safeguarding of the intangible cultural heritage. Windhoek, 30 November–4 December 2015

UNESCO (2015j) Decision 10.COM 6.a. The tenth session of the intergovernmental committee for the safeguarding of the intangible cultural heritage. Windhoek, 30 November–4 December 2015

UNESCO (2016c) ITH/16/6.GA/7. The sixth session of the general assembly of the states parties to the convention for the safeguarding of the intangible cultural heritage. Paris, 30 May–1 June 2016.
UNESCO (2016d) ITH/16/11.COM/9.a. The eleventh session of the intergovernmental committee for the safeguarding of the intangible cultural heritage. Addis Ababa, 28 November–2 December 2016.
UNESCO (2017d) ITH/17/12.COM/4. The twelfth session of the intergovernmental committee for the safeguarding of the intangible cultural heritage. Jeju Island, 4–9 December 2017
UNESCO (2017e) ITH/17/12.COM/11. The twelfth session of the intergovernmental committee for the safeguarding of the intangible cultural heritage. Jeju Island, 4–9 December 2017
UNESCO (2017f) ITH/17/12.COM/8.b Rev. The twelfth session of the intergovernmental committee for the safeguarding of the intangible cultural heritage. Jeju Island, 4–9 December 2017
UNESCO (2018f) ITH/18/13.COM/4. The 13th session of the intergovernmental committee for the safeguarding of the intangible cultural heritage. Port Louis, 26 November–1 December 2018
WIPO (2003) WIPO/IP/TIP/03/12. WIPO national seminar on intellectual property. Tripoli, 29–30 April 2003

Chapter 7
Conclusion

The international community has developed various legal frameworks to protect different types of cultural heritage, and six international conventions analyzed in this book—the 1954, 1970, 1972, 1995, 2001, and 2003 Conventions—are the results of its efforts to address new challenges for the protection of cultural heritage nationally and globally. In addition, as complementary and supplementary tools to facilitate effective implementation of the conventions, concrete operational guidelines have been developed after the adoption of the conventions. Unlike the texts of the conventions, it has been possible to update these guidelines continuously to ensure flexible application of the conventions in a changing environment. This book conducted, additionally to a statutory analysis of the provisions of international cultural heritage law and the relevant documents, an empirical analysis in order to get a closer look at actual cases at courts and statutory meetings of the conventions, with a view to identifying possible disjunctions between the texts and practice.

All of the international conventions for the protection of various types of cultural heritage have shown the existence of the considerable status and roles of NSAs. Many aspects of the status and roles of NSAs according to their categories, and the changes as well, can be observed. For example, important roles of experts can be seen in certain conventions, and NGOs and local communities have expanded their roles in those conventions' implementation. As for the status of NSAs, it was witnessed that the rights and obligations of local communities and individuals in particular have been increasing in some areas of cultural heritage. However, there exist discrepancies between the provisions of the conventions (with their operational documents) and actual practice. In other words, NSAs' status and roles vary according to their different categories as well as the applicable conventions, both in the texts and in practice.

Herein, for the purpose of providing different angles from which to view and better understand the status and roles of NSAs in international cultural heritage law, a summary of findings will be compiled for each category of NSA. Doing so will be helpful in finding ways forward for the protection of cultural heritage by the

J. Kim, *Non-State Actors in the Protection of Cultural Heritage*, Creativity, Heritage and the City 3, https://doi.org/10.1007/978-981-16-6659-9_7

international community with the participation of NSAs having proper status and roles. Finally, in these pages, the remaining challenges to the future thus envisioned will be identified.

7.1 Assessment and the Ways Forward

Heritage is about social and cultural processes that aim to create links between people. Therefore, participation of different NSAs brings diverse perspectives on heritage identification, interpretation, preservation, and promotion. It also enriches and supplements the efforts of the States for the protection of heritage. However, various NSAs—UNESCO, experts, NGOs, local communities, and individuals—have different mandates and capacities, and their status and roles also differ according to the specific convention context. When each NSA is placed well according to its genuine characteristics based on the provisions stipulated in the text of conventions or their operational documents, their contribution to the implementation of the conventions can be maximized.

Indeed, Ahmed Skounti, UNESCO facilitator for intangible cultural heritage,[1] stressed that that the non-recognition of any legal status of NSAs and the absence of a clear procedure for their involvement are the biggest obstacles to promoting their participation in international cultural heritage protection.[2] For example, he pointed out that only specific advisory bodies of the 1972 Convention have clear and binding roles according to its text, while the 'local community,' which can and should play many roles in the Convention's implementation, is not mentioned at all in that text.

In order to make a general assessment of the status and roles of NSAs in international cultural heritage law, closer attention to each of their categories will be paid based on the findings made in the foregoing chapters of this book. To compare differences among the conventions, the assessment will focus on just a few of the common NSA rights, obligations and roles set out in several of those conventions. It is hoped that thereby, this review will discover several practical ways of moving forward to enhance NSAs' participation in the implementation of the cultural heritage conventions.

UNESCO

As an international organization established on inter-state consent, UNESCO has a dual identity in relation to international cultural heritage law: one as a secretariat that functions as a depository of the conventions, and the other as a specialized agency offering its unique expertise. In other words, in addition to its basic roles in providing an open forum wherein States participate in international law,

[1] UNESCO trains experts in the field of intangible cultural heritage to be familiar with the 2003 Convention so that they can support States Parties and other stakeholders seeking guidance and training for the protection of such heritage.

[2] Email interview conducted on the 28th of December, 2020.

UNESCO also conducts its own specialized mandates as an independent NSA (Collins 2011, p. 312). However, the oscillation of its status between these two different characteristics has varied by convention.

For example, several parts of the texts of the 1954 Convention and its Second Protocol adopted in 1999 empowers UNESCO to take its own initiative. The 1970 Convention also has similar articles concerning the active participation of UNESCO in the implementation of the Convention. However, contrary to the 1954 and 1970 Conventions, the 1972, 2001 and 2003 Conventions, where a separate advisory body exists to perform highly specialized functions (maintaining the Lists, most notably), the roles of UNESCO appear to be rather limited. In fact, in those three conventions, there is no provision demonstrating roles for UNESCO other than assisting the intergovernmental committees and States Parties. And yet, the roles of UNESCO have gradually expanded, with the development of their Operational Guidelines and Directives, to contribute to implementation in more practical ways, such as conducting missions and providing capacity-building and awareness-raising activities for States Parties. It seems that the success of the conventions with listing mechanisms entailed more cooperation between UNESCO and the States; moreover, more technical roles beyond its functions as a Secretariat of the conventions are expected from UNESCO in the future. UNESCO has played conciliatory and mediatory roles as well. In particular, the Second Protocol of the 1954 Convention added capacities to lend good offices or function as a conciliator or mediator in cases where no Protecting Powers are appointed. The Operational Guidelines of the 1970 Convention adopted in 2015 developed the good offices roles of UNESCO in more concrete terms, endowing it with an additional, active capacity to intervene in controversial auctions to raise awareness of their potentially negative impacts. A mediatory role for UNESCO concerning disputes among States Parties (at their request) also was set out in the 2001 Convention. It is noteworthy that the cases related to the roles of UNESCO as a facilitator are increasing recently.

As Kishore Rao, the former Director of UNESCO World Heritage Center emphasized, one of the most important aspects for UNESCO to have is the highest maintained level of integrity and technical competence in dealing with various agendas of the conventions in impartial ways.[3] Therefore, it is important to have at least minimal provisions to ensure UNESCO's roles, both as an organization supporting the implementation of cultural heritage conventions in technical ways and as a neutral body facilitating cooperation among States Parties through mediation and coordination. In this vein, relevant provisions in certain conventions and operational documents concerning the active roles of UNESCO mentioned above can be re-established in other conventions and their operational documents as well.

[3] Email interview conducted on the 28th of December, 2020.

Experts

In general, the roles of experts in the implementation of the international cultural heritage conventions, whether for the formal advisory groups or for individuals,[4] have been well noted both in the texts of the conventions and their operational documents. Those provisions have generally been implemented well at the national and international levels. For example, they are invited to the meetings of States Parties or intergovernmental committees in their advisory capacity, and many conventions recognize them as one of the important stakeholders for their implementation. In particular, those conventions with international Lists, such as the 1972 and 2003 Conventions, require a pivotal contribution of expert groups for the maintenance of those Lists, especially for evaluation of nomination files.[5]

However, without any listing system stipulated in a convention, the roles of experts in its implementation are rather limited. The 1954 Convention, wherein there exists a unique system of appointing a Commissioner-General by States Parties to deal with all matters related to the application of the Convention for the protection of cultural property during wartime, yielded the roles of individual experts to NGOs only later. For the 2001 Convention, the roles of the expert body have been expanded after the Meeting of States Parities asked for more roles for their evaluation of the List of Best Practices of underwater cultural heritage,[6] but the scope of those roles is narrow relative to the 1972 and 2003 Conventions with their listing mechanisms.

It is important to note that in practice, changing political environments for intergovernmental committees in some conventions have allowed lobbies to help ensure the success of States' nominations or management agendas. This tendency of the politicization of committee decisions has reduced experts' latitude for exercising of their expertise. This disjunction between text and practice is especially evident in the 1972 Convention, and there are possibilities that the 2003 Convention will follow a similar track.

The involvement of experts in the implementation of cultural heritage conventions is highly important, in that their knowledge and experience are crucial to the maintenance of conventions' scientific and technical profiles. In addition, as Marina Schneider, Treaty Depositary of the 1995 Convention, pointed out in an interview, lack of knowledge of the benefits of conventions is one of the biggest challenges,[7] and experts play a pivotal role in raising awareness of conventions among the various stakeholders.

---

[4] Differences concerning their characteristic exist. For example, advisory bodies for the 1972 Convention are specifically named in the text of the Convention, while those for the 2001 and 2003 Conventions are nominated and selected by States Parties.

[5] For the nomination files for the Lists of the 2003 Convention, NGOs can also work as experts to evaluate them.

[6] However, specific provisions on the List of Best Practices are set out neither in the text of the 2001 Convention nor its Operational Guidelines. The List of Best Practices under the 2001 Convention is created by the decision of the Meeting of the States Parties and therefore it is very different from the international Lists under the 1972 and 2003 Conventions that are created by their own provisions.

[7] Email interview conducted on the 28th of December, 2020.

To enhance the participation of experts in conventions' implementation, having an explicit mechanism for their participation as a separate advisory body, as seen in the 1972, 2001 and 2003 Conventions, is highly recommended. However, in practice, there exists a danger of committee politicization that would adversely impact conventions' credibility and lead to questioning of their very sustainability (Meskell 2013; Keough 2011). Committees are aware of this problematic phenomenon, but call only for soft remedies.[8] Therefore, additional tools should be explored to rectify the situation and secure the respect of experts' technical and scientific authority. Of course, committees cannot always decide all matters in full compliance with experts' recommendations, just as experts cannot always consider all of the committees' agenda items and related information. However, setting a rule whereby, at minimum, the recommendations of expert bodies are not dramatically overturned by committees, can be at least an initial procedural solution. For example, not changing more than two stages of recommendations of experts for nominations to the List of the 1972 Convention,[9] or not changing experts' recommendations on items without meeting more than two criteria for the nominations to the Lists of the 2003 Convention,[10] can be considered. Although, as noted in Chap. 4, these Conventions are developing an 'Upstream Process' type of mechanism to facilitate communication between experts and States Parties concerning nominations, it is still important to have written rules to allow experts to exert their full capacity to facilitate conventions' purposes and uphold their credibility.

NGOs and Local Communities

NGOs have a dual identity as experts as well as advocates of the interests of local and international communities. In the former identity, they play a role similar to that of the advisory body or individual experts, as seen in the 1954 Convention. The latter identity of NGOs, as advocates representing the interests of communities, is outlined in the 1972 and 2003 Conventions in particular. In fact, the Operational Guidelines or Directives of these two Conventions have further developed the roles of both local and international communities in the implementation of the Conventions, and many cases of NGOs advocating the rights or practical influence of such communities have been demonstrated.

The status and roles of NGOs and local communities are especially well set out in conventions managing international Lists. In conventions without active nomination mechanisms, such as the 1954 and 2001 Conventions, not many concrete rights, obligations or roles of NGOs and communities can be found.[11] The reason is that

[8] For example, most recently, UNESCO (2019g), para. 14 reads: "...Recalls that, in order to uphold the sustainability of the listing system, the credibility of the process for inscription must be ensured at all stages, and hence, underlines the importance that the decisions of the Committee shall be based only on experts' recommendations and evidence-based considerations."

[9] Such as, from non-inscription to referral or from deferral to inscription.

[10] The decision of the committee can change the recommendation from referral or non-inscription to nomination.

[11] The Lists of the 1954 Convention, its Second Protocol, and the 2001 Convention are not very actively managed compared with those of the 1972 and 2003 Conventions.

the nomination of heritage and its protection necessarily require the participation of NSAs. While emphasizing the obligations *erga omnes* conferred to NGOs and local communities to protect the common heritage of humanity, the 1972 Convention has gradually added more provisions to its Operational Guidelines on the participation of local communities in the nomination and management processes of the World Heritage Sites in cooperation with the States Parties. The related statistics on the participation of NGOs and communities in committee sessions support this assertion.

Indeed, the rights of NGOs and communities have been expanded further. Especially, consent of the relevant communities is mandatory criterion for a successful nomination in the 2003 Convention. This stems from the unique characteristic of intangible cultural heritage, for which communities play irreplaceable safeguarding and transmitting roles. The 1972 Convention can refer to these criteria of the 2003 Convention to strengthen the rights of communities to participate in the nomination process of World Heritage properties.

Recent cases have shown the growing influence of local communities, often as represented by NGOs in intergovernmental committees, where the nomination of new sites and authorization of state-led management plans are discussed. However, in spite of the development of the relevant provisions of the operational documents of the conventions, in practice, in particular at the national level, the participation of NGOs and local communities has been rather limited. One possible solution to this problem is the creation of a mandatory process of hearings for the representatives of local people and the relevant NGOs during the evaluation process by expert bodies or committee discussion. The involvement of NGOs in the WTO Dispute Settlement System, which allows them to participate in the process of dispute settlement through *amicus curiae* briefs, could be a good point of reference.[12] A new process of hearings for NGOS and local communities would enhance the transparency of nominations as well as the credibility of the conventions. This, additionally, would exert more pressure on the States Parties *not* to take a top-down approach in the nomination or management of cultural heritage, and would also enable the NGOs and local community to check and monitor governments' actions. As Francesco Bandarin, the former Assistant Director-General of UNESCO and now one of the principals of an international NGO named Our World Heritage noted, heritage conservation is increasingly seen as "a joint venture" of States and NSAs.[13]

Individuals

The tendency to imposing more obligations on individuals to protect cultural heritage is especially evident in the implementations of the 1954 and 1970 Conventions in particular. The destruction of cultural property has come to be considered as a war crime, with a growing, accompanying understanding of it as an attack on the common heritage of humanity. As witnessed in judicial exercises in ICTY and the Statute of the ICC, the accretion of the burden on individuals for the protection of cultural heritage

---

[12] Since 1998, WTO Panels and the Appellate Body have accepted *amicus curiae* briefs and NSAs of widely varying type have submitted numerous briefs (Boisson de Chazournes 2004).

[13] Email interview conducted on the 28th of December, 2020.

during armed conflicts is in line with development of international humanitarian law, which has gradually imposed more criminal responsibility on individuals as the understanding of 'war crime' has expanded. More responsible behavior of individuals as participants in the art market has been increasingly required as well. The provisions of the 1995 Convention, and the Operational Guidelines of the 1970 Convention adopted in 2015, support this tendency, and certainly in recent years, there have been many cases illustrative of it.

Now, as regards the rights of individuals, a tendency toward stronger protection of property right has been observed. Further to the 1954 Convention, which enabled *bona fide* acquirers' requests for indemnity, the 1970 and 1995 Conventions ensured the rights of individuals to bring actions for recovery of their cultural property or reasonable compensation. In the 1995 Convention respecting recovery actions, special attention was paid to indigenous people.

At first glance, the rights and duties of individuals seem in balance. With the growth of human rights and indigenous people's rights, individuals have found more ground for their property rights in terms of tangible and movable cultural heritage. However, it should be considered that local communities also can be included in the 'individual' category, unlike other categories of NSA such as UNESCO and experts. The problem is that putting individuals and communities together extends the coverage of cultural heritage conventions to intangible and immovable cultural heritage, with the result that common assessment becomes more problematic. Whereas there exist common responsibilities required of individuals and communities for protection of cultural heritage, their substantive and procedural rights in the implementation of the relevant conventions are limited in practice. This kind of imbalance of rights and duties for individuals and local communities can endanger the sustainability of heritage protection, because they live with the heritage and are directly influenced by the decisions of States on the matters regarding its protection.

There can be many ways to ensure the rights, obligations and roles of NSAs for further, sustained contributions to the implementation of the cultural heritage conventions. However, due to the variety of contents, governance systems and any of the other mechanisms of each convention, there is not one, single option that fits for all of them. In spite of the difficulties of finding proper and common solutions to the problems of the participation of NSAs, it is evident that change should be in the direction of strengthening their status and roles. It is important that any new measures need to be added to the texts of conventions or their operational documents to facilitate States Parties' follow-ups in due course. Considering the complex processes of amending conventions, the Operational Guidelines or Directives that guide their implementation are the best places to reflect changes. Information sharing among States Parties and different NSAs on their follow-ups in practice will be another tool to strengthen the participation of NSAs, and UNESCO is the right actor to coordinate it.

7.2 Challenges and the Future Ahead

Threats against the protection of cultural heritage are growing with the spread of globalization. The value of cultural heritage, sadly, is easily played down in the name of development. According to statistics on the State of Conservation (SOC) of World Heritage Sites in 2017, 417 of 547 sites (76%) are under threat of development activities such as construction, resource exploitation, tourism, and pollution; and certainly, one of the major factors putting the 86 sites on the World Heritage in Danger List is development pressure (Kim 2017, p. 99). This kind of pressure from development-minded governments and their industrial partners can harm cultural spaces, as witnessed in many cases before domestic courts and international tribunals (Chechi 2015, p. 469).[14]

Especially in an atmosphere of global economic competitiveness and development prioritization, the top-down approach is common to the implementation processes of the cultural heritage conventions reviewed in this book. NSAs, and especially local communities, are easily left out of the domestic nomination process (Millar 2006, p. 38), by the over-emphasis on the 'global value' of cultural heritage. For the tangible sites of cultural heritage, for example, the 'local value' of the cultural place is created by the ideas, traditions, and associated practices that are perceived and appreciated by the local community who have a strong attachment to it, and the way people relate to such places is pursued through their collective perceptions not by the physical features of those places (Salazar 2015, pp. 122–123).

The danger of the top-down approach has been witnessed in the field of intangible cultural heritage as well. Due to their intrinsic form, items of intangible cultural heritage cannot be transmitted without its bearers. However, State-led safeguarding measures can easily pull the heritage subject out of its original context and into the realm of taxidermy. Without close communication and cooperation among the individuals and communities bearing the intangible cultural heritage for the nomination as well as management processes, the heritage item may exist only on the 'list' of the 2003 Convention.

At the same time, technological advancement has enabled freer and less restricted flow of assets and properties, which phenomenon can accelerate illicit trafficking of cultural property. Clandestine excavation and illegal transportation of cultural property will not end, if museums, art dealers and individual purchasers lack scruples about participating in art transactions without proper provenance. States' regulations on commercial activities directed to underwater cultural heritage, for example, are important, but exploitation of heritage cannot be halted without active participation of individuals who appreciate the value of in situ conservation of underwater cultural heritage. The illegal import and export of cultural property due to the chaos

---

[14] Exemplary cases are *Coal Contractors Limited v. Secretary of State for the Environment and Northumberland County Council* [1993] EGCS 218, *Bulankulama and Others v. Secretary, Ministry of Industrial Development and Others* (2000), LKSC 18, *Parkerings-Compagniet AS v. Republic of Lithuania*, ICSID Case No. ARB/05/08, Award of 11 September 2007, and *Glamis Gold Ltd. v. United States*, Award (NAFTA Arb. Trib. 2009).

of destruction during armed conflict also is difficult to tackle by States' actions alone. In addressing these challenges, the specialized roles of UNESCO and experts in facilitating cooperation between States and various non-state stakeholders by provision of their guidance and advice should not be forgotten.

As assessment of the provisions and cases related to the status and roles of NSAs in different international cultural heritage law settings has shown, it is worth noting that international cultural heritage law has made various attempts to address the challenges to cultural heritage protection, such as by expanding the status and roles of different NSAs in the provisions of the conventions. Through revision of the operational texts of the conventions, NSAs' status and roles have steadily grown. And whereas it cannot be said that their call for participation has been heard very well in practice, growing appreciation and recognition of their status and roles are apparent.

It is difficult to say whether or not the state-centric approach to the protection of cultural heritage will be changed dramatically in the near future. Notwithstanding, the Westphalian-inspired notions of state-centricity are no longer capable of capturing the significant status and roles of NSAs (Cutler 2009, p. 20), particularly those that relate to the protection of cultural heritage. As Francesco Francioni pointed out some years ago, "the concept of cultural heritage…requires a radical shift in perspective from the national interests of the State to which the property belongs, to the general interest of humanity in identifying and preserving a cultural or natural site so exceptional as to be of universal value (Francioni 2007, p. 229)." Although the States have the supreme power to conclude treaties, conventions and agreements in international law and have been a major actor in enforcing them at the domestic and international levels, protection of cultural heritage remains a common concern of the international community. Therefore, it is important for the various NSAs to be involved actively in the implementation of cultural heritage conventions to ensure heritage's sustainable conservation. As stated in the Sustainable Development Goal (SDG), "strengthening efforts to protect and safeguard the world's cultural and natural heritage" cannot be achieved only by the actions of States,[15] and sustainable human and economic development of societies through the protection of cultural heritage cannot be reached without participation of the various actors of society (Bandarin et al. 2011).

For their parts, NSAs seem to be ready in this regard. A common understanding of the necessity of the sustainable protection of cultural heritage has been widely spread thanks to the development and promotion of the various international conventions. NSAs, sharing the responsibility for the protection of cultural heritage in various aspects, are calling for more engagement in the international legal and political regimes for the protection of cultural heritage. Conversely too, more innovative and practical mechanisms to ensure the rights, obligations and roles of NSAs should be explored continuously to facilitate their contribution to the enforcement of cultural

---

[15] SDG 11 pledges to "make cities and human settlements inclusive, safe, resilient and sustainable." The "world's cultural and natural heritage" referred to in target 11. 4 is not only confined to 'World Heritage' under the 1972 Convention, but includes various types of cultural heritage from movable to immovable, or from tangible to intangible (UN 2018).

heritage law. It is time for States to appreciate the participation of NSAs and to reflect the necessity of their enhanced status by endowing them with concrete roles in the efforts to achieve the central goal of international cultural heritage law: sustainable protection of cultural heritage.

References

Bandarin F, Hosagrahar J, Albernaz FS (2011) Why development needs culture. J Cult Herit Manag Sustain Dev 1(1):15–25

de Chazournes B, Laurence, (2004) Transparency and Amicus Curiae briefs. J World Invest Trade 5(2):333–336

Chechi A (2015) Non-state actors and cultural heritage: friends or foes? AFDUAM 19:457–479

Collins R (2011) Non-state actors in international institutional law: non-state, inter-state or supra-state? The peculiar identity of the intergovernmental organization. In: d'Aspremont J (ed) Participants in the international legal system: multiple perspectives on non-state actors in international law. Routledge, Abingdon

Cutler AC (2009) Critical reflections on the Westphalian assumptions of international law and organization: a crisis of legitimacy. In: Bianchi A (ed) Non-state actors and international law. Ashgate, Farnham

Francioni F (2007) A dynamic evolution of the concept and scope: from cultural property to cultural heritage. In: Yusuf AA (ed) Standard setting in UNESCO vol. 1: normative action in education, science and culture. Martinus Nijhoff, Leiden

Keough EB (2011) Heritage in peril: a critique of UNESCO's world heritage program. Wash Univ Glob Stud Law Rev 10(3):593–615

Kim J (2017). Dosiwa Yusan (City and Heritage). In: Hyunmook L et al (eds) Hankook Sahoewa SDG 11: Uriui Jisokganeunghan Dosi (Korean Society and SDG 11: Our Sustainable City). Korean National Commission for UNESCO, Seoul

Meskell L (2013) UNESCO's world heritage convention at 40: challenging the economic and political order of international heritage conservation. Curr Anthropol 54(4):483–494

Millar S (2006) Stakeholders and community participation. In: Leask A, Fyall A (eds) Managing world heritage sites. Butterworths, Amsterdam

Salazar NB (2015) The local-to-global dynamics of world heritage interpretation. In: Bourdeau L, Gravari-Barbas M (eds) World heritage, tourism and identity: inscription and co-production. Ashgate, Farnham

UN, (2018) SDG 11 synthesis report: tracking progress towards inclusive, safe, resilient and sustainable cities and human settlements: SDG 11 synthesis report for the high level political forum. UN, New York

UNESCO (2019g) Decision 14.COM 10. The 14th session of the committee of the intergovernmental committee for the safeguarding of the intangible cultural heritage. Bogotá, 9–14 December 2019

The manufacturer's authorised representative in the EU is Springer Nature Customer Service Centre GmbH, Europaplatz 3, 69115 Heidelberg, Germany. If you have any concerns regarding our products, please contact ProductSafety@springernature.com

Printed and bound by CPI Group (UK) Ltd, Croydon, CR0 4YY
30/09/2026
02225290-0003